WARS
Then & Now

By Rick Waddell

Jacksonville, Florida ♦ Herndon, Virginia
www.Fortis-Publishing.com

Wars

Then & Now

By Rick Waddell

ISBN: 978-0-9846371-8-8

Published by Fortis Publishing

Jacksonville, Florida—Herndon, Virginia

www.Fortis-Publishing.com

Manufactured in the United States of America

ACKNOWLEDGMENTS

Like most successful men, I married way above myself. In the 31 years since I met my wife, Donna, she has been a constant source of stability, support, and encouragement. Little that I have done would have been possible, or meaningful, without her, including this book.

My West Point classmate, Kerry Kachejian, a fellow Engineer officer, was in the midst of publishing his own book about his time in Iraq. Kerry was kind enough to introduce me to his publisher, Fortis, a soon as I asked for his help.

To my delight, the editor, Dennis Lowery, at Fortis is also a native Arkansan. He quickly set me on the path to producing this book, nudging me forward with each email and edited chapter file.

My oldest son, Gerald, provided timely research in the home stretch, and useful editing throughout.

To these go the credit; any errors are entirely my own.

TABLE OF CONTENTS

A NOTE ON SOURCES

The raw material for the vignettes and quotes comes primarily from secondary historical sources and news reporting. Many of these sources are now available on the internet. Most of the photographs come from the online database of the National Archives. Where this is not the case, I have sought to use photos from other open and free sources. Any use of photographs that may be copyrighted is inadvertent.

INTRODUCTION

On Monday, 8 December 1941, the cows got milked, the eggs got collected, steel was milled, and cars rolled off the assembly lines. The ships still smoked in Pearl Harbor, and the dead and missing were being counted, but the US economy and population, still heavily agricultural, did not stop. The enemy had crippled one of America's fleets, but did little else.

In contrast, on Wednesday, 12 September 2001, the financial engine of the modern US economy was shuttered as the rescue crews picked vainly through the debris of the collapsed World Trade Center. The modern economy depends on near instant transfer of financial and equity instruments, and the ease of personal travel. The transfers and travel rely simply on trust, that planes fly on time and safely, that financial centers are secure places to work, that rules and contracts will be enforced, that transactions will take place from anywhere on the globe, that brokers and analysts will be at their desks covering all markets in any time zone, 24/7. The enemy in this new era turned the instruments of modern travel – the ease of access to airports and airplanes - into deadly effective weapons against the primary instruments of the financial and stock markets – human capital and trust. The enemy did not merely topple a couple of buildings or shut down a city, but shut down the American airline industry, the primary stock market of the world, and many of America's most prominent banks for several days. Unlike Pearl Harbor, the direct effects of 9-11 were not local, but nationwide in scope.

This view is not in any way unanimous. In the days after the 9-11 attacks, former Senator Daniel Patrick Moynihan said, "This, after all, was not Pearl Harbor. We have not lost the Pacific fleet." The conservative columnist Robert Novak wrote that "the second day of infamy was not perpetrated by an enemy that at that time was militarily superior and seemed to put this

1

nation's very existence in question."[1] Yet, the Pacific Fleet was not destroyed at Pearl Harbor, despite the grievous losses, and went on the offensive a few months thereafter. As strong as Japan was on 7 December 1941, it was not strong enough to transport the millions of troops that would have been required to directly threaten the existence of the United States. In the aftermath of Pearl Harbor, creating the view that our entire Pacific Fleet was destroyed and that the nation's very existence was at stake may have been necessary to the mobilization of manpower and industry that proved necessary to wage war simultaneously in North Africa, Italy, France, Burma, the South Pacific, Central Pacific, and North Atlantic. Despite the greater damage done to our economy on 11 September 2001, America did not respond in the same manner.

The America of December 1941 was still suffering from the Great Depression. Of its 132 million citizens, 43.5 % still lived in rural areas. Only slightly more than half the dwellings had complete plumbing. Life expectancy was less than 63 years, and 47 of every 1000 children died in infancy. Despite these social statistics that would be considered Third World today, America had the world's strongest industrial base, with more than 32 million motor vehicles on the road; 37% of households had a telephone and 73% had radios. It was on this foundation that America set out to change the map of the world.

The America of 2001 was incomparably better off in ways that would have been inconceivable to those called on to become the Greatest Generation. The population was more than twice as large at 282 million, of which only 21% was rural, and fulltime farmers were less than 1%. Life expectancy had risen to 76.5 years, while infant mortality had fallen to 7 of every 1000. Material abundance had transformed the quality of American life, especially

---

[1] Both quotes from Robert Novak, "This Is No Pearl Harbor," 13 September 2001, http://www.townhall.com/columnists/robertnovak/rn20010913.shtml, accessed 30 May 2011.

for the poorest segments – 94% of American households had fixed telephone service, 98% had at least one television, 99% had radio, 51% had a home computer, 41.5% had internet service; the country also had over 100 million cell phone subscribers and 210 million motor vehicles were on the road.[2] The American Gross Domestic Product (GDP) in 2001 was about seven-and-a-half times larger in real terms than it was in 1941. Contrary to popular belief, America continued to be the leading manufacturing nation, producing about 20% of the world's goods.[3] By 2001, the GDP of individual American states was often comparable to large nations. Even a relatively poor American state, like Arkansas, had a GDP per capita roughly equal to Germany's.[4] In

---

[2] For statistics in this section see U.S. Census Bureau, ""20th Century Statistics," *Statistical Abstract of the United States: 1999* (Washington, D.C.: US Government Printing Office, 1999) pp. 874, 879, 881, 885; See also US Census Bureau, "Households With a Computer and Internet Use: 1984 to 2009," *Computer and Internet Use*, http://www.census.gov/hhes/computer/, accessed 10 June 2011, and Daniel E. Sullivan, "Recycled Cell Phones – A Treasure Trove of Valuable Metals," U.S. Geological Survey, 2006, http://pubs.usgs.gov/fs/2006/3097/fs2006-3097.pdf, accessed 13 June 2011, and U.S. Census Bureau, "Mini-historical Statistics," *Statistical Abstract of the United States: 2003* (Washington, D.C.: US Government Printing Office, 2003).

[3] Some sources have indicated that China surpassed the U.S. in 2011 in manufacturing output. If accurate, this would be the first time in more than a century that the U.S. was not the leading manufacturing nation. For example, see "China Became the World's Top Manufacturing Nation, Ending 110 Year US Leadership," *MercoPress*, 15 March 2011, http://en.mercopress.com/2011/03/15/china-became-world-s-top-manufacturing-nation-ending-110-year-us-leadership, accessed 13 June 2011. For a contrasting view, see Mark J. Perry, "The Truth About U.S. Manufacturing," *The Wall Street Journal*, 25 February 2011, http://online.wsj.com/article/SB10001424052748703652104576122353274221570.html, accessed 13 June 2011.

[4] "Europe vs. America: Germany Edges Out Arkansas in Per Capita GDP,"*The Wall Street Journal Opinion Journal*, 19 June 2004, cited at http://www.freerepublic.com/focus/f-news/1156731/posts, accessed 12 June 2011; Daniel Mitchell, "Fiscal Policy Lessons from Europe, Heritage Institute, Backgrounder 1979, http://www.heritage.org/research/reports/2006/10/fiscal-policy-lessons-from-europe, accessed 12 June 2011; By 2011, three years into the Great Recession, California's GDP was still roughly equivalent to Italy's, and Texas' GDP was close to

the war that began on 11 September 2001, we have used a fraction of our national strength, with about 1% of our population serving in uniform, and little more than 1% of our annual GDP employed directly in the war effort.

This war – the Global War on Terror - has had several combat fronts, most notably Afghanistan and Iraq, but also the Philippines and the Horn of Africa. In 2011, America also became involved in a war in Libya, unconnected to the other on-going fronts. Of all the areas where American forces have been engaged, the Iraqi front in the Global War on Terror dominated the news from 2003 until early 2009, while action on the other fronts rarely broke through. War coverage in general dropped precipitously from early 2009 onwards. As previously in American history, the conduct of the current war by generals, bureaucrats, and politicians has become entangled in electoral politics. In every set-back, in every mishap lies a possible domestic political advantage. The 24-hour news cycle and the internet have only exacerbated this trend. Perhaps worse is the American thirst for instantaneous, almost bloodless victory. As memories of the horrors of WWII fade, hope springs eternal that warfare might one day be abolished. If not abolished, then maybe warfare can be sanitized or made much more legalistic in order to reduce the death and destruction.

Tens of millions of Americans are still alive who lived through some of the historical events described herein. Images from photos, films, movies, and earlier governmental information efforts linger from our past – particularly from World War II - conditioning our response to today's wars. With the benefit of hindsight, the earlier wars are clearer than the current one. History is only written afterwards, with the benefit of reflection, but it is worth remembering what was thought and done at the time. America's current efforts are better understandable in the context of the efforts

---

Russia's; see "Comparing US States with Countries," *The Economist*, 13 January 2011, http://www.economist.com/blogs/dailychart/2011/01/comparing_us_states_countr ies, accessed 12 June 2011.

Americans in earlier generations made in similar circumstances. That is the only point of this book.

Since the current wars are not ones where front lines move slowly across maps, but rather are of the sort that is primarily dependent on small unit actions against shadowy insurgent and terrorist cells, with support provided by high-tech electronic equipment and high-flying aircraft, this book will not focus on grand strategy, operational art, or tactical developments better left to in-depth analysis. This book will instead follow many of the themes common in the journalism of the Global War on Terror, which inevitably reflect, and feed, the themes of US politics. These key themes have been playing out around dinner tables, on college campuses, in bars, and certainly in political campaigns. War is a political act, both internal to the belligerent countries, and externally. Politics and war are inseparable. This book does not seek to be comprehensive or exhaustive, but rather illustrative. Consequently not every American war is covered and not every notable historical event during our major wars is described. America has been at war before, and the lessons are worth learning. The quotes and vignettes appearing in this book serve to illustrate those lessons.

PREPAREDNESS

A common cliché holds that the government in general and the military in particular prepares for the last war, which is why America often seems unprepared for a new war, especially when the new wars happen as surprises. Public expressions about military preparedness come and go, sometimes driven by political campaigns, sometimes driven by real fears of US military inferiority, and sometimes, like at Pearl Harbor, driven by concrete facts brought home in bloody fashion. For most of its history, America has had small standing forces, augmented by state militia that required mobilization in time of crisis. During the Civil War, and both World Wars, the mobilization went beyond calling state militias into Federal service, and required conscription and conversion of civilian industries to arms manufacturing. While the needs of the Cold War meant that America maintained relatively large standing forces, the historical pattern remains one where the public is skeptical of standing forces, where policy makers reflect that skepticism in trying to keep active forces to a minimum, and therefore where participation of part-time citizen soldiers is still crucial in times of crisis.

CURRENT SITUATION

"As you know, you go to war with the Army you have. They're not the Army you might want or wish to have at a later time."

- Secretary of Defense Donald Rumsfeld, 8 December 2004, town hall meeting with soldiers, Camp Buehring, Kuwait, in response to a question on quality and availability of US equipment by Specialist Thomas Wilson [5]

WORLD WAR I

"We are ruled by an arbitrary and irresponsible popular opinion which, through a certain sublimated optimism which is at once benevolent and baleful, treats military service as inconsequential and renders it well-nigh impossible to maintain that vigorous discipline with is indispensable to an effective army."

- Editorial from The Army and Navy Journal[6]

In 1915, with Europe already deep into its bloodbath, the U.S. had only 174,100 men under arms, with 106,800 in its Army, and with pacifists as both the Secretary of War and Secretary of State – Newton Baker and William Jennings Bryan respectively.[7] Preparing for a potential war was the opposite of U.S. national policy. Upon US entry into World War I in April 1917, America's Regular Army had grown to 127,588, deployed mainly along the string of frontier posts it had garrisoned during the Indian campaigns. A few thousand troops served overseas in the Panama Canal Zone, the Philippines, and in China. Another 80,446 National Guardsmen and 5,523 Reservists were in Federal service for the punitive expedition then underway against Pancho Villa in Mexico.[8]

---

[5] Thomas E. Ricks, "Rumsfeld Gets Earful from Troops," *The Washington Post*, 9 December 2004, http://www.washingtonpost.com/wp-dyn/articles/A46508-2004Dec8.html, accessed 2 August 2011.

[6] No date given, but the author portrays it as from an edition on the eve of World War I. See Russell F. Weigley, *History of the United States Army* (New York: Macmillan, 1967) 336.

[7] U.S. Census Bureau, "20th Century Statistics" Section 31, *Statistical Abstract of the United States: 1999* (Washington, D.C.: US Government Printing Office, 1999) 22. Bryan resigned in June 1915 over fears that President Wilson would use the sinking of the *Lusitania* as a pretext to enter the war.

[8] Weigley 357-358.

To meet Allied demands for an early deployment of help, the U.S. pulled four Regular regiments from the Mexican campaign, assembled them into the 1st Division, and shipped them hastily to France, where they began arriving in June 1917. The Regiments had been under strength, and borrowed from other units to fill their ranks. Their equipment was that issued for the frontier, including cowboy hats. They had no howitzers, mortars, or 37mm guns - standard issue weapons for the Western Front armies - nor did they have any training on the use of such weapons.[9]

African-American troops exercising in cantonment near the Marne.[10]

The American forces required extensive training upon arrival in France, and would not enter combat in large numbers until spring 1918. Meanwhile,

---

[9] Weigley 356.
[10] National Archives, ARC Identifier 533502 / Local Identifier 165-WW-127(18) Still Picture Records Section, Special Media Archives Services Division, College Park, MD;Item from Record Group 165: Records of the War Department General and Special Staffs, 1860 – 1952.

mobilization brought in very large numbers of troops in only 18 months. President Wilson had hoped to avoid large numbers in the war, but GEN Pershing's first report in July 1917 called for a million troops in France by the end of 1918, which must have seemed astounding to a country which had never deployed such numbers before. Once Pershing came to the conclusion that Britain and France were worn out, he raised his estimate of American troops required to 3 million in France by May 1919.[11] To the country's credit, America responded rapidly to the changing situation. Almost 2 million troops were in France by the end of the war on 11 November 1918 versus the 1 million originally requested less than 18 months earlier, and the Army's strength was 3,685,458.[12] The United States had recovered from an almost total lack of preparation for war to send a formidable field army into the main theater of conflict to engage successfully in modern mass warfare in which it had had no relevant experience.

WORLD WAR II

"...blind leading the blind, and officers generally elsewhere."
- MG Lesley McNair's comment on training new conscripts and mobilized Guardsmen in 1940-1941.[13]

After World War I, demobilization was conducted with the same speed as the build-up. By 1920, the armed forces numbered 343,300, and the winning slogan in the Presidential campaign was Warren G. Harding's "Return to Normalcy."[14] Soon America was into the Roaring Twenties, and military concerns slipped again into the background, even though small forces continued to serve on the Caribbean islands, in Central America, in the Philippines, and at Tientsin in China.

---

[11] Weigley 358-360.
[12] Weigley 358.
[13] Weigley 428.
[14] Statistical Abstract 1999, 22.

GEN MacArthur, the Army Chief of Staff, would report in 1934 that the entire U.S. Army had only 12 functioning post-World War I tanks.[15] By the time war broke out again in Europe in September 1939, the Regular Army had 190,000 officers and men, with 140,000 of those stationed Stateside in the same string of battalion-sized frontier posts. The troops were armed with the 1903 Springfield rifle (so-named because it debuted in 1903), and had only one 37mm anti-tank gun in the inventory. The National Guard had another 200,000 on its rolls.[16]

As the new European war turned into the Phony War, the danger seemed remote. The anti-war, anti-preparedness, and isolationist movements remained very strong in the United States. Any move to a war footing was seen as a move to war. Consequently, although the armed services conducted contingency planning, mobilization planning did not begin in earnest until after the stunning fall of France in June 1940. Even then, neither the Roosevelt Administration nor the armed services asked publicly for conscription for fear of igniting a backlash in an election year. Congressional leaders themselves undertook to pass conscription without direct leadership from the White House, withstanding the political heat by first agreeing to a mobilization of the National Guard in late August 1940, and passing the Burke-Wadsworth conscription bill in mid-September, but the effect of the laws was limited to a mere year.[17]

During the year of partial mobilization, re-armament began slowly. By the end of the fiscal year in 1940, the armed forces had grown to 458,400, but no major new equipment was produced for the Army.[18] Training quality was hindered by the rapid increase in strength and the lack of weapons. The military had insufficient weapons even for rudimentary training, often using weapons fashioned out of wood or broomsticks.

---

[15] Weigley 414.
[16] Weigley 419.
[17] Weigley 426-7.
[18] Statistical Abstract 1999, 22. Weigley 432.

Even as the war in Europe worsened with the Battle of Britain and the German invasion of the Soviet Union, America resisted re-armament such that the renewal of Burke-Wadsworth passed the House of Representatives in 1941 by a single vote, and the President ordered a drawdown of the mobilized National Guard to begin in early 1942.

A wooden fifty-caliber anti-aircraft machinegun during the 1941 Louisiana Maneuvers.[19]

In the Louisiana Maneuvers of September 1941, a year after the mobilization began, the ground forces were still missing "10 percent of the mortars, 40 percent of the 37-mm guns, 18 percent of the 155-mm howitzers, and 87 percent of the .50-caliber machine guns," and the 1st Armored Division had only sixty-six US-produced medium battle tanks on hand.[20] On 7 December 1941, the Army had grown to over 1.6 million, but only one division and one anti-aircraft regiment were rated fully combat ready.[21] In early 1943, some

---

[19] From http://www.usmilitariaforum.com/forums/index.php?showtopic=60390.
[20] Martin Blumenson, *Kasserine Pass* (Boston: Houghton Mifflin Company, 1966), cited in http://www.militaryphotos.net/forums/showthread.php?14893-The-Battle-of-Kasserine-Pass, accessed 13 June 2011.
[21] Weigley 435.

Army divisions were still complaining about a lack of training ammunition, and the continued use of broomstick machineguns in training.[22]

As in World War I, once America entered the war, changes came rapidly. In the three years and nine months of its participation in the war, the U.S. inducted 16.1 million into its armed forces.[23] At the close of Fiscal Year 1945, the U.S. had just over 12 million under arms, with 8.27 million in the Army and Army Air Forces, 3.32 million in the Navy and 470,000 in the Marine Corps.[24] World War II thus followed the long-standing American pattern: resist large standing forces, resist rearmament, conduct a rapid build-up of manpower and industry when required, then conduct a rapid demobilization and "return to normalcy." Expressing this sentiment, the Republican's winning slogan in the 1946 Congressional campaign was, "Had enough?"

KOREA

On 31May 1945, the Army had stood at 8,291,336, including 2,354,210 in the Army Air Corps.[25] Following the pattern of rapid mobilization followed by rapid demobilization, by 1950, despite occupation duties across the world, the total strength of U.S. armed forces had declined to less than 1.5 million, and the Army to less than 600,000.[26]

---

[22] Major Benjamin L. Bradley, USAF, "Searching For Competence: The Initial Combat Experience Of Untested U.S. Army Divisions In World War II – A Case Study Of The 90th Infantry Division, June-July 1940," U.S. Army Command and Staff College, 2005, at http://www.dtic.mil/cgi-bin/GetTRDoc?AD=ADA506897&Location=U2&doc=GetTRDoc.pdf.

[23]Anne Leland and Mari-Jana "M-J" Oboroceanu, *American War and Military Operations Casualties: Lists and Statistics*, Congressional Research Service, 15 September2009, 2. Hereafter "CRS."

[24] Statistical Abstract 1999, 22.

[25] Weigley 435.

[26] Statistical Abstract 1999, 22.

When North Korea invaded South Korea on 25 June 1950, the U.S. hastily assembled a combat force of 403 men from the skeletonized units on occupation duty in Japan – Task Force Smith. Four days after the Task Force landed, on 5 July 1950, the North Korean forces rolled through them, causing the unit to disintegrate into a chaotic retreat. The Communists pushed U.S. and South Korean forces back to the Pusan Perimeter, comprising just 10 percent of the South Korean territory, capturing the commander of the U.S. 24th Division, MG William Dean, in the process. Many historical commentaries on this action point to outmoded U.S. weapons in addition to the troops and units softened by easy occupation duties.[27] However, the weapons available in 1950 were the same ones that had defeated the Axis powers only five years before. Moreover, the American weapons were pitted against Soviet-supplied weapons of exactly the same vintage. The real cause of the disaster of Task Force Smith and the retreat back to Pusan was the unpreparedness of the American troops to use the weapons against a determined foe.[28]

As in 1917 and 1941, America rallied. GEN MacArthur marshaled forces inside the Pusan Perimeter, and then mounted the surprise amphibious counterattack at Inchon. When Communist China entered the war the fighting turned into a brutal WWI-style stalemate with fixed flanks and frontal assaults. Substituting firepower for manpower, the US fired more shells in the 37 months of Korea than it had in the 45 months of its participation in WWII.[29] The U.S. fought in Korea without the full mobilizations launched in the World Wars, leading some to call Korea, "The

---

[27] For example, see Weigley 502-503, who points out that although the weapons were from WWII, some of their designs dated from WWI. See also Max Hastings, *The Korean War* (New York: Simon and Shuster, 1987) 15-22. Hereafter "Hastings."

[28] In the early 1990s, as the post-Cold War "drawdown" was underway, the Chief of Staff of the Army, GEN Gordon Sullivan, was fond of using the phrase "No more Task Force Smith's" to describe his goals for the sort of Army he wanted to emerge from the cut-backs

[29] Weigley 524.

Forgotten War." Even without full mobilization, the U.S. inducted over 5.7 million into the Armed forces during the conflict, and active duty strength peaked at over 3.6 million.[30] The fighting in the Korean War ended with an official stalemate – the Armistice of 27 July 1953 – and the battle lines remain today essentially unchanged. As the war has not ended, crises still occasionally flare up, as is happening at the time of writing with the recent sinking of the South Korean ship, *Cheonan*, on 26 March 2010, by a North Korean torpedo, and the North Korean shelling of an offshore South Korean island in November 2011.

THE COLD WAR

The Bomber Gap

In the aftermath of Korea, the U.S. established a new pattern. In the 1950s, with Communism contained in Korea, but apparently still aggressive, the U.S. opted to maintain large standing forces in peacetime, which remained above 2 million through the decade.[31] Containment became the official U.S. policy until the end of the Cold War. Confronting potential ground attacks across the "Inter-German Border" in Europe or the Demilitarized Zone in Korea became the two principal missions. Sufficient forces were deployed forward to act as a deterrent, while rapid reinforcement of the two fronts would be required in the event of crisis. Additionally, confronting a growing Soviet and then Chinese nuclear threat caused an increase in force structure, both as a deterrent and as a rapid response. In the nuclear stalemate of the Cold War, with Western and Communist forces able to see each other across boundaries in Europe and Korea, lack of preparedness could lead to surprises that would make Pearl Harbor pale in comparison. "Readiness" to fight and reinforce on the two fronts, or readiness to respond to a nuclear threat

---

[30] Statistical Abstract 1999, 22; CRS 3.
[31] Statistical Abstract 1999, 22. The active duty strength would not again fall below 2 million until the early 1990s.

became a critical requirement, and a constant political issue until the final Western victory came with the ultimate collapse of the Soviet Union.

In 1957, the Soviets began flying nuclear-capable bombers near the borders of the US and western allies. This caused the fear that the Soviets had leaped ahead of the US in bomber production and capability, creating a "bomber gap" – a fear that the U.S. would not be prepared despite the large standing forces and continued high defense spending. The political response was a demand for more U.S. bomber production, and the beginning of U-2 spy plane overflights of the Soviet Union to determine their true capabilities.[32]

The Missile Gap

Almost at the same time as the emergence of the feared Bomber Gap, the Soviets launched the first orbiting satellite, Sputnik, on 4 October 1957. This surprise was followed closely by the launch of the second Sputnik on 3 November, which carried a dog into space. These successes helped create a new readiness, or preparedness, fear – the Missile Gap. The combination of the two Gaps helped tarnish the national defense reputation of President Eisenhower and Vice President Richard Nixon as they headed into the 1960 elections. One of the leading proponents of the Missile Gap, Senator John F. Kennedy, would use this fear of not being prepared with particularly sharp effect in his successful presidential campaign against Nixon.[33]

1980s and the Gulf War

---

[32]"Bomber Gap," The Coldwar Museum, at
http://www.coldwar.org/articles/50s/bomber_gap.asp.
[33] Christopher A. Preble, "'Who Ever Believed in the Missile Gap?': John F. Kennedy and the Politics of National Security," *Presidential Studies Quarterly*, Vol. 33, 2003, at http://www.questia.com/googleScholar.qst?docId=5002052634. The author argues that Kennedy really did believe in the Missile Gap, and was only informed that it did not really exist in the first weeks of his administration in early 1961. Kennedy continued to use the Missile Gap, though, as an argument for increased military spending.

After withdrawal and self-imposed defeat in Southeast Asia, the U.S. focused on the defense of South Korea and Western Europe as the least politically divisive defense policy. Simultaneously, it ended the draft, even while maintaining more than 2 million, now all volunteers, under arms. In the post-Vietnam gloom of the waning countercultural movement, the first few years of the all-volunteer forces produced units of questionable quality. At his first press conference on 17 September 1979, upon assuming the position of Chief of Staff of the Army, GEN Edward C. Meyer called attention to the difficulties of manning the force with quality soldiers. Units that existed on paper were undermanned and under equipped for the tasks at hand, a phenomenon that would become known as the "hollow Army." Even for the main missions of defending along the Inter-German Border or along the Korean DMZ, Meyer said he had a "prudent risk force" – one that could still do the job, but at an uncomfortable level of risk.[34]

Even as Meyer was making his case, a series of international events was happening that underscored the continued risk to the U.S., its citizens, and its broader interests in the world. In July 1979, the Marxist-led Sandinistas overthrew the Somoza regime in Nicaragua, and quickly invited in Soviet-bloc advisers. On 15 October, the regime in El Salvador was likewise overthrown, and a Marxist insurgency ensued against the new government. Twenty days later, on 4 November, radicals seized the American embassy in Tehran, taking 52 American hostages. On 21 November, radicals burned the US embassy in Pakistan, killing two American servicemen. On 2 December, mobs sacked the US embassy in Libya. On 27 December, the Soviets invaded and occupied their neighbor, Afghanistan.[35] As the new decade dawned, Marxist-inspired M19 guerillas seized the Dominican embassy in Bogota, Columbia,

---

[34] Rick Waddell, "The Army and Peacetime Low Intensity Conflict, 1961-1993: the Process of Peripheral and Fundamental Military Change," dissertation, Columbia University, 1994, 232.
[35] Waddell 229-230.

on 27 February 1980, taking the American ambassador and other diplomats hostages.

Spread over seven months, these events highlighted the weakened nature of American prestige. On 24 April 1980, an attempt to rescue the American hostages in Tehran failed miserably, and served to confirm GEN Meyer's comments on America's hollow military capabilities, the ugly handmaiden to damaged prestige. As the hostage crisis dragged on through 1980 with daily updates on the nightly news, America turned to a new President, widely decried by his critics as a war-monger. President Reagan, though, harkened back to the days of WWII, when America rose above the Depression to save the world; his view was of an America that was confident and active abroad. The resulting Reagan military build-up raised active duty strength by 200,000, from 2.159 million in 1980 to 2.359 million in 1986, or about 9.3%, although the total had decreased by 50,000 by the time he left office.[36] More important than the small increase in troop strength was the continued funding of new equipment – the M1 Abrams tank, the M2 Bradley infantry fighting vehicle, the F-18 Navy fighter jet, the F-117 and B-2 Stealth planes, the Blackhawk and Apache helicopters, and new classes of ships – all equipment still fighting today. Even more important was a new willingness to confront adversaries, whether in the skirmishes along the Cold War perimeter in Lebanon, Grenada, and Libya, or in the conflicts in Central America and Afghanistan, or in the deployment of Cruise and Pershing missiles to NATO bases despite vociferous domestic opposition in the U.S. and Europe.

The Reagan build-up also helped spawn a "Defense Reform Movement." Some in the movement sought to produce more combat power more efficiently, arguing that the new equipment was too expensive per unit, and too complicated. Some critics questioned whether the threat was all that important, preferring to believe in peaceful coexistence. Critics pointed to

---

[36] CRS 7.

outlandishly expensive toilet seats or hammers as indicators of inherently wasteful procurement practices. By the end of the Reagan era in the late 1980s, the Reform narrative held that the American military could not deploy, could not sustain, and could not fight, armed as it was with overpriced equipment that would not work well in combat.[37]

"Readiness" was again the political debating point, given the continued need to deploy additional forces rapidly to either West Germany or South Korea. Annual exercises were held to test Active, Reserve, and National Guard units – Return of Forces to Germany (REFORGER) and Team Spirit (for South Korea). The expected invasions across the two interior borders of the divided nations were likely to be rapid; U.S. and allied forces were outnumbered, and geographical depth was limited. No time would be available for general mobilization as had happened in the two World Wars. Some Reserve and Guard units received more money and better equipment, and were due to deploy within a matter of days. The main reinforcements, though, would be active duty forces that drew equipment from pre-positioned stocks. Given the dominant thinking in the 1980s about the quality of American troops and equipment, "readiness" was a constant concern, and drove armed services reporting of statistics and political and academic arguments over the veracity of the reports.

In the early Autumn of 1989, while doing the coursework for my doctorate at Columbia, one classroom discussion centered around the imbalance of NATO and Warsaw Pact forces, and the political and economic difficulty the Western democracies had in maintaining adequate forces. Accepted wisdom was that the US was already in steep decline, with a recent best-seller titled, *The Rise and Fall of the Great Powers*, making this very point.[38] This

---

[37] For examples of the sentiments, see James Fallows, *National Defense* (New York: Random House, 1981) and Arthur T. Hadley, *The Straw Giant* (New York: Random House, 1986).

[38] Paul Kennedy, *The Rise and Fall of the Great Powers* (New York: Random House, 1987).

discussion was led by an adjunct professor whose day job was in the Defense Department, and three of the students were serving officers doing their graduate work. When one of the officers advanced the notion that the quality of the new American equipment – the Abrams tank and the Bradley Fighting Vehicle – was actually much superior to the competing Soviet models, the professor quickly shot down this notion because as he put it, "Even so, that equipment will still be maintained and used by American enlisted men." To this Defense Department official, equipment quality may have been debatable, but the continued low quality of American soldiers was almost an article of faith. The Reform narrative reigned supreme.

Ironically, the Social Science Department at West Point also used such thinking in its required International Relations classes in 1990 and 1991, even as the TV screens in the classrooms were showing the American military deploying, sustaining, and then fighting in superb fashion during the Gulf War, upending a decade of defense policy and defense journalism thinking. The classroom material at West Point came from Hedrick Smith, *The Power Game*, and the accompanying PBS mini-series of the same name.[39]

The American military in the Gulf War used the equipment, the training, the procedures for deployment, and the sustainment infrastructure that had been developed for reinforcement of NATO and South Korea over the previous four decades of the Cold War. American forces defeated the fourth largest army in the world, considered by some critics as superior to our own since it had been trained with Soviet doctrine and armed primarily with

---

[39] Hedrick Smith, *The Power Game: How Washington Works* (New York: Random House, 1988). As Hedrick Smith's website says even now: "Praised by scholars and policymakers as the definitive work on Beltway politics, The Power Game is used in college courses around the country." Of course, the material has no doubt been revised. See http://www.hedricksmith.com/topics/theWashingtonPowerGame.shtml. I was an instructor of International Relations at West Point in this period, and we led off one of our key blocks of instruction with this mini-series.

Soviet equipment, and possessed eight years of recent bloody combat experience in mass warfare. Doing so in only four days of ground combat, and with so few casualties was a surprise made all the grander because it ran directly contrary to the major currents of U.S. political and policy thinking, and the expectations derived of such thinking, dating back to the creation of the All-Volunteer military of the mid-1970s. In the Gulf War, America was prepared.

GLOBAL WAR ON TERROR

"What a disgrace that their families have to hold bake sales to buy discarded Kevlar vests to stuff into the floorboards of the Humvees! Bake sales for body armor."

- Al Gore, Jr., 26 May 2004[40]

"As president, I will see to it that we don't have to have bake sales and bargain-basement sell-offs, yard sales by parents and buy on the Internet to supply the troops of the United States of America."

- Senator John F. Kerry, 3 June 2004, while campaigning for President[41]

"You know, I've heard from an Army captain who was the head of a rifle platoon -- supposed to have 39 men in a rifle platoon....Ended up being sent to Afghanistan with 24 because 15 of those soldiers had been sent to Iraq. And as a consequence, they didn't have enough ammunition, they didn't have enough Humvees. They were actually capturing Taliban weapons, because it was easier to get Taliban weapons than it was for them to get properly equipped by our current commander in chief."

---

[40] "Remarks by Al Gore," 26 May 2004, at http://www.moveon.org/pac/gore-rumsfeld-transcript.html.
[41] Dan Balz, "Kerry Says He Would Add 40,000 to Army," *The Washington Post*, 4 June 2004, at http://www.washingtonpost.com/wp-dyn/articles/A11971-2004Jun3.html.

- Senator Barack H. Obama, 22 February 2008 during a Democrat presidential primary debate.[42]

Specialist Wilson's question to the Secretary of Defense in December 2004 was driven by the lack of light armored vehicles capable of withstanding roadside bombs – the Improvised Explosive Devices, or IEDs, which were already the major killers of US and allied soldiers – and by the lack of adequate "bullet-proof vests" to provide personal protection against these homemade weapons. One author could find no instance where a bake sale was held to buy body armor for deploying troops, although some police departments did collect used bullet-proof vests and sent them to deployed units to place on the floorboards of thin-skinned vehicles.[43] Nonetheless, the political charges of lack of preparedness played an early, and enduring, role in the criticism of the U.S. response to the attacks on 9-11.

In the 1990s, America searched for the Peace Dividend, even as it engaged in the Clinton Wars, often billed as humanitarian interventions. Active duty strength declined to 1.38 million by 2001.[44] Both recruiting and retention lagged, and new recruit quality suffered a serious decline.[45] This was the military force available to America on the day the current war began. As American political cycles progressed after 2001, a new narrative emerged and is reflected in the comments made by the major political figures above: the stresses of multiple deployments with inadequate equipment to Iraq and

---

[42] Jake Tapper, "Obama's Army Anecdote," ABC News, 22 February 2008, http://blogs.abcnews.com/politicalpunch/2008/02/from-the-fact-3.html, accessed 2 August 2011.

[43] Eliana Johnson, "Where's the Yeast?" *National Review*, 14 July 2004, at http://www.nationalreview.com/comment/johnson200407140956.asp.

[44] Jim Garamone, "Clinton Signs Authorization Act, Pay, Tricare Affected," Armed Forces Press Service, 31 October 2000, at http://usmilitary.about.com/library/milinfo/milarticles/blfy2001payact.htm.

[45] RAND National Defense Research Institute, "Have Improved Resources Increased Military Recruiting and Retention?" RAND Research Briefs, 2004 at http://www.rand.org/pubs/research_briefs/RB7556/index1.html.

Afghanistan were causing problems with recruiting and retention, and contributing to a higher suicide rate, resulting in a "broken army."[46]

Following the pattern begun in the Korean War, America went to war after 9-11 without mobilizing either society or industry. Roughly one percent of Americans are serving on active duty or in the Reserves and National Guard. Aside from family members of these servicemen, the vast majority of Americans have felt no direct impact of the war on their lives. Rather than call forth a concerted effort of the ingenuity of the private sector as the Wilson and Roosevelt Administrations did (and neither of these administrations were particularly fond of large private businesses), procurement since 9-11 has adhered mostly to established channels. Rather than mass mobilization after an attack on the homeland, the approach under both the Bush and Obama Administrations has been "just-in-time, and only just enough."

Nonetheless, America has responded to the shifting needs of the war. Ground force strength has been allowed to grow, from 480,000 in the Regular Army to a targeted end strength of 569,000, and from 172,000 to 189,000 in the Marine Corps.[47] On the politically contentious issue of armor against the IED threat, the Pentagon had begun deploying improved body armor including ceramic chest and back plates (called Small Arms Protective Inserts, or SAPI plates) to frontline troops in Bosnia only in 1999, each weighing an average 31 pounds.[48] Troops on staffs or in support units did not

---

[46] See Bruce Auster, "Series Overview: America's Broken Army," 9 January 2009, at http://www.npr.org/templates/story/story.php?storyId=99154498.

[47] "Gates Increases U.S. Army End Strength," 23 July 2009, at http://www.janes.com/news/defence/land/jdw/jdw090723_1_n.shtml. For Fiscal Year 2009 authorizations, see "Title IV – Military Personnel Authorizations, at http://www.dtic.mil/congressional_budget/pdfs/FY2009_pdfs/SASC_110-335_MILPERS.pdf.

[48] Major General Stephen M. Speakes, "Statement Before the Tactical Air and Land Forces Subcommittee House Armed Services Committee United States House of Representatives on Army Force Protection Programs," Second Session, 109th

get the SAPI plates until later.[49] When the IED threat became acute in Iraq upon the end of the ground war and the start of the insurgency, in mid-2003, the Pentagon responded by ordering vests and plates for all deployed troops in Iraq. More than 160,000 vests were produced by nine companies and shipped by January 2004.[50]

The author, heavily laden with Interceptor Body Armor, crossing the Tigris in January 2006. Note the flimsy life preserver strips around our necks.

Even heavier ceramic armor issued to the author as part of the Improved Outer Tactical Vest in September 2009.

Traditionally before the Iraq and Afghanistan campaigns, military transport and other light vehicles were not armored. Yet these thin-skinned vehicles were prime targets for Iraq and Afghan insurgents. Consequently, the Pentagon also moved first to place armor on existing vehicles, and then to produce new variants with factory-installed armor, and finally to design and produce entirely new classes of mine- and IED-resistant vehicles. In the early

Congress, 15 June 2006, at http://www.globalsecurity.org/military/library/congress/2006_hr/060615-speakes.pdf, 1-3.

[49] When I deployed to Iraq in January 2004 to work on the staff of the Coalition Provisional Authority, I was issued only the Kevlar vest, without the SAPI plates.

[50] Lisa Burgess, "Armor On Its Way To Iraq Bound Troops," *Stars and Stripes*, 14 January 2004, at http://www.military.com/NewsContent/0,13319,FL_armor_011404,00.html.

months of the Iraqi insurgency, innovative units installed self-fabricated "hillbilly armor" while awaiting government-issued equipment.

Left: A typical soft-skinned HMMWV in 2005, Forward Operating Base Speicher, Tikrit, Iraq. Such vehicles were only used inside the base. Right: A HMMWV with "hillbilly armor" in February 2004, Presidential Palace, Baghdad, Iraq.[51]

In May 2003, only 235 armored High Mobility Multi-purpose Wheeled Vehicles (HMMWVs) were in the theaters of war, but production continued to rise, reaching 450 per month in October 2004, and more than 1000 per month in June 2006. By July 2005, 9727 up-armored HMMWVs were in the theaters; by June 2006, the number had risen to 12,179, and another 6490 HMMWVs had been converted with government-issue add-on armor kits, and these were scheduled to be replaced by mid-2007 with factory-built models. Moreover, another 12,425 transport and support vehicles had been

---

[51] Author's personal photos.

converted with add-on armor. Meanwhile, any military vehicles without government-issue armor were prohibited from leaving base.[52]

As the strength of IEDs grew in response to vehicle armor, the Pentagon procured a new class of vehicles especially designed to protect against mines and IEDs – the Mine Resistant Ambush Protected vehicles (MRAPs) – composed of several different designs from different manufacturers. Thousands were rushed into order for delivery to Iraq, with large numbers arriving in 2007 and 2008. As the MRAPs are very large vehicles, a lighter variant was sought for the more rugged off-road terrain in Afghanistan –the MRAP- All Terrain Vehicle (MATV). In late 2009, the Pentagon ordered 6600 MATVs from the Oshkosh Corporation for use in Afghanistan.[53]

An up-armored M1114 HMMWV[54]

---

[52] Speakes 4-5.
[53] DOD News Briefing, 4 November 2009, at
http://www.defense.gov/Transcripts/Transcript.aspx?TranscriptID=4506.
[54] M1114 photo from http://www.militaryfactory.com/armor/imgs/hmmwv-m1114uah_3.jpg.

Even as Specialist Wilson entered history with his question in December 2004, the Pentagon procurement system was well into its ramp-up. Hundreds of thousands of ballistic armor vests were produced and shipped, and more than 50,000 vehicles would be produced or re-armored. The scale of the effort was small in comparison to those in earlier generations, but it was not insignificant.

A Cat 1 MRAP prototype by Navistar[55]

---

[55] Photo from http://defense-update.com/images_new/MRAP_Cat_1_navistar.jpg.

A MATV prototype by Oshkosh[56]

CONCLUSION

American history proves Secretary Rumsfeld to have been correct about going to war with the army you have, however impolitic and tone-deaf his answer was. Just as the vast majority of Americans have no direct connection to those fighting in the current war, most Americans will not know of the production effort for this war because unlike the mobilization efforts of earlier generations, the Bush and Obama Administrations have engaged in little media fanfare. Rather than call on the mighty forces of American science and industry, the Administrations have preferred a slow, sedate approach to procurement, perhaps with the intent of avoiding accusations of waste and corruption (accusations which were made anyway). Like the war effort for Korea and later Vietnam, the "just-in-time and only just enough" mentality in the Global War on Terror seems calculated to exact the minimum amount of attention and cause the minimum disruption to domestic American life.

---

[56] Photo from
http://www.oshkoshdefense.com/defense/products~matv~photo5.cfm.

FIGHTING BACK

One current of popular thought making the rounds since the 9-11 attacks is that the United States did not have to respond so aggressively. One can find political and journalistic commentators arguing that despite US efforts in Iraq, Afghanistan or elsewhere, the terrorists continue to get stronger, or that our aggressive operations are in fact breeding new terrorists or that our efforts are making the enemy more fanatical, thus making the enemy stronger. In other words, fighting back only serves to enrage and embolden the enemy thereby making America less safe. Rarely do these commentators offer a coherent alternative to fighting back.

As the following vignettes and historical examples highlight, the current war is not the first time in our history where the enemy gained in strength or fanaticism after America decided to go to war.

CURRENT SITUATION

"Rather than reducing the number of terrorists worldwide and lessening the motivation of terrorists to attack the United States, the war in Iraq is having precisely the opposite effect...[There] is no question that many of our policies have inflamed our enemies' hatred toward the U.S.... we're less safe today because the war in Iraq has hindered our ability to make progress in combating terrorism."

- Speaker of the House Nancy Pelosi, September 2006[57]

---

[57] "Iraq a 'Cause Celebre' for Extremists, Intel Report Says," http://www.foxnews.com/story/0,2933,215920,00.html, 27 September 2006.

"[T]his war is lost and the surge is not accomplishing anything...."

- Senate Majority Leader Henry Reid, April 2007, about two months after the Surge was launched in Iraq[58]

"Guantánamo makes us less safe...."

- Senate Majority Leader Harry Reid, May 2009[59]

"The Taliban in Pakistan is training jihadis to attack New York, belying again W.'s chuckleheaded contention that we have to wage war against terrorists abroad so we don't have to face them at home. Our battles meant to diminish enemies replenish them. The inept Times Square bomber was infuriated by U.S. drone attacks in Pakistan."[60]

- Maureen Dowd, 11 May 2010

Dowd's is the crowning irony. An immigrant to America uses the weak laws and lax enforcement of those laws to travel to Pakistan to be trained as a terrorist. In the meantime, he is granted US citizenship, but is allegedly driven to homicidal rage by US military operations against the lairs of the terrorists who trained him. Dowd's implications are presumably that US actions abroad are breeding even more terrorists, as in this case, so it would be better somehow to wait until the enemy comes to the US rather than try to stop them abroad, although she leaves unsaid how such a strategy might work in practice.

Beginning with the premise that fighting back makes America less safe, perhaps by enraging the enemy into greater fanaticism and greater efforts,

---

[58] Associated Press, "Reid: Iraq War Lost, U.S. Can't Win," http://www.msnbc.msn.com/id/18227928/ns/politics/page/2/, 20 April 2007.
[59] David M. Herszenhorn, "Democrats in Senate Block Money to Close Guantanamo," http://www.nytimes.com/2009/05/20/us/politics/20detain.html, 19 May 2009.
[60] Maureen Dowd, "The Evil of Lesser Evilism," *The New York Times*, 11 May 2010, at http://www.nytimes.com/2010/05/12/opinion/12dowd.html?hp.

we should consider the example of the two World Wars and Cambodia, where the current pattern emerges.

WORLD WAR I

The US declared war on Germany on 6 April 1917 and began its build-up and deployment overseas. The US Navy went into immediate action against the German submarine fleet and assisted the general blockade of Germany, thereby tightening the economic noose. The first American troops in divisional strength began arriving in France in June 1917. The American troops went into quiet sectors as they trained.[61] By early 1918, America had 318,000 men in France.[62]

In March 1918, though, despite the US naval and land force aid, Germany accumulated enough military might to launch the "Ludendorff Spring Offensives." The Germans used 192 divisions of troops, 50 of which had been moved from the Eastern Front when the Communists took over Russia in 1917 and Russian military efforts collapsed, an event which America's entry into the war earlier in 1917 failed to relieve.[63] The Russian collapse was a stupendous victory for Germany and its allies. The Germans launched five major attacks between March and June 1918, and almost cracked the Western Allies' defensive front. American forces were particularly useful only later in the fighting during the Second Battle of the Marne when German forces were within 35 miles of Paris, earning the 3d Infantry Division its nickname, "Rock of the Marne." American casualties, though, were heavy

---

[61] The sector most used by US forces was the Vosges Mountains. See The Great War Society, "Sector Occupation," The Doughboy Center, http://www.worldwar1.com/dbc/sector.htm.
[62] "The Ludendorff Offensives, 21 March-18 July 1918," http://www.historyofwar.org/articles/battles_ludendorff.html
[63] "The Ludendorff Offensives, 21 March-18 July 1918," http://www.historyofwar.org/articles/battles_ludendorff.html.

(see the Chapter on casualties). The deaths per day were some of the heaviest ever sustained by American forces in combat.

It is safe to say that Germany and its allies were stronger militarily a year after American entry into World War I due to the stunning German victory over Russia. From the vantage point of March 1918, the US effort would have looked feeble – too little, too late.[64] Another view from March 1918 might have been that American entry into the war drove Germany to make the harsh peace with Russia, and launch the deadly attacks in France, making US entry the cause of the increased bloodshed. In hindsight, it is also safe to say that that German military strength was brittle, and that the corrosive effects of high casualties and economic blockade undermined the enemy at home. America and its allies withstood the Spring Offensives, although at times their prospects appeared bleak, and persevered. And, they won the war in the Allied counteroffensive that ensued. As the next vignette also demonstrates, in American history the enemy often gets stronger militarily after America finally decides to fight back, and before the final enemy defeat.

WORLD WAR II: Germany

In 1939, Germany went to war without a fully mobilized economy. Full mobilization came only after America's entry, and after it became clear that a quick German victory against the Soviet Union was impossible. In the spring of 1942, Hitler appointed Albert Speer as Minister of Armaments and War Production, and full mobilization began; however "total war" was only declared in 1943.[65]

---

[64] In an attempt to keep Russia in the war and fighting, the U.S. sent a mission under the lead of Elihu Root, former Secretary of War and Secretary of State, to Russia, "designed to try to salvage that country and its war effort." The mission clearly failed. Weigley 378-379.

[65] Marcel Baudot, et al, eds., *The Historical Encyclopedia of World War II* (New York: Greenwich House, 1984) 186, 192-198.

Consequently, German war production increased rapidly despite the efforts of the American and Allied bombing campaign, and the Allied victories in North Africa, Sicily, and Italy. Output from the German chemical industry grew 30%, automotive fuel production increased 85%, and electric power production grew by 26% from 1941 to 1944; in general, German armaments production more than doubled between 1941 and 1943.[66] Surprisingly, given the horrendous bombing raids, annual tank production more than quintupled from 5200 in 1941 to 27,300 in 1944.[67] Similarly, aircraft production more than tripled from 12,401 in 1941 to 40,593 in 1944.[68] By 1945, the German armed forces had suffered almost 4 million killed or missing, but still stood at 7.83 million at the end of the war, versus 7.3 million available at the end of 1941.

Aside from dramatically increasing its war production, Germany also came to rely more on fanatical devotion of shock troops beholden to the Nazi Party directly, rather than to the German State. These were the Schutzstaffeln, or SS, and its military units, the Waffen-SS. More than 30 divisions of these troops were raised and deployed after 1941, often being sent to the most critical spots on the fronts, where recklessness, brutality, and a willingness to commit mass sacrifice might be necessary.[69]

In short, Germany was stronger near the end of the war in manpower and production than it was when America began fighting back after the Pearl Harbor attacks. After suffering years of battlefield defeats, Hitler was still able to launch the Ardennes Offensive in December 1944 with 30 divisions and 1000 aircraft (including new jet fighters), causing 77,000 US casualties,

---

[66] Baudot 197-198.
[67] I.C.B. Dear and M.R.D. Foot, eds., *The Oxford Companion to World War II* (New York: Oxford University Press, 1995) 459.
[68] Baudot 397.
[69] Dear 1946, 1049. Baudot 435.

of which 19,000 were killed.[70] Like the critics of today's wars, one could have argued in December 1944 that America's willingness to fight back caused Germany to get stronger and more determined, as well as more fanatical in its actions.

WORLD WAR II: Japan

Like Germany, Japan only fully mobilized its economic resources after Pearl Harbor.[71] During the long American campaigns across the wide expanses of the Pacific, and the Allied campaigns in the remote China-Burma-India Theater, Japanese war production and manpower grew, despite the accumulating defeats on land, air, and sea. Japanese aircraft production more than quintupled from 5,090 in 1941 to 28,180 in 1944.[72] In 1944, Japan launched 72 warships versus 27 launched in 1941.[73] On 7 December 1941, the Japanese Army had a total of 51 combat divisions.[74] In August 1945, Japan had 55 divisions and 26 independent brigades totaling 1.9 million troops just in the home islands to defend against any Allied invasion.[75] After the surrender, the Allies would repatriate 3.5 million Japanese troops from abroad.[76]

Japan, therefore, also grew in strength despite US and Allied war efforts. As in the German case, US efforts made the Japanese more fanatical in their approach to war. American battlefield victories led the Japanese to launch suicidal *banzai* charges, with any survivors often committing suicide afterwards. On Saipan in 1944, only 1780 of more than 24,000 Japanese were taken prisoner; on Iwo Jima in early 1945, only a few hundred of the

---

[70] Dear 50; Baudot 72.
[71] Baudot 279.
[72] Baudot 397.
[73] Dear 610.
[74] Baudot 46.
[75] Dear 623.
[76] Baudot 261.

more than 20,000 Japanese defenders survived; on Okinawa, only 7400 of 97,000 Japanese troops surrendered.[77] Additionally, hundreds of civilians committed suicide on Saipan and Okinawa rather than submit to occupation. The Japanese also resorted to *kamikaze* waves – as many as 5000 suicide airplane pilots were used during the last year of the war – and to suicide boats, human torpedoes, and human aerial bombs that sank or damaged dozens of ships, thirty-six during just the Okinawa campaign.[78]

CAMBODIA

"Maybe we underestimated the anger $7 billion in bombing would unleash."
- Sydney Schanberg, *The Killing Fields* (1984)

Perhaps there is no better comparative historical vignette for this type of thinking than the single line coming from the character portraying the journalist Sydney Schanberg in the film, *The Killing Fields*, as he attempts to explain why the Communists of the Khmer Rouge would commit genocide against their own countrymen. In a few words, Schanberg absolves the mass murdering Communists and their ideology of any culpability, as well as absolving anyone, like himself, who opposed US efforts to stop Southeast Asian communism. To Schanberg, the Khmer Rouge's desire to create a peasant-based utopia, no matter the body count required, was a result of US military efforts. Akin to the Iraqi citations above, for Schanberg US efforts to stop the Khmer Rouge and their allies drove the communists into greater fanaticism and became the cause for their crimes.

CONCLUSION

Following Maureen Dowd's or Sydney Schanberg's formulation, the more we bombed Germany and Japan in World War II, the more we drove the enemies to produce and the stronger and more angrier they got, or so it

---

[77] Baudot 424-425; Dear 826.
[78] Dear 642.

would have seemed from a vantage point relatively late in the war. Fighting the Axis powers "over there" to keep them from being able to attack the U.S. at home might have seemed a chuckleheaded failure in December 1944 as the Nazi's launched the Ardennes Offensive and as the Marines and the Army began their suffering on Iwo Jima and Okinawa in 1945, especially as Japanese fanaticism increased almost beyond human understanding. After years of hard fighting, the enemy was materially stronger than at the beginning, and the US still suffered more than 38,000 killed in only a few months of fighting in these three battles near the end of the war.

Among the American military, it's a commonplace to say that the enemy gets a vote. American leaders and planners can control our own actions, but can only guess at the enemy's likely response. Consequently, we are frequently surprised by the enemy's ingenuity and tenacity, or the enemy's ability to gain in strength despite our best efforts. The vital question, then, is our own ability to adapt, to be flexible. The enemies in the current war are no different. When faced with an enemy surprise, or a change in enemy tactics, we expect the American military to adapt and overcome. Our military history is replete with successful battlefield and campaign adaptations.

Our history is also replete with those seeking to gain from every military setback. We should understand such rhetoric as having its roots in our domestic politics, and the search for even temporary domestic political advantage, sad as that may be.

ALLIES

Since WWI America has had long-term foreign allies who have assisted us in our wars, even in the absence of formal alliances. Indeed, in both World Wars the coalitions to which America belonged were simply known as "the Allies." The high point of the alliances was the treaty systems arising from the ashes of WWII – The North Atlantic Treaty Organization (NATO), the Southeast Asian Treaty Organization, and the Rio Treaty.

Despite treaties, relations with our long-term allies have not always been smooth. Not all interests and not all fears are common. France withdrew from NATO's integrated military command in 1966 due to disagreements over US control of the alliance, and only returned in March 2009. Moreover, NATO may have been the defender of the West against Soviet expansionism, and a defender of democracy, but the alliance comfortably sheltered dictatorships in the member states of Turkey, Portugal and Greece for many years.

The current narrative theme widely accepted is that "the US has gone it alone" in the War on Terror, particularly in Iraq. "Going it alone" is essentially identical to another frequently heard criticism that "the US has acted unilaterally." As usual in American politics, such themes develop in major election years.

CURRENT SITUATION

"The greatest position of strength is by exercising the best judgement in the pursuit of diplomacy, not in some trumped-up, so-called coalition of the bribed, the coerced, the bought and the extorted, but in a genuine coalition."
- Senator John Kerry, 9 March 2003[79]

---

[79] Mickey Kaus, "Two Hail Marys", *Slate*, 10 March 2003, http://www.slate.com/id/2079923/, accessed 16 June 2011.

"This president says he is a leader. Well Mr President, look behind you. There's hardly anyone there. It's not leadership if we haven't built the strongest alliance possible and America is going almost alone."
- Senator John Kerry, 21 October 2004[80]

*Dean's candidacy has been powered by his attack on what he calls **"the president's unilateral intervention in Iraq...."***

*Dean, who many polls show is the front-runner for the Democratic nomination, also charged that Bush "is about to be responsible for the fact that North Korea has become a nuclear power." He said, "There is no disgrace in having the most powerful nation on earth negotiate **bilaterally** with North Korea, while we also pursue a **multilateral** track."*

Dean assailed "the hard-liners in the Bush administration" for spurning the possibility of engaging in bilateral negotiations with the regime of Kim Jong II.

*In the speech, Dean blasted what he called Bush's **"go-it-alone approach** to every problem," as well as what he said was its **"radical unilateralism"** and "brash boastfulness."*

*"We find ourselves, too often, isolated and resented," he declared, charging that Bush administration officials **"seem to believe that nothing can be gained from working with nations that have stood by our side as allies for generations."** (emphasis added)[81]*

---

[80] Jamie Dettmer, "Candidates Clawing for Lead in Midwest as Kerry Cites Israel," *New York Sun*, 21 October 2004, http://www.nysun.com/national/candidates-clawing-for-lead-in-midwest-as-kerry/3526, accessed 16 June 2011.
[81] Tom Curry, "Dean Assails Bush 'Unilateralism,'" MSNBC.com, 15 December 2003, http://www.msnbc.msn.com/id/3718010/, accessed 16 June 2011.

In 2003, Democrats found a theme that they thought would resonate with voters – that the Bush Administration had adopted a "go-it-alone" approach, or unilateralism, that left America alone, isolated in world affairs. Consider the quote above where Howard Dean criticized President Bush for being simultaneously too unilateral and too multilateral, and saw both as a manifestation of a go-it-alone approach.

The criticism of "going it alone" and "unilateralism" became a constant through the 2004 and 2008 presidential campaigns, as the example below illustrates. This consistent narrative was accepted as common wisdom until the Obama inauguration of January 2009.

SENATOR CLINTON:
*"… [W]e have failed to reach out to countries, we have alienated our friends, and we have emboldened our enemies....I want to send a very clear message to the rest of the world that **the era of unilateralism**, preemption and arrogance of the Bush administration is over …."*(Emphasis added)

SENATOR OBAMA:
*"…I think it is absolutely true that either of us would step back from some of **the Bush unilateralism** that's caused so much damage."[82]* (Emphasis added)

HISTORICAL CONTEXT

What follows are brief descriptions of some of the more famous post-World War II coalitions that have gone to war with the US, and a comparison to the coalitions aiding the US in Iraq and Afghanistan.

---

[82] Both quotes come from Transcript, Democrat Presidential Primary Debate, 21 February 2008, Austin, TX, http://www.cnn.com/2008/POLITICS/02/21/debate.transcript/.

KOREA

Allied nations contributed about 40,000 troops to the US-led UN effort in the Korean War. In total, sixteen nations provided combat troops, five others provided medical units, and one provided critical basing support.[83]

Combat troops:

Australia	Netherlands
Belgium	New Zealand
Canada	Philippines
Colombia	South Africa
Ethiopia	Thailand
France	Turkey
Greece	United Kingdom
Luxembourg	United States

Naval Support, Air Bases, and Military Servicing and Repairs: Japan

Countries providing medical staff: Denmark, Italy, Norway, India, Sweden

---

[83] Max Hastings, 365-8. See also SparkNotes, *"The Korean War (1950-1953),"* http://www.sparknotes.com/history/american/koreanwar/section4.rhtml. The War Memorial of Korea in Seoul, just outside Gate 1 of the U.S. base at Yongsan, pays tribute to 21 UN members sending troops to the Korean War.

American GI giving a class to Ethiopian troops in Korea, May 1951
[84]

VIETNAM WAR

Most Americans would be surprised that Allies provided substantially more troops to the effort in Vietnam than to the Korean War. Allied troop strength peaked at 68,889 in 1969, with 31 Allied maneuver battalions deployed, plus support troops. South Korea maintained the equivalent of a corps in Vietnam for several years, with 50,000 troops deployed at the peak. In total, more than 40 nations supplied some level of assistance to South Vietnam, of which the eight below provided troops.[85]

US	South Korea
Australia	Spain
New Zealand	Taiwan
Philippines	Thailand

---

[84] ARC Identifier 541957 / Local Identifier 306-PS-51(9709)

Still Picture Records Section, Special Media Archives Services Division, College Park, MD. Item from Record Group 306: Records of the U.S. Information Agency, 1900 - 2003

[85] L.S. Collins, *Allied Participation in Vietnam* (Washinton, DC: Department of the Army, 1985) v, 23.

GULF WAR: DESERT STORM

The coalition-of-the-willing assembled by President George H.W. Bush in 1990-1991 was the largest American-led combat coalition since World War II, with 29 allies supplying 259,600 troops to the theatre. Even subtracting the 100,000 Saudi Arabian forces that were primarily defending their own territory where the Coalition mobilized, the 159,600 is still the largest contingent of allied troops supplied to a US-led post-WWII combat operation.[86]

US	Australia
Saudi Arabia	Niger
UK	Netherlands
Egypt	Spain
France	Senegal
Syria	Bahrain
Morocco	Belgium
Kuwait	Argentina
Oman	Afghanistan
Pakistan	Greece
United Arab Emirates	South Korea
Qatar	Poland
Bangladesh	Denmark
Canada	Hungary
Italy	Norway

---

[86] "Military Statistics: Gulf War Coalition Forces (most recent) by Country," http://www.nationmaster.com/graph/mil_gul_war_coa_for-military-gulf-war-coalition-forces.

THE CLINTON WARS

Below are examples from two of the US-led UN-sponsored operations of the mid-1990s, in what was hoped would be a new era of collective security born of the end of the Cold War, the collapse of the Soviet Union, and an apparently reinvigorated United Nations.

Somalia (UNISOM II), March 1993-March 1995

This coalition had 28,000 troops and police coming from 34 nations. Most of this total came from other coalition members, as only a small number of US logistical troops were provided to UNISOM II. An additional 17,700 US troops remained under the command of a US Joint Task Force separate from the UN command.[87]

Australia	Indonesia	Pakistan
Bangladesh	Ireland	Philippines
Belgium	Italy	South Korea
Botswana	Kuwait	Romania
Canada	Malaysia	Saudi Arabia
Egypt	Morocco	Sweden
France	Nepal	Tunisia
Germany	Netherlands	Turkey
Ghana	New Zealand	United Arab Emirates
Greece	Nigeria	United States
India	Norway	Zambia
		Zimbabwe

---

[87] See R. J. Norton, "Somalia II," in David A. Williams,ed., *Case Studies in Policy Making and Implementation* (Newport, Rhode Island: Naval War College, 2002) 167-182. See also UN Department of Peacekeeping – Somalia, *Somalia - UNOSOM II Facts and Figures*, http://www.un.org/Depts/dpko/dpko/co_mission/unosom2facts.html.

WARS THEN & NOW

United Nations Mission in Haiti (UNMIH), September 1993-June 1996

Thirty-five nations contributed troops and policemen to the occupation of Haiti, although each contribution was small, as the total number authorized was only 6065 troops and 847 policemen.[88]

Algeria	France	New Zealand
Antigua	Guatemala	Pakistan
Barbuda	Guinea Bissau	Philippines
Argentina	Guyana	Russia
Austria	Honduras	St Kitts and Nevis
Bahamas	India	St Lucia
Bangladesh	Ireland	Suriname
Barbados	Jamaica	Togo
Belize	Jordan	Trinidad and Tobago
Benin	Mali	Tunisia
Canada	Nepal	United States
Djibouti	Netherlands	

GLOBAL WAR ON TERROR

Below are the members of the go-it-alone "coalition of the bribed, the coerced, the bought and the extorted" that was presumably the fruit of President Bush's unilateralism that squandered alliance unity. Note than many of these nations sent troops to both Iraq and Afghanistan simultaneously.

First below is the list of 40 countries, including 16 NATO allies, sending troops to Iraq since 2003, as well as those countries providing critical support bases. The numbers peaked at more than 42,987 during the ground war in

---

[88] UN Department of Peacekeeping – Haiti, *Haiti: Facts and Figures*, http://www.un.org/Depts/dpko/dpko/co_mission/unmihfacts.html.

March-April 2003.[89] As late as December 2008, on the eve of the end of occupation after almost 6 years of warfare, there were still 24 allied nations and 6350 allied troops present.[90]

Iraq Coalition:

Countries providing basing or transit support without which the war effort would have been impossible:

- Jordan
- Kuwait
- Qatar
- Bahrain
- Saudi Arabia
- Germany
- Ireland

Other countries had large numbers of citizens working in Iraq as security or service contractors. One should consider these countries as unofficial members of the coalition:

- Peru
- Uganda
- South Africa
- Bangladesh

---

[89] Out of a total of 466,985 assembled for the invasion. See Adam J. Herbert, "Total Force in a Search for Balance," in *Warfighting*, Book 1, 14th edition (Maxwell AFB: Air University, December 2003), 188.

[90] The list of countries was compiled by reference to the almost 6 years of Iraq Weekly Status Reports issued by the US State Department, as well as the authors own notes and observations taken over five deployments to Iraq. For the December 2008 figures see State Department,"*Iraq Weekly Status Report,*" *3 December 2008,* http://2001-2009.state.gov/documents/organization/112944.pdf.

WARS THEN & NOW

Countries that provided troops, or "boots-on-the-ground" in Iraq:

Europe:
Albania
Britain*
Bosnia
Bulgaria*
Czech Republic*
Denmark*
Estonia*
Hungary*
Italy*
Latvia*
Lithuania*
Macedonia
Netherlands*
Norway*
Poland*
Portugal*
Romania*
Slovakia*
Spain*

Asia-Pacific:
Australia
Fiji**
Japan
Mongolia
New Zealand
Philippines
Singapore***
South Korea
Thailand
Tonga

Central Asia:
Armenia
Azerbaijan
Georgia
Kazakhstan
Moldova
Ukraine

Latin America:
Dominican Republic
El Salvador
Honduras
Nicaragua

Middle East:
Jordan****

* NATO members ** Under UN control *** Ship only ****Independently deployed

Nations sending troops to Afghanistan:

At least 49 allied nations have provided troops to Afghanistan in addition to the U.S., with peak allied troop strength at about 42,400.[91] Some of these nations had troops simultaneously in Iraq and Afghanistan.

Albania	El Salvador	Latvia	Singapore
Armenia	Estonia	Lithuania	Slovakia
Australia	Finland	Luxembourg	Slovenia
Austria	France	Macedonia	South Korea
Azerbaijan	Georgia	Malaysia	Spain
Belgium	Germany	Mongolia	Sweden
Bosnia	Greece	Montenegro	Switzerland
Bulgaria	Hungary	Netherlands	Tonga
Canada	Iceland	New Zealand	Turkey
Croatia	Ireland	Norway	Ukraine
Czech Republic	Italy	Poland	UAE
Denmark	Jordan	Portugal	UK
		Romania	

CONCLUSION

"Freedom is not free."

> - A common expression among the senior officers of our long-time allies, the Republic of Korea

America fought beside Western European allies for almost 100 years in WWI, WWII, Korea, and the Balkans. In earlier times, we celebrated those allies, as the World War I and II posters below illustrate.

---

[91] Ian S. Livingston, Heather L. Messera, and Michael O'Hanlon, *Afghanistan Index*, Brookings Institution, 31 May 2011, p. 4, for the current contributing nations.

In the 20 years since the Western victory in the Cold War, America has increasingly fought beside allies from other parts of the world beyond Western Europe, some of them nations experiencing a new freedom after the collapse of Soviet totalitarianism. This enduring pattern of behavior continues in Iraq and Afghanistan, contrary to the reigning narrative that comes across in the daily papers and on the news shows. Sadly, this narrative, required by domestic American politics, slights or insults the contributions of the allied nations in the War on Terror, denying those allies the attention and the accolades they deserve.

Alliance poster from World War I

World War II posters[93]

---

[93]All posters are from the National Archives Digital Records, available on-line: World War I: "Our Flags. Beat Germany. Support every flag that opposes Prussianism. Eat less of the food Fighters need, Deny yourself something. Waste Nothing.": ca. 1917 - ca. 1919, ARC Identifier 512685 / Local Identifier 4-P-247 Still Picture Records Section, Special Media Archives Services Division, College Park, MD. Item from Record Group 4: Records of the U.S. Food Administration, 1917 – 1920; THIS MAN IS YOUR FRIEND. CANADIAN: 1941 - 1945; ARC Identifier 515798 / Local Identifier 44-PA-2097F; Still Picture Records Section, Special Media Archives Services Division, College Park, MD; Item from Record Group 44: Records of the Office of Government Reports, 1932 - 1947. THIS MAN IS YOUR FRIEND. ENGLISHMAN: 1941 - 1945 ; ARC Identifier 515792 / Local Identifier 44-PA-2097; Still Picture Records Section, Special Media Archives Services Division, College Park, MD; Item from Record Group 44: Records of the Office of Government Reports, 1932 – 1947. THIS MAN IS YOUR FRIEND. AUSTRALIAN: 1941 - 1945, ARC Identifier 515796 / Local Identifier 44-PA-2097D; Still Picture Records Section, Special Media Archives Services Division, College Park, MD; Item from Record Group 44: Records of the Office of Government Reports, 1932 – 1947.

CASUALTIES

No fighting between individuals or between small groups of men – combat – is ever truly of low intensity. Wars, though, can be described as such, normally by the amount of death they produce on one or both sides. Two social scientists defined "war" as an armed conflict between nation-states that produces 1000 or more battle-connected deaths per year.[94] For conflicts like Iraq and Afghanistan, though, where the enemy is an elusive insurgent, no good name exists. One author counted more than fifty names for such conflicts.[95] The most commonly used names of the past few decades are "small wars" or "low intensity conflict," but no such name does justice to those fighting and dying.[96]

Like pornography, people know war when they see it. For most days during Operation Iraqi Freedom, the American people got to see a lot of the war as the media maintained a daily body count (at least during the Bush administration). Consequently, the nation collectively shuddered with the count-of-the-day as the cumulative total killed flashed across the page or the screen. So much death, it seemed.

Casualties in Afghanistan had no such prominence. Only in 2009, with the Obama administration's new emphasis on Afghanistan, and the dramatic reduction in violence in Iraq, did the media begin to focus some attention on the rising casualties in Afghanistan. By August 2011, though, the media still had not begun the daily drumming of the number killed since the war's inception as they had done in Iraq.[97]

---

[94] Melvin Small and J. David Singer, "Patterns in International Warfare, 1816-1980," *International War*, ed. Melvin Small and J. David Singer (Homewood, IL: Dorsey, 1985) 8-9.
[95] Howard Lee Dixon, *Low Intensity Conflict Overview, Definitions, and Policy Concerns* (Langley Air Force Base, VA: Center for Low Intensity Conflict, 1989) 50.
[96] For a discussion on categorizing and naming conflicts, see Waddell, , 2-12.
[97] As Byron York put it at the end of September 2009, "So far this month, 38 American troops have been killed in Afghanistan. For all of 2009, the number is 220 -

Historically, both the Iraq and Afghanistan campaigns are of relative low intensity, whether looking at the initial, brief ground maneuver wars, or the longer occupation phases. Perhaps it is easier for a democracy to face and absorb large-scale casualties that come in a brief period, than to face the burden of slow, protracted death played out publicly on each night's newscast.

Below are comparative descriptions of some of the bloody days and bloody battles in American history.

CIVIL WAR: Antietam

Union: 2108 killed in action, 9540 wounded, 753 missing
Confederate: 1674 killed in action, 8039 wounded and missing

The total casualties for this battle were 22,114, almost all of which occurred on 17 September 1862. With 3782 Americans killed on both sides, this is the bloodiest single day in American military history.[98]

WORLD WAR I

The US entered the war by Congressional declaration on 6 April 1917, only 5 months after President Wilson won re-election with the campaign slogan, "He kept us out of war." In today's vernacular, this would have been

---

- more than any other single year and more than died in 2001, 2002, 2003, and 2004 combined. With casualties mounting, the debate over U.S. policy in Afghanistan is sharp and heated. The number of arrivals at Dover is increasing. But the journalists who once clamored to show the true human cost of war are nowhere to be found." Byron York, "Without Bush, Media Lose Interest in War Caskets," *The Examiner*, 29 September 2009, http://www.washingtonexaminer.com/politics/Without-Bush-media-lose-interest-in-war-caskets-8310113-62427012.html.
[98] "The Battle of Antietam," http://www.nps.gov/anti/historyculture/upload/Battle%20history.pdf; "Antietam: Casualties," http://www.history.army.mil/StaffRide/Antietam/Casualties.htm

President's Wilson's "war of choice, not necessity." In less than a year of combat, the US suffered the following casualties:

Killed in action: 53,402
Non-battle deaths: 63,114
Wounded: 204,002[99]

Over a year, these casualties resulted in a rate of more than 319 deaths **per day**, and 559 per day wounded. Since most of the US fighting occurred after March 1918, the rate per day during the heaviest fighting was considerably higher. In the Meuse-Argonne offensive in October 1918, just a few weeks before the war ended, American casualties peaked at 6000 killed in a single week, and two other weeks in October 1918 exceeded 5000 killed each.[100]

Civilians killed in the Japanese attack, eight miles from Pearl Harbor[101]

WORLD WAR II: Pearl Harbor

Servicemen and civilians killed: 2403. Wounded: 1178.[102]

---

[99] CRS, 2.
[100] Gary Mead, *The Doughboys: America and the First World War* (New York: The Overlook Press) 348.
[101] "Captured: The Pacific and Adjacent Theaters in WWII," PLOG: Photo Blogs From the Denver Post, *Denver Post*, 18 March 2010, http://blogs.denverpost.com/captured/2010/03/18/captured-blog-the-pacific-and-adjacent-theaters/1547/?source=ARK_plog.

WORLD WAR II: Continual Slaughter: The Bulge, Iwo Jima, Okinawa

After three years of already bloody warfare in two Pacific theaters, the China-Burma-India Theater, North Africa, Italy, and France, American casualties soared in 1945. Three battles stand out for their ferocity as more than 38,000 American soldiers died in the few weeks that these battles encompassed.

The Battle of the Bulge, 16 December 1944-25 January 1945

By mid-December 1944, Germany had suffered months of defeats on both the Western and Eastern Fronts since the Normandy invasion of 6 June. Yet they secretly assembled a force of 30 divisions and 1000 aircraft to launch a surprise counter-offensive against the Western allies in the thinly guarded area of the Ardennes Forest of Belgium.

Killed in action: 19,000
Wounded, captured, missing: 62,000[103]

This was the costliest battle in American history in terms of total casualties, with a death rate of 463.4 per day. Consider the combination of failed planning, failed intelligence gathering, and underestimating of the enemy that led to this reversal. Using today's exacting political and journalistic standards, the Battle of the Bulge would be seen as a monumental disaster, leading to calls for the dismissal of the many generals we now consider heroes, and certainly to a crescendo of vilification of President Roosevelt for his failed leadership so many years into an expensive and bloody war. Moreover, to paraphrase a criticism so frequently heard about the Iraq

---

[102] Dear 872.
[103] Veterans of the Battle of the Bulge, http://www.battleofthebulge.org/; see also Donna Miles, "Battle of the Bulge Remembered 60 Years Later," American Forces Press Service, http://www.defense.gov/news/newsarticle.aspx?id=24591.

campaign and the 9-11 attacks, during this battle we were occupying Belgium and fighting Germans, nations in no way connected to the 7 December attack at Pearl Harbor. As the slaughter in the Ardennes was ending, a slaughter in the Pacific was days away from beginning.

Iwo Jima, 19 February-26 March 1945

In the fighting on the tiny island of Iwo Jima, near the end of World War II, US forces suffered horrendous casualties in a five-week battle. The planning indicated a 14-day campaign that ultimately lasted 36 days.[104] About one-third of the invasion forces hitting the beaches became casualties. American deaths were about 700 per square mile of territory conquered.[105]

Killed in action: 6,821,
Wounded: 19,217
Battle fatigue: 2648[106]

The 2nd Battalion, 28th Marine Regiment, was almost wiped out. Of 1688 Marines in the battalion, originals and replacements, 1511 were killed or evacuated due to wounds. Of the 177 that re-deployed from the island, 91 had been wounded and returned to duty.[107]

Even though these figures for such a short battle astound, the death rate per day is less than 190, compared to the 319 per day in World War I. Those killed in the five-week battle in 1945 compare to about eight days of losses in

---

[104] Dear 604.

[105] Colonel Joseph H. Alexander, U.S. Marine Corps (Ret), "CLOSING IN: Marines in the Seizure of Iwo Jima," *Marines in World War II Commemorative Series*, http://www.nps.gov/archive/wapa/indepth/extcontent/usmc/pcn-190-003131-00/sec7.htm.

[106] Richard F. Newcomb, *Iwo Jima* (New York: Henry Holt, 1965) 296-297.

[107] James Bradley with Ron Powers, *Flags of Our Fathers* (New York: Bantam, 2000) 246.

October 1918, and were less than half of the 463 killed per day in the Battle of the Bulge. Nonetheless, so many deaths for so little terrain at a time when Americans could sense the coming end of the war provoked outrage at home. The Hearst newspapers ran editorials denouncing the losses even as the battle was on-going, and clippings reached Marines still fighting.[108]

An even bigger bloodbath, though, was beginning. The first kamikaze struck off the coast of Okinawa on 18 March, as the mopping up was still underway on Iwo.

Graves on Iwo Jima, April 1945[109]

Okinawa, 1 April 1945-29 June 1945

Okinawa was the largest and deadliest battle in the Pacific campaigns, for both sides. It gave a preview of what could be expected in any invasion of the Japanese home islands.

Killed in action: 12,513
Wounded: 36,631
Battle fatigue and other non-battle casualties: 26,000[110]

---

[108] Alexander, http://www.nps.gov/archive/wapa/indepth/extcontent/usmc/pcn-190-003131-00/sec7.htm.

[109] PLOG, Denver Post.

[110] For killed and wounded, see Dear 836; for fatigue and non-battle casualties, see "Battle of Okinawa," http://www.globalsecurity.org/military/facility/okinawa-battle.htm.

Of the dead, 4900 were sailors killed mostly by the suicide of the *kamikaze* pilots, which sank 36 ships and damaged 368. Also killed was the invasion commander, LTG Simon Buckner.

We remember Iwo Jima more than Okinawa or any other Pacific battle because of the iconic flag-raising photograph, which the Roosevelt and Truman administrations immediately seized upon as the theme of the "Mighty 7th" war-bond tour, which raised $26.3 billion even as the slaughter on Okinawa was proceeding.[111] It was a useful response to the Hearst editorials.[112]

VIETNAM: LZ X-ray and LZ Albany

US Army forces came up against the People's Army of Vietnam (PAVN) in a large-scale battle for the first time in November 1965. The popular political narrative about Vietnam encountered frequently even today is that the conflict in Vietnam pitted US and South Vietnamese forces against a home grown insurgency armed with cast-off weapons that the insurgents picked up on the battlefield. The truth is that North Vietnamese regulars were present in regimental strength before US arrival, and many of the fiercest battles were fought between regular soldiers of both sides.

From 14 through 20 November 1965, US soldiers of the 1st Battalion and 2nd Battalion, 7th Cavalry and the 2nd Battalion, 5th Cavalry, all belonging to the 1st Air Cavalry Division fought the 66th and 33rd PAVN regiments, first at Landing Zone (LZ) X-ray, 14-17 November, and then at LZ Albany, 17-20 November. The LZ X-ray battle was immortalized by the movie, *We Were Soldiers*, based on the book, *We Were Soldiers Once... and Young*, by LTG (Ret) Harold G.

---

[111] Bradley, *Flags*, 294.
[112] Alexander, http://www.nps.gov/archive/wapa/indepth/extcontent/usmc/pcn-190-003131-00/sec7.htm.

Moore and Joe Galloway. Moore commanded the 1st Battalion during the battle, and Galloway was present as a correspondent.

Killed in action: 234 (including four originally listed as missing)
Wounded: 242[113]

PEACE, 1980-2001, vs. WAR, 2001-2008

During the last decade of the Cold War, 1980-1989, US forces lost a total of 81 killed in hostile actions, and another 294 killed in terrorist attacks. On average in this decade, with an average of 2.2 million on active duty, the average number of deaths per year due to accidents was 1320.8; the average per year due to homicide was 109.2, and the average for suicides per year was 248.2.[114]

In the "Peace Dividend" years of the 1990s when most of our military actions were renamed "Peace Operations," the strength of the armed forces declined to about 1.4 million on active duty. In this decade, the US lost 148 to hostile action, and 89 to terrorist attacks.[115] The average deaths due to accidents declined to an annual average of 604.2.

In the war-plagued first decade of the new millennium, during the first three years of the War on Terror, accidental deaths continued to be greater than deaths from either hostile action or terrorists attacks. In the first year of the Iraq campaign, 2003, with its ground invasion, military accidents claimed 576 lives worldwide, versus 343 lost to enemy contact in both Iraq and Afghanistan combined. By 2008, after the success of the Surge in Iraq, accidents again surpassed combat and terrorist-caused deaths worldwide,

---

[113] LTG Harold G. Moore (Ret.) and Joseph L. Galloway, *We Were Soldiers Once...And Young,* http://www.lzxray.com/day3.htm and http://www.lzxray.com/albany2.htm.
[114] All casualty figures from 1980 onwards from CRS.
[115] The CRS lists the deaths in the Somalia intervention as terrorist attacks. Of the 148 lost to hostile action in the 1990s, 147 were lost in 1991 in the Gulf War.

470 to 352. Average annual deaths due to accidents continued to fall to 528.9 during the decade, despite the higher operations tempo due to combat deployments. The average annual deaths due to hostile fire and terrorism during the Global War on Terror from 2001 to 2008 was 428.6, substantially less than the average annual loss to accidents, but with peak combat deaths of 739 in both 2004 and 2005, 761 in 2006, and 847 in 2007 at the height of the Iraqi Surge.[116] In 2010, as the Afghan Surge reached its peak troop deployment, fatalities in Operation Enduring Freedom peaked at 499, or which 34 were from non-hostile causes.[117]

Suicides in Peace Dividend Years of the 1990s v. War Years of the 2000s[118]

Despite the hardship of war and multiple deployments from home, average annual suicides continued to fall in the first eight years of the 2000s, with an average 183.8 per year, compared to an average of 209.7 in the far more peaceful 1990s. However, suicides rose sharply in 2007 and 2008 to 211 and 235, respectively. While these two years are significantly higher in absolute and percentage terms from the preceding war years, the 2007 total is still less than the totals for 1990-1995 after the Cold War was clearly won, a period punctuated by the comparatively brief combat deployments for Desert Shield, Desert Storm, and Somalia, and by the general downsizing of all the services. Even the 2008 total of 235 is still less than the total suicides in 1991, 1992, 1993 and 1995.

The Terrorist Attacks of 11 September 2001
Killed: 2975[119]

---

[116] CRS does not list any deaths due to terrorism in these years. The most recent CRS report before printing – 26 February 2010 – did not update the data for accidents or terrorist deaths for 2009 or 2010.

[117] Ian S. Livingston, Heather L. Messera, and Michael O'Hanlon, *Afghanistan Index*, Brookings Institution, 31 May 2011, p. 11

[118] CRS 7, 8.

Iraq: Operation Iraqi Freedom and Operation New Dawn (as of 16 June 2011)

Killed: 4466 (3514 killed in action, 952 non-battle deaths)
Wounded: 32,120

Afghanistan: Operation Enduring Freedom (as of 16 June 2011)[120]
Killed: 1610 (1264 killed in action, 346 non-battle deaths; includes those killed in adjacent areas)
Wounded: 12,002

In both Iraq and Afghanistan, the main killer of US troops has been improvised explosive devices (IEDs) made in the early years from left-over munitions such as artillery shells and mines. In the last three years, greater quantities of homemade explosives (HME) have been used.

CONCLUSION

At the time of writing (June 2011), the US has lost about 11% less killed in Iraq and Afghanistan combined in the almost ten years since the 9-11 attacks – 6076 - than were lost in the five weeks on Iwo Jima - 6821. The total US deaths from the past ten years are equivalent to a mere nineteen days of US combat in World War I. Advances in military protective equipment, medical evacuation, military medicine, and military tactics have certainly contributed to lower casualties. The nature of the enemy and of the war, though, has been the major factor. The Iraqi and Afghan campaigns have not seen anything remotely like the fixed flanks, massed artillery and machine guns and frontal assaults of WWI or Iwo Jima, or the large battles of Korea and

---

[119] "Official 9/11 Death Toll Climbs by One," CBS News, 10 July 2008, http://www.cbsnews.com/stories/2008/07/10/national/main4250100.shtml.
[120] Iraq and Afghanistan casualty figures come from "Defenselink Casualty Report," 16 June 2011, http://www.defense.gov/news/casualty.pdf.

Vietnam. Although savage, the combat has occurred between small groups of combatants in brief engagements normally measured in hours – small scale, or "low intensity." For a nation with the size and wealth of the U.S., losing in the current campaigns is not a question of ability to raise and maintain forces, and sustain casualties, but rather one of political volition.[121] You cannot win in combat, a battle, a campaign, or a war if you simply give up.

---

[121] In April 2007, the Senate Majority Leader, SEN Harry Reid of Nevada, declared the war in Iraq was lost, before the Surge had even been implemented. Similarly, in November 2009, former Senator Fred Thompson declared the war in Afghanistan lost although the US had lost only 923 killed. See "Reid: Iraq War lost, US can't win," http://www.msnbc.msn.com/id/18227928/, 20 April 2007; Ben Smith, "Fred Thompson: Afghan war 'has been lost,'" http://www.politico.com/blogs/bensmith/1109/Fred_Thompson_Afghan_war_has_been_lost.html, 19 November 2009.

VICTORY

To a soldier engaged in individual combat, winning is a matter of life, death, or serious injury. Better you win and the other guy lose. To a soldier in a small unit engagement, the same is true, although his buddies' lives are also at risk. For larger units engaged in a battle, losing involves death and injuries, and can mean dishonor, capture, and retreat. Losing at this level harms those friendly units on your flanks, and can damage your overall cause. At the highest levels of military strategy, victories in engagements small to large determine whether you can deliver the desired outcome of the war. In short, to soldiers from privates to generals, winning is paramount. At the level of relationships between nations managed by political leaders, it is all but impossible to win strategically by choosing to lose on the battlefield. The contrasting quotes below speak for themselves.

THE CURRENT SITUATION

"I'm always worried about using the word 'victory,' because, you know, it invokes this notion of Emperor Hirohito coming down and signing a surrender to MacArthur."

- President Obama, July 2009 [122]

HISTORICAL CONTEXT

WORLD WAR II

"You ask, what is our aim? I can answer in one word: It is victory, victory at all costs, victory in spite of all terror, victory, however long and hard the road may be; for without victory, there is no survival."

---

[122] Note: Emperor Hirohito was not present at the signing ceremony for the surrender of Japan. "Obama: 'Victory' Not Necessarily Goal in Afghanistan," http://www.foxnews.com/politics/2009/07/23/obama-victory-necessarily-goal-afghanistan/.

- Churchill on the question of victory[123]

"From the Far East I send you one single thought, one sole idea--written in red on every beachhead form Australia to Tokyo--There is no substitute for victory!"

- MacArthur's message from the Far East[124]

Korea

"...there is a right kind of victory and a wrong kind of victory...."

- From Truman's statement explaining his 11 April 1951 relief of GEN MacArthur, for "rank insubordination."

"The American tradition had always been that once our troops are committed to battle, the full power and means of the nation should be mobilized and dedicated to fight for victory – not for stalemate or compromise."

- From MacArthur's response to his relief. [125]

"The only thing that can defeat us is our own state of mind. We can lose if we falter....The things we believe in most deeply are under relentless attack. We have the great responsibility of saving the basic moral and spiritual values of our civilization. We have started out well——with a program for peace that is unparalleled in history. If we believe in ourselves and the faith we profess, we will stick to that job until it is victoriously finished....We must reject the

---

[123] From Churchill's first speech as Prime Minister, http://library.thinkquest.org/CR0212881/wcfirspe.html.

[124] This famous quote was learned by all Plebes at West Point for decades.

[125] The two preceding quotes come from an email from James Zobel of the MacArthur Center, Norfolk, VA, to COL Rick Waddell, 6 October 2009; excerpted from the MacArthur exhibits reference Truman's relief of MacArthur.

counsels of defeat and despair. We must have the determination to complete the great work for which our men have laid down their lives."

- Truman's State of the Union Speech, 9 Jan 1952:

Vietnam

"It is very difficult to tell a young soldier, 'Go out there and fight, perhaps die, for a good bargaining position.'"[126]

- John P. Roche, special assistant to President Johnson, writing in 1968 that the basic issue in Vietnam was whether a free society could fight a limited war for limited objectives.

The Global War on Terror

"As the central front in the global war on terror, success in Iraq is an essential element in the long war against the ideology that breeds international terrorism. Unlike past wars, however, victory in Iraq will not come in the form of an enemy's surrender, or be signaled by a single particular event -- there will be no Battleship Missouri, no Appomattox."

- President George W. Bush, November 2005[127]

CONCLUSION

In the current wars, a paramount domestic American political question is the definition of victory – the "right kind of victory" - and whether we will "stick to that job until it is victoriously finished" consistent with our oft-stated national interests and worthy of the sacrifices that our armed forces have made. Or, do the efforts now underway in Iraq and Afghanistan and the

---

[126] "No Substitute for Victory," *The Washington Times*, 27 July 2009, http://www.washingtontimes.com/news/2009/jul/27/no-substitute-for-victory/.
[127] "No Substitute for Victory," *The Washington Times*, 27 July 2009, http://www.washingtontimes.com/news/2009/jul/27/no-substitute-for-victory/.

casualties sustained seek only stalemate, compromise or a good bargaining position? Sadly, as a nation, we still seem deeply ambivalent.

PRISONERS

Dealing with prisoners has been controversial in several of America's wars, either during the war or afterwards, or both. Since the current war began on 9-11, allegations have arisen that the U.S. has routinely used torture and abuse, and this became a major theme during the 2004 presidential campaign. Closing the prison camp for terrorists at Guantanamo was a major issue in the 2008 campaign. Like those opposing the Iraq Campaign, opponents of the Global War on Terror often referred to Guantanamo as the No. 1 recruitment tool for terrorists, as if the terrorists had had major problems recruiting and mounting attacks before 9-11.

Treatment of prisoners after a battle has a long history. In ancient times, many such prisoners simply became slaves to the conquerors, when left alive. With the advent of chivalry came the custom of yielding to a foe with the prisoner later being ransomed or swapped. Paroles, ransoms, or swaps gave an incentive for surrender, thus avoiding the costs of an assault for both sides, and the prospect of a long imprisonment for the losers. Additionally, paroling prisoners relieved the capturing force of the cost of maintaining prisoners. Like parole, the exchange of prisoners allowed the return of one's countrymen held by the enemy, and served as an incentive for foes to treat prisoners well in captivity in hopes of similar treatment for their fellow soldiers in enemy hands.

Customs for the treatment of prisoners of war (POWs) were later codified in the Hague Conventions (1899 and 1907) and in the Geneva Conventions (1929 and 1949). As seen in the recent debates in the United States, gaps still exist with respect to individuals from armed groups that are not members of organized national armed forces from countries or territories and those that do not adhere to either the customary restraints or the formal Geneva treaty requirements; so -called "illegal combatants."

The issues faced in the current war are not unique. The following vignettes serve to illustrate the changing nature of how Americans have treated prisoners, and the politics that went with such treatment. This is not merely the province of JAG lawyers, civilian activists, and Federal judges, but is of concern to all American soldiers, and the citizen families that send their loved ones off to war.

CURRENT SITUATION

"If I read this to you and did not tell you that it was an FBI agent describing what Americans had done to prisoners in their control, you would most certainly believe this must have been done by Nazis, Soviets in their gulags, or some mad regime —Pol Pot or others— that had no concern for human beings. Sadly, that is not the case. This was the action of Americans in the treatment of their prisoners."

- Senator Durbin, referring to treatment of prisoners at Guantanamo[128]

"While a Pentagon investigation acknowledged patterns of abuse at Abu Ghraib, it sought to characterize these incidents as isolated and the actions of a small group of rogue soldiers. National leaders and the media, however, sought to determine if these incidents were based on a larger policy of permissible torture as defined by the Department of Defense (and possibly emanating from the White House) in regard to the war on terror."

- Elizabeth Jewell, "George W. Bush," *U.S. Presidents Factbook*[129]

---

[128] The Congressional Record – Senate, S6594, 14 June 2005, http://frwebgate.access.gpo.gov/cgi-bin/getpage.cgi?dbname=2005_record&page=S6594&position=all.

[129] Jewell 458.

REVOLUTIONARY WAR

"Major André ought to be considered a spy from the enemy, and that agreeable to the law and usage of nations, it is their opinion he ought to suffer death."

> - Verdict against British Major John André, captured after meeting Benedict Arnold to plot the surrender of West Point to the British Army[130]

Well before the winning of the American Republic, treatment of prisoners was already embedded in international custom. George Washington himself had been a prisoner in the French and Indian War, and had received a parole along with his men.[131]

Major André was "somewhat disguised" in civilian clothes and traveled under an assumed name after his meeting with Arnold and before his capture on 23 September 1780. General Washington quickly appointed a military tribunal to try André. Among the members were the European officers Lafayette and Steuben. After a quick trial, the tribunal convicted André and sentenced him to death on 29 September. André was considered a gentleman and a model prisoner. His only request was to be shot like a soldier; however, Washington denied this request and hanged André on 2 October strictly in accordance with the treatment customarily meted out to spies under the "law and usage of nations."[132]

---

[130] William Roscoe Thayer, *George Washington* (originally published 1922, Amazon Kindle edition), location 1033-1035.

[131] Thayer, locations 167-169.

[132] The arch-Nazi Herman Göring also requested the honor of being shot as a soldier. Upon denial of his request, he committed suicide rather than suffer the indignity of being hanged.

André's treatment seems summary in comparison with modern standards that require many years of deliberation over process and perhaps years more for trial of the 9-11 terrorists.

CIVIL WAR

"...it is hard on our men held in Southern prisons not to exchange them, but it is humanity to those left in the ranks to fight our battles. Every man released on parole or otherwise, becomes an active soldier against us at once, either directly or indirectly. If we commence a system of exchange which liberates all prisoners taken, we will have to fight on until the whole South is exterminated. If we hold those caught they amount to no more than dead men."

- General Grant in a letter to General Butler, 18 August 1864[133]

85. War-rebels are persons within an occupied territory who rise in arms against the occupying or conquering army, or against the authorities established by the same. If captured, they may suffer death, whether they rise singly, in small or large bands, and whether called upon to do so by their own, but expelled, government or not. They are not prisoners of war; nor are they if discovered and secured before their conspiracy has matured to an actual rising or to armed violence.

- Article 85 of General Orders No. 100 (the Lieber Code) of the Union Army, 24 April 1863.[134]

In the American Civil War, both sides accused the other of mistreatment of prisoners. The fate of both Union and Confederate prisoners worsened after

---

[133] Jerry Staub, "Sherman's Inability to Liberate the South's Most Notorious Prison," eHistory Archive, Ohio State University, 2011, http://ehistory.osu.edu/uscw/features/articles/ArticleView.cfm?AID=69.

[134] See "The Lieber Code of 1863," Air War College, http://www.au.af.mil/au/awc/awcgate/law/liebercode.htm#section4.

the Union refused further prisoner exchanges in 1864. Shipments of medicine and food to the South were under blockade restrictions, and this worsened the lot of all Southerners and their prisoners. Union territory experienced no such privations, but Southern prisoners in the North nonetheless suffered, especially during winter. In late 1864, in response to Southern treatment of prisoners at Andersonville, the Union Secretary of War, Edwin M. Stanton, ordered retaliation and some Union prison camps reduced their POWs to only bread and water, further weakening them in the coming winter. Consequently, some 26,000 Southern prisoners died in Union hands, whereas some 22,500 Union prisoners died in the South. Sources vary, but only about 8% of all of the Union prisoners in Southern hands died despite the widespread privations in the South, most notoriously at Andersonville where the death rate was 30% and about 12,000 of the Andersonville inmates died (more than 50% of the total deaths of Union POWs). In the North, 12-13% of all Southern POWs died, despite the material abundance of the North. The worst Union prisons included Elmira, New York (or "Hellmira" to its inmates), where 24-25% died, and Camp Douglas near Chicago, and Rock Island, Illinois where 16-20% died.[135]

In the North, President Lincoln suspended the writ of habeas corpus, and empowered his generals to use military tribunals to silence or mute opposition to the war. Thousands of his opponents went to jail.[136] In perhaps

---

[135] "Prisoner Exchange," Spartacus Educational, http://www.spartacus.schoolnet.co.uk/USACWexchange.htm. The Congressional Research Service reports 26,000-31,000 deaths of Confederate prisoners, versus an estimated 74,524 Confederate battle deaths. See CRS, 3. This debate was acrimonious during the Civil War, and in the decades afterward. The Union figures quoted seem to have come from an 1866 report to Congress by the Secretary of War Stanton, but the Army's Chief of the Record and Pension Office reported in 1903 that 30,218 Union prisoners had died in Southern prisons. See James Ford Rhodes, *History of the United States of America: From the Compromise of 1850 to the McKinley-Bryan Campaign of 1896*, vol 5: 1864-1866, Chapter XXIX (New York: Macmillan, 1904; 1920 edition), cited at http://tigger.uic.edu/~rjensen/prisons.htm.
[136] John S. Bowman, ed., *The Civil War Almanac* (New York: W. H. Smith, 1983) 353.

the most notorious case that rose to the Supreme Court, a military tribunal appointed by Major General Ambrose Burnside convicted a former Ohio Congressman, Clement Vallandigham, for treason for his outspoken opposition to the war, and sentenced him to confinement in a military prison. The Supreme Court rejected Vallandigham's request for review on the grounds that the military commissions were not among the enumerated list of courts over which the Supreme Court had the power of judicial review.[137] In another notorious case, Union General Benjamin Butler ordered a civilian, William Mumford, tried by military tribunal, and then hanged him for tearing down a U.S. flag in Union-occupied New Orleans. Being an irregular combatant of any kind caught behind the lines was perilous, as the Lieber Code (quoted above) makes clear. Article 82 of the Lieber Code allowed for summary treatment of irregulars as "highway robbers or pirates." Summary treatment usually meant swift death by the captors.

Issuing Rations at Andersonville[138]

---

[137] Ex Parte Vallandigham, 68 U.S. 1 Wall. 243 243 (1863), http://supreme.justia.com/us/68/243/case.html.
[138] Pictures of the Civil War, Select Audiovisual Records, National Archives and Records Administration, "Prisoners and Prisons," No. 72, Issuing rations.

After the war, in an example of victors' justice, the Confederate commandant of Andersonville, Major Henry Wirz, was tried by a Union military tribunal for war crimes, and hanged. He is the only American convicted of war crimes to ever suffer this fate in the United States.[139] No Union commandant was ever tried.

WORLD WAR II

"I've interviewed well over 1,000 combat veterans. Only one of them said he shot a prisoner….Perhaps as many as one-third of the veterans I've talked to, however, related incidents in which they saw other GIs shooting unarmed German prisoners who had their hands up."
- Stephen E. Ambrose, *Citizen Soldiers*[140]

"The American aircraft which destroyed the convoy reinforcing the Lae garrison in New Guinea, 3 March 1943, machine-gunned the survivors swimming in the water, reporting: 'It was a grisly task, but a military necessity since Japanese soldiers do not surrender and, within swimming distance off shore, they could not be allowed to land and join the Lae garrison.'"
- Paul Johnson, *Modern Times*[141]

Lawful combatants are subject to capture and detention as prisoners of war by opposing military forces. ***Unlawful combatants are likewise subject to***

Andersonville Prison, Ga., August 17, 1864. Photographed by A. J. Riddle. 165-A-445, http://www.archives.gov/research/military/civil-war/photos/images/civil-war-072.jpg.
[139] "Andersonville," The History Channel, http://www.history.com/topics/andersonville. See also Bowman, 392.
[140] Stephen E. Ambrose, *Citizen Soldiers: The U.S. Army from the Normandy Beaches to the Bulge to the Surrender of Germany, June 7, 1944 to May 7, 1945* (New York: Simon and Schuster, 1997) 352.
[141] Paul Johnson, *Modern Times* (New York: Harper Perennial, 1992) 428-429. Hereafter "Johnson."

capture and detention, but, in addition, they are subject to trial and punishment by military tribunals for acts which render their belligerency unlawful. The spy who secretly and without uniform passes the military lines of a belligerent in time of war, seeking to gather military information and communicate it to the enemy, or an enemy combatant who without uniform comes secretly through the lines for the purpose of waging war by destruction of life or property, are familiar examples of belligerents who are generally deemed not to be entitled to the status of prisoners of war, but to be offenders against the law of war subject to trial and punishment by military tribunals. (Emphasis added)

> - U.S. Supreme Court, *Ex Parte Quirin*, rejecting an application for writ of habeas corpus by eight German spies caught infiltrating the United States (including one American citizen). The prisoners sought to be tried in civil court, alleging that the President had no authority to try them in a military tribunal. President Roosevelt's order creating the tribunal had denied the prisoners access to civilian courts; the tribunal proceedings were conducted partially in secret.[142]

World War II is considered the "good war" even by many in the perpetual anti-war, anti-U.S. crowd because the evil confronted was so manifest and clear. The generation that fought the war is commonly referred to as the "Greatest Generation." Yet, some of the behavior of this generation, whose experience is within living memory and which still impacts heavily on our understanding of war in general, toward prisoners would be shockingly unacceptable by the standards to which we hold America's forces today.

Only .7% of the Americans prisoners in the hands of the Germans died in captivity. Surprisingly, a higher percentage - 1% - of Germans POWs in American hands died, even though 400,000 Germans were sent to camps in

---

[142] Ex Parte Quirin, 317 U. S. 1 (1942), http://supreme.justia.com/us/317/1/.

the U.S. where there was no lack of shelter, food, and medical care. Many of the deaths presumably came with the large influx of Germans taken prisoner in the last few months of the war who were placed in large makeshift camps. The official Army historian came to describe the American treatment of German POWs near the end of the war as "inhumanity." [143] The brutality against Americans in the Pacific was far worse, with 34-38% of Americans dying in Japanese camps.[144] Conversely, few Japanese soldiers chose to surrender, as culturally this was seen as unacceptable disgrace. Historians, though, record that Allied treatment of those Japanese that did surrender was often deadly.[145]

Malmedy

On 17 December 1944, during the Battle of the Bulge, a unit of the 1st SS Panzer Division murdered 84 American prisoners. When the battle lines shifted, American forces found the frozen corpses. The Americans used German prisoners to help dig out and recover the dead. Any German prisoners in the area found wearing American paratroop boots - indicating that at a minimum they had robbed dead Americans - were then made to march in the snow barefooted until their feet were frozen solid, thus requiring amputation. After the war, U.S. military tribunals tried 73 of the

---

[143] Ambrose, 361, 363.

[144] Percentages of prisoner deaths from Ambrose, 361; number of Germans sent to the U.S. from Ambrose, 362.

[145] For a recent example, see Niall Ferguson, "Prisoner Taking and Prisoner Killing in the Age of Total War: Towards a Political Economy of Military Defeat," *War in History*, 2004, 11 (2): 148–192. The historian William Manchester, a veteran of the Okinawa campaign, noted in *Goodbye, Darkness: A Memoir of the Pacific War* (Boston: Little Brown and Company, 1980), p. 184, that after Marines on Guadalcanal heard that Japanese troops were beheading Marine POWs, "From then until the end of the war, neither side took prisoners except under freakish circumstances."

former SS troopers for the Malmedy massacre.[146] The U.S. convened no courts-martial for the shooting of German prisoners.[147]

The Dostler Trial

In one of the earliest war crimes trials after the Axis surrender, a German general was tried by the victors in the same region as his offense and then shot. From 8 to 12 October 1945, an American military tribunal in Rome tried German General Anton Dostler, commander of the 75th German Army Corps, and sentenced him to death by firing squad for ordering the execution of 15 American soldiers caught behind enemy lines in Italy while conducting a sabotage raid – that is, for mistreatment of POWs under the Hague Convention of 1907 and the customs of war. The American tribunal was established under the provisions of a local circular published by the commander of U.S. forces in the Mediterranean Theater of Operations. Dostler's defense council argued that the tribunal did not conform to the requirements of the Geneva Convention, but his objection was overruled by the tribunal itself relying on longstanding practice and custom.[148] Dostler was shot in Italy on 1 December 1945.

---

[146] Ambrose 356.

[147] Ambrose 352.

[148] "Case No. 2, The Dostler Case: The Trial of General Anton Dostler, Commander of the 75th German Army Corps," Law-Reports of Trials of War Criminals, The United Nations War Crimes Commission, Volume I, London, HMSO, 1949, http://www.ess.uwe.ac.uk/wcc/dostler.htm#REGARDING.

German General Anton Dostler just before his execution in Aversa, Italy. [149]

Other Trials

The Dostler trial occurred under U.S. Army standing practice for the prosecution of war crimes. In 1942, the Allies decided to prosecute enemy war criminals after the war, aiming for larger prey, and the International War Crimes Tribunals were the mechanism established, and the main trials were those at Nuremberg and Tokyo.[150] These trials were in addition to those carried out by individual countries or on a multilateral regional basis.

Winston Churchill and other British leaders had argued that certain of the Nazi leaders should be dealt with summarily – in other words, shot on sight – but only the topmost leaders.[151] At the late 1943 Teheran Conference, Stalin proposed shooting the top 50,000 German officers and specialists. In the ensuing banter, President Roosevelt offered 49,000; Churchill took Stalin at his word and left the room in anger. In reconciliation Stalin brushed off his

---

[149] "Pictures of World War II: Prisoners," No. 171, Blomgren, December 1, 1945. 111-SC-225295, National Archives,
http://www.archives.gov/research/military/ww2/photos/#prisoners.
[150] Dear 1258.
[151] "Churchill: Execute Hitler Without a Trial: Newly Released Government Documents from 1942 Reveal the War Cabinet's Debates," *The Sunday Times*, 1 January 2006, http://www.timesonline.co.uk/tol/news/uk/article784041.ece, accessed 13 August 2011.

offer as "only playing."[152] Eventually, the main allies agreed to put the principal surviving Nazi leaders on trial. The resulting Nuremberg International Military Tribunal met from November 1945 to October 1946 composed of judges and prosecutors from the US, UK, France, and the Soviet Union. The tribunal tried 22 Nazi defendants of which 10 were hanged on 16 October 1946. Subsequently U.S. military tribunals tried another 200 Nazis in the US Zone of Occupation with another 24 executed.[153]

In the International Military Tribunal in the Far East, 11 Allied powers were involved in the trials and prosecution of 28 Japanese leaders from 3 May 1948 until 4 November 1948 in Tokyo. Of these, 7 were executed on 23 December 1948 after approval by General MacArthur as the Supreme Commander Allied Powers, and after the US Supreme Court rejected jurisdiction over the Tribunal[154]. Allies also conducted more than 2000 regional trials trying 5700 defendants, resulting in 920 additional executions, mainly for mistreatment of Allied POWs. The most controversial of these regional trials may have been the case of General Tomoyui Yamashita in October 1945 in Manila by a U.S. military tribunal, the first Japanese official to stand trial. In circumstances similar to the Dostler case, MacArthur established a military tribunal and preferred charges within days of Yamashita's surrender, giving the defendant only three weeks to prepare a defense, and a swift trial ensued. The U.S. Supreme Court also denied review of the case, and Yamashita was hanged on 23 February 1946.[155]

The military tribunals of World War II were not without critics. For some, the tribunals were not truly neutral; for others, the basis of the trials of the

---

[152] Sergei Kudryashov, "Stalin and the Allies: Who Deceived Whom?" *History Today,* (vol. 45 no. 5), May 1995, at http://www.mtholyoke.edu/acad/intrel/kudrya.htm.
[153] Dear 824-828.
[154] Hirota V. MacArthur, 338 U. S. 197 (1948), http://supreme.justia.com/us/338/197/case.html.
[155] In ReYamashita, 327 U.S. 1(1946), http://supreme.justia.com/us/327/1/. For the general account of the Far East trials, see Dear 347-350.

major leaders at Nuremberg and in Tokyo were examples of retrospective reasoning, since no customary or codified law existed for crimes against international peace or the waging of aggressive war. Other critics pointed out that the international tribunals and the national tribunals did not consider alleged crimes committed by Allied powers, particularly the Soviets. The Chief Justice of the Supreme Court, Harlan Fiske Stone, criticized Associate Supreme Court Justice Robert H. Jackson's participation as a prosecutor at Nuremberg as a "high-grade lynching party."[156] Associate Supreme Court Justices William Francis Murphy and Wiley Rutledge dissented from the Court's decisions not to review the cases against General Yamashita and Lieutenant General Masaharu Homma, contending that MacArthur's military tribunals were not properly constituted, were willing to consider coerced evidence and hearsay, and allowed insufficient time for the defense to prepare, as well as dissenting from the view that certain U.S. Constitutional rights did not apply to those enemy belligerents on trial for war crimes. Perhaps echoing the views of the Chief Justice on Nuremberg, Justice Murphy would famously write in his dissent on the Homma case, "Today the lives of Yamashita and Homma, leaders of enemy forces vanquished in the field of battle, are taken without regard to due process of law. There will be few to protest. But tomorrow the precedent here established can be turned against others. A procession of *judicial lynchings* without due process of law may now follow." (emphasis added)[157] Justice Rutledge concurred in the dissent.

---

[156] Wiley Rutledge, "Executive Detention, and Judicial Conscience at War," *Washington University Law Review*, Vol. 84:99: 2006, p99 -177, 2006, p. 111, at http://lawreview.wustl.edu/inprint/84-1/p99Green2.pdf. Multiple sources also allege that Chief Justice Stone at one point called the Nuremberg trials a "fraud."
[157] Application of Homma, 327 U.S. 759 (1946), http://caselaw.lp.findlaw.com/scripts/getcase.pl?court=us&vol=327&invol=759. For general criticism, see Dear, 1258.

KOREA

"Many American officers and men interviewed for this book admitted knowledge of, or participation in, the shooting of Communist prisoners when it was inconvenient to keep them alive."

- Max Hastings, *The Korean War*[158]

POWs were a critical issue in the Korean War. The North Koreans frequently shot any prisoners taken on the battlefield, whereas the Chinese rarely did. UN prisoners that made it to Communist camps, though, were subjected to brutal treatment and used as propaganda tools. American prisoners fared the worst, with 2701 of 7140 dying in the camps, whereas only 50 of 1188 Commonwealth prisoners died.

The issue of POWs also postponed the termination of hostilities from February 1952 until July 1953. The UN allies wanted to avoid what had happened only a few years before at the close of World War II when hundreds of thousands of Soviet POWs were forcibly repatriated to the Soviet Union, only to be sent to gulags – and to further years of deprivation and death - for having surrendered in the first place. In the first survey of Communist POWs held in South Korea, the UN discovered that as many as 72,000 of the 132,000 held did not want to return to the North. Such a refusal rate was unacceptable to the Communist negotiators because of what it might say about the Communist system as a whole. About 45% of American casualties occurred after the Armistice talks began.[159]

---

[158] Hastings 287.
[159] Statistics on American, Commonwealth and Communist POWs and American casualties from Hastings 287, 306, 329.

Koje-Do

In the UN camps in South Korea, many of which were run by U.S. forces, British historian Max Hastings reports that the Communist POWs suffered a "casual brutality." American enlisted MPs frequently ran the camps.[160] A potent mixture of leniency, incompetence and politicized media made these POW camps one of the major scandals of the war. U.S. military leadership of the Korean POW camps failed to control either the excesses of the guards, or the behavior of the prisoners.

When the armistice talks stalled in 1952 partly over the issue of forced repatriation of prisoners, Communist agents infiltrated the main POW camps in South Korea. This infiltration led directly to the agents' murder of POWs not wanting to return, with the murders serving as an example to other POWs. The agents also led the POWs to manufacture weapons, dig defensive positions, and drilled the POWs for eventual battle with their guards. On 7 May 1952, the Communist agents in one compound on Koje-Do Island captured Brigadier General Francis Dodd, the Koje-do commander, when he unwisely entered the compound to negotiate. The agents then proceeded to "try" Dodd for his abuse of the POWs before releasing him on 9 May. The Communist allegation was that UN Command was abusing POWs to force them to reject repatriation. These POW events gave the enemy a major propaganda coup at a time when many Western intellectuals were still inclined to look positively upon the march of "socialism," even when enforced by military subjugation. In June 1952, UN Command moved in combat units and assaulted one of the compounds with troops and tanks. Opposition in the other camps collapsed, but the propaganda victory had already been won.

---

[160] Hastings 306-307.

President Rhyee's Unilateral Action

To express his dislike for certain aspects of the Armistice negotiations, on 18 June 1953, South Korean President Syngman Rhee ordered his troops to release more than 25,000 North Korean POWs under his control in contravention of the terms of the Armistice. His troops and policemen helped the North Koreans to hide, and only 1000 were ever rounded up. Another 22,604 POWs that had refused repatriation were turned over by the UN to the "Neutral Nations Repatriation Commission" as agreed in the Armistice; of these, only 137 chose to return North. More than 75,000 Communist POWs had chosen repatriation, and were shipped back on 5 August 1953.[161]

GLOBAL WAR ON TERROR

Let me just say this. I believe the services have a -- look, the kids did bad things. But the notion that it's all just these kids....The officers are "in loco parentis" with these children. We send our children to war. And we have officers like that general, whose job is to be mother and father to these kids, to keep them out of trouble.

- Seymour Hersh, 4 May 2004[162]

...we have destroyed our credibility when it comes to rule of law all around the world, and given a huge boost to terrorist recruitment in countries that say, "Look, this is how the United States treats Muslims."

- Senator Barrack Obama, presidential candidate, 16 June 2008[163]

---

[161] For statistics, see Hastings 323, 328.

[162] "Bill O'Reilly: Inside Iraq's Abu Ghraib Prison," Fox News, 4 May 2004, http://www.foxnews.com/story/0,2933,118955,00.html.

[163] "Transcript: Jake Tapper Interviews Barack Obama, Presumptive Democratic Nominee on Gay Marriage, Education and the General Election," ABC News, 16 June 2008, http://abcnews.go.com/print?id=5178123.

"On November 13, 2001, I signed an executive order establishing military tribunals to try captured terrorists. The system was based closely on the one created by FDR in 1942, which tried and convicted eight Nazi spies who had infiltrated the United States. The Supreme Court had unanimously upheld the legality of those tribunals."

- Former President George W. Bush, *Decision Points*[164]

"Today, for the first time in our Nation's history, the Court confers a constitutional right to habeas corpus on alien enemies detained abroad by our military forces in the course of an ongoing war."

- Justice Antonin Scalia, dissent in *Boumediene v. Bush*, 12 June 2008[165]

Among the most emotive issues in the current war have been the prison camps at Abu Ghraib, Iraq, and Guantanamo, Cuba. One could be forgiven for thinking that the only prisoners in the current war were those at these two camps. In fact, tens of thousands in Afghanistan and Iraq have been captured, detained, processed, and tried in local courts where applicable; a large number have also been released. The proportionately few cases of abuse or violence at detention facilities housing this large number of detainees have been reported, generally by soldiers, and then investigated by proper military authorities, with resulting punishment meted out.

Abu Ghraib

Seymour Hersh's "kids" included Army Reservists Staff Sergeant Ivan "Chip" Frederick (age 36 at the time of the offense), and Specialist Charles Graner

---

[164] George W. Bush, *Decision Points* (New York: Crown, 2010, Kindle version) location 3307-3313.

[165] Scalia, J., Dissenting, Supreme Court of The United States, Nos. 06–1195 and 06–1196, Lakhdar Boumediene, Et Al., Petitioners 06–1195 *V.* George W. Bush, President of The United States, Et Al, http://docs.justia.com/cases/supreme/slip/553/06-1195/dissent3.pdf.

(age 35 at the time), the two principal ringleaders of the abuse that occurred on multiple occasions from October to December 2003. Frederick and Graner both had a background in civilian corrections. This background undercut another favorite media theme of Abu Ghraib, that the Reserve Military Police unit assigned to Abu Ghraib lacked sufficient training for dealing with prisoners. Frederick and Graner certainly had such training in their past civilian careers. Moreover, Military Policemen routinely deal with arrests and detainees – in short, prisoners – and all soldiers are trained generally in the laws of armed conflict. No special training was required for the Reservists involved to know that "the numerous incidents of sadistic, blatant, and wanton criminal abuses" they perpetrated were wrong.[166]

In January 2004, almost four months before the journalistic accounts and photos appeared in late April 2004, the Army had begun investigating the Abu Ghraib incidents, because another soldier sent the incriminating photographs to authorities. The Army eventually prosecuted and convicted 11 soldiers for the abuses at Abu Ghraib.

The Abu Ghraib story led U.S. and international news reporting for several weeks. While much media commentary and congressional investigations sought to determine whether the abuses were somehow official policy, as the Army defendants claimed, no evidence of such a policy could be found.[167] The notion that higher-ranking generals or officials in the Defense

---

[166] For this description of the abuses, see Major General Antonio Taguba, "Article 15-6 Investigation of the 800th Military Police Brigade," p. 16, at www.npr.org/iraq/2004/prison_abuse_**report.pdf**.

[167] In his Senate testimony on 11 Mat 2004, MG Taguba, the official investigating officer, would state in direct response to Senator Byrd's goading on the issue of "policies and planning" for abusive interrogation techniques, "Sir, we did not find any evidence of a policy or a direct order given to these soldiers to conduct what they did. I believe that they did it on their own volition." Senate Armed Services Committee, "Review of Department of Defense Detention and Interrogation Operations," S. Hrg. 108-868, May 7, 11, 19; July 22; September 9, 2004, p. 339, at

Department or the White House spent their time communicating detailed instructions for abuse to Staff Sergeants or Specialists should have been treated as bizarre.[168] Seeking to find the roots of Abu Ghraib in the Oval Office or the Office of the Secretary of Defense would be akin to seeking some sort of secret set of orders for My Lai in the Oval Office of Democrat President Johnson or in the office of Secretary of Defense McNamara. As it was, My Lai happened in March 1968, in a presidential election year, but only appeared in the media more than a year later after the elections were safely over; Abu Ghraib, by contrast, became one of the key events of the early 2004 election season. Had it not been for the lurid nature of the photographs showing abusive humiliation and hinting at far worse, especially acts by American female soldiers against male Muslim prisoners, and the fact that the pictures arrived in the midst of the 2004 presidential campaign, Abu Ghraib might not have become quite the media phenomenon that it did, although the events certainly would still have attracted substantial attention.

The actions of low-ranking soldiers may not have received much attention in America's previous wars, but in the modern media age, even the humblest soldier can have a strategic effect.

Guantanamo

Part of the long-running opposition to the War on Terror revolves around the use of the Guantanamo Naval Base to house some of the terrorists picked up on the battlefield in Afghanistan or in other operations. In the first few months of the war, pictures of prisoners who were hooded, shackled, and in

---

http://frwebgate.access.gpo.gov/cgi-bin/getdoc.cgi?dbname=108_senate_hearings&docid=f:96600.pdf.

[168] For an expression of the expectation, or the hope, that the events could be linked to the highest echelons of government, see Seymour M. Hersh, "Torture at Abu Ghraib: American Soldiers Brutalized Iraqis. How Far Up Does the Responsibility Go?" *The New Yorker*, 10 May 2004, http://www.newyorker.com/archive/2004/05/10/040510fa_fact.

orange jumpsuits elicited a strange sympathy from many in the U.S. and in other countries. A lack of basic understanding of the requirements of the Geneva Conventions among journalists and the public increased the anxiety when the Bush Administration announced that prisoners sent to Cuba would not be treated as prisoners-of-war and were not entitled to the protections of Common Article 3 of the Geneva Conventions of 1949. The Administration argued that the provisions of the Conventions did not apply to "illegal combatants" from non-state actors that were not signatories to the Convention, and in any case did not adhere to any of the recognized laws of war; moreover, Common Article 3 applied only to persons engaged in "armed conflict not of an international character occurring in the territory of one of the High Contracting Parties," whereas both al Qaeda and their principle allies, the Taliban, were clearly engaged in international actions that crossed multiple borders. Nonetheless, on 7 February 2002, President Bush issued orders that "the United States Armed Forces shall continue to treat detainees humanely and, to the extent appropriate and consistent with military necessity, in a manner consistent with the principles of the Geneva Conventions...."[169] The Bush Administration did an abysmal job of explaining any of its stances and decisions.

A gullible and partisan press exacerbated the problems of Guantanamo. In one famous incident, a magazine, *Newsweek*, reported that the Koran had been desecrated by American guards, leading to riots, deaths, and injuries in the Islamic world, particularly in liberated Afghanistan. The magazine's

---

[169] "Senate Armed Services Committee Inquiry into the Treatment of Detainees in U.S. Custody: Executive Summary," p. 3, 20 November 2008, at http://levin.senate.gov/newsroom/supporting/2008/Detainees.121108.pdf;full report at http://armed-services.senate.gov/Publications/Detainee%20Report%20Final_April%2022%202009.pdf.

subsequent apology for its shoddy reporting did not repair the damage done to American prestige nor restore the dead to living.[170]

According to press accounts in Reuters, as of February 2011, only 7 of the more than 800 prisoners that have passed through Guantanamo have died – one from an apparent heart attack after using an elliptical trainer to exercise, another from colon cancer, and five from apparent suicides. This would be a death rate of slightly less than 1%, or about the rate experienced by German prisoners in U.S. hands during World War II.[171] Indeed, prisoners at Guantanamo, or "Club Gitmo" as some called it, gained weight from the diet and had access to exercise facilities, various video game devices, DVDs, books, and other amenities. None of this, nor the frequent visits to the facilities by American and international officials, stopped domestic and foreign critics from decrying the prison as a blot on America's good standing in the world, or as one Democrat Congressman put it, "[I]ts very existence stains and defies the moral fiber of our great nation."[172] Denouncements of and calls to close the Guantanamo prison were regular features in U.S. election campaigns in 2004, 2006, and 2008. Critics frequently alleged that Guantanamo was a major recruiting tool for terrorists, or even the Number 1 recruiting tool for terrorists (when they were not arguing that the Coalition operations in Iraq were Number 1), without any supporting evidence, and as if terrorists had had trouble recruiting suicidal adherents before Guantanamo was opened.

---

[170] Dan Glaister and Declan Walsh, "After Week of Riots, Newsweek Admits It Got Qur'an Story Wrong," *The Guardian*, 16 May 2005, http://www.guardian.co.uk/media/2005/may/16/pressandpublishing.usnews.

[171] Jane Sutton, "Guantanamo Prisoner Dies After Exercising," 3 February 2011, http://www.msnbc.msn.com/id/41410814/ns/us_news-security/.

[172] "Obama Signs Order to Close Guantanamo Bay Facility," CNN Politics, 22 January 2009, http://articles.cnn.com/2009-01-22/politics/guantanamo.order_1_detention-guantanamo-bay-torture/2?_s=PM:POLITICS.

Senator Obama, as the Democrat presidential nominee in 2008, made the immediate closure of the prison one of his most repeated campaign promises. Rarely detailed were the alternatives. Two days after his inauguration, President Obama signed an Executive Order to close the Guantanamo prison facility in order to reclaim the "moral high ground." The Order called for the "prompt and appropriate disposition of the individuals detained at Guantanamo" and declaimed that these individuals had "the constitutional privilege of the writ of habeas corpus" to challenge their detention.[173] However, this order did not result in the immediate closure of Guantanamo, as its many critics wanted, or as the many campaign promises led its critics to expect. Instead, the Order set a time limit for closure not to exceed one year – or 22 January 2010. As of this writing in August 2011, Guantanamo is still open, and has no foreseeable date for closure.

Lofty rhetoric and solemn promises were more useful as political campaign tactics than as tools in military campaigns. The Obama-mandated review of the conditions at the prison facilities concluded that they met the standards of the Geneva Convention, contrary to the expectations set by years of reporting on torture and abuse, but in accordance with President Bush's original order from 7 February 2002.[174] On the issue of habeas corpus the Obama Administration argued , a mere 31 days after taking office, that while habeas corpus somehow applied at Guantanamo, it did not apply at other detention facilities such as the one at Bagram Airbase, Afghanistan.[175] By

---

[173] "Closure of Guantanamo Detention Facilities: Executive Order -- Review and Disposition of Individuals Detained at the Guantánamo Bay Naval Base and Closure of Detention Facilities," 22 January 2009, http://www.whitehouse.gov/the_press_office/ClosureOfGuantanamoDetentionFacilities/ .

[174] Peter Finn and Del Quentin Wilber, "Review Finds Detainees' Treatment Legal," *The Washington Post*, 21 February 2009, http://www.washingtonpost.com/wp-dyn/content/article/2009/02/20/AR2009022002191.html.

[175] Charlie Savage, "Obama Upholds Detainee Policy in Afghanistan," *The New York Times*, 22 February 2009, http://www.nytimes.com/2009/02/22/washington/22bagram.html.

May 2009, the new administration was considering indefinite detention of the illegal combatants at Guantanamo without trial, if that became necessary.[176] The Administration has so far dealt with the issue of the illegal combatants at Guantanamo and elsewhere in a manner roughly identical to the policies followed by the much maligned Bush Administration.

Other prisoner controversies that have rankled and are still to be resolved include the release program and recidivism of detainees at all facilities, and trials of the illegal combatants remaining at Guantanamo.

Catch and Release

In a new form of the old parole system, many thousands of detainees and prisoners in Iraq and Afghanistan have been released. At Guantanamo, of the more than 800 prisoners sent there, all but 172 have been released in one form or another.[177] The population of detainees under Coalition control in Iraq peaked at 26,000 in 2007. That year, more than 8900 were released and more than 10,000 were released in 2008, even as new detainees came in from on-going military operations.[178] Those detainees designated as moderates were given a chance at rehabilitation coupled with vocational training; often the detainees were released to leaders of their tribes or communities who offered pledges for the good behavior of those released. Similar screening, rehabilitation, and reconciliation programs exist in Afghanistan.[179]

---

[176]Peter Finn, "Obama Endorses Indefinite Detention Without Trial for Some," *The Washington Post*, 22 May 2009, http://www.washingtonpost.com/wp-dyn/content/article/2009/05/21/AR2009052104045.html.
[177] Sutton, MSNBC.
[178] "Rise in Iraqi Detainee Releases," BBC Mobile News, 2 August 2008, http://news.bbc.co.uk/2/hi/middle_east/7538681.stm.
[179] See for example, "Afghan Leaders Call for Peace as 14 Detainees Released at Helmand Shura," United States Central Command, 4 November 2010, at http://www.centcom.mil/press-releases/afghan-leaders-call-for-peace-as-14-detainees-released-at-helmand-shura.

Some soldiers and other critics refer derisively to these programs as the "catch-and-release" program, since some of those released return to the battlefield, which has been a challenge for as long as paroles have been used in war (see Grant's comment above).[180] With respect to Guantanamo, in late 2010, the Director of National Security reported that 150 of the 598 detainees – 25% - released as of 1 October 2010, were confirmed or suspected of having returned to the fight.[181] The most notorious example in Iraq was the Obama Administration's release of the brothers Laith and Qais al-Khazali in June and December 2009 respectively in what looked like a de facto prisoner swap for the British civilian hostage, Peter Moore, who was freed hours after the release of Quais. The al-Khazali brothers were leaders of the Iranian-aligned Shiite faction, Asa'ib Ahl al-Haq, and had been the alleged masterminds behind the capture of Moore and four of his colleagues (subsequently murdered), as well as the capture of five American soldiers (also murdered). The objective of the release was reconciliation of the faction with the Maliki administration in Iraq.[182]

---

[180] See for example, Sara A. Carter, "Catch-And-Release of Taliban Fighters in Afghanistan Angers Troops," *The Washington Examiner*, 6 December 2010, http://washingtonexaminer.com/news/world/2010/12/catch-and-release-taliban-fighters-afghanistan-angers-troops.

[181] Director of National Intelligence, "Summary of the Reengagement of Detainees Formerly Held at Guantanamo Bay, Cuba," http://www.dni.gov/electronic_reading_room/120710 Summary of the Reengagement of Detainees Formerly Held at Guantanamo Bay Cuba.pdf.

[182] See Timothy Williams, "U.S. Transferred Detainee Before Hostage Release," *The New York Times*, 31 December 2009, http://www.nytimes.com/2010/01/01/world/middleeast/01iraq.html, and Bill Roggio, "Did the Obama Administration Violate an Executive Order by Releasing Qais Qazali [sic]?" *The Weekly Standard*, 31 December 2009, http://www.weeklystandard.com/weblogs/TWSFP/2009/12/did the obama administration v.asp?page=2.

Trials

Our laws change. Our courts, their judges, and their opinions change. A majority of the Supreme Court has now arrived where the minority was in the 1940s. In a series of cases, the most important of which were *Hamdan v. Rumsfeld* (2006) and *Boumediene v. Bush* (2008), the Court found that the procedures for military tribunals in the War on Terror, similar in almost all respects to those used in earlier eras to try violators of the laws of war, violated the procedural requirements of the latest Uniform Code of Military Justice, and the procedural requirements of Common Article 3 of the Geneva Conventions (1949), even though Article 3 explicitly did not apply to conflicts of an international character. In *Boumediene*, the Court also extended constitutional habeas corpus protections to the Guantanamo detainees. [183]

The significance of the Court's shifting position is highlighted by the dissenters. In his dissent to *Hamdan*, Associate Justice Clarence Thomas condemned the decision's "unfamiliarity with the realities of warfare and its willful blindness to our precedents," and continued,

> "Those Justices who today disregard the commander-in-chief's wartime decisions, only 10 days ago deferred to the judgment of the Corps of Engineers with regard to a matter much more within the competence of lawyers, upholding that agency's wildly implausible conclusion that a storm drain is a tributary of the waters of the United States…. It goes without saying that there is much more at stake here than storm drains"[184]

As a result of the 9-11 attacks, and to provide legal basis for imprisonment and military trial of detainees, Congress passed the Authorization for Use of

---

[183] *Hamdan v. Rumsfeld* - 05-184 (2006), http://supreme.justia.com/us/548/05-184/; *Boumediene et al v. Bush et al*, No. 106-1195 (2008), http://docs.justia.com/cases/supreme/slip/553/06-1195/index.pdf .
[184] Thomas, J., dissenting, *Hamdan v. Rumsfeld*.

Military Force (2001), the Detainee Treatment Act (2005) and the Military Commissions Act (2006). The Supreme Court cases found fault with procedures in all of them, and ultimately with the denial of habeas corpus to enemy combatants (legal or not), such denial being a practice consistently used in past wars and just as consistently upheld by previous Supreme Court cases. As Chief Justice John Roberts noted in his dissent in Boumediene, "Today the Court strikes down as inadequate the most generous set of procedural protections ever afforded aliens detained by this country as enemy combatants."[185]

The cumulative weight of the various decisions was to apply judicial reasoning to circumscribe the powers of the Commander-in-Chief in the midst of war in ways contrary to the history of Supreme Court decisions on very similar cases in previous conflicts. As a result, Al Qaeda and Taliban prisoners will now be treated far better than the "law and usage of nations" has hitherto required, and certainly better than their Nazi or Japanese militarist predecessors ever were. Military tribunals were used throughout American history, but now are suddenly insufficient to try terrorists picked up on the battlefield.

Soon after assuming office in 2009, the Obama Administration suspended the work of military tribunals at Guantanamo. In November 2009, the Administration announced its intention of trying Khalid Shaikh Mohammed and four others connected directly to the 9-11 attacks in a Federal civilian court in New York City. In January 2010, the Administration indicated that it wanted to bring as many as 80 of the Guantanamo prisoners to the U.S., some to stand trial in civilian courts and some to be tried in the still suspended military tribunals, although the process for designating which detainees would be tried by the two different trial formats remained a

---

[185] Roberts, C.J., dissenting, *Boumediene V. Bush*.

mystery.[186] The consequent political uproar, and congressional actions to prohibit such transfers, retarded the entire process further. In the first detainee trial, held in a civilian court in New York in late 2010, the all-civilian jury convicted the detainee on a single charge of conspiracy, acquitting him of more than 280 other charges related to the deaths of 224 people in the 1998 al-Qaeda bombing of U.S. embassies in Africa.[187] Despite this, President Obama stated emphatically in early January 2011 that he still favored civilian trials for the detainees despite widespread congressional and public opposition; however, by the end of the same month, the Obama Administration was planning to resume the military commissions which had been stalled for more than two years by presidential order.[188]

CONCLUSION

In the popular movies *Saving Private Ryan* (1998) and *The Patriot* (2000) one of the subthemes is the killing of prisoners after their surrender. Indeed a key scene in the *Patriot* is the redemptive one where the main character, himself a war criminal, orders his militia to offer quarter to surrendering

---

[186] Charlie Savage, "Accused 9/11 Mastermind to Face Civilian Trial in N.Y.," *The New York Times*, 13 November 2009, http://www.nytimes.com/2009/11/14/us/14terror.html; "US Officials: 35 Guantanamo Detainees Face Trial or Commission," *The Independent*, 23 January 2010, http://www.independent.co.uk/news/world/americas/us-officials-35-guantanamo-detainees-face-trial-or-commission-1876772.html.

[187] Jonathan Dienst and Alice McQuillan, "Jurors Deliver Mixed Verdict in Guantanamo Detainee Trial," NBC New York, 18 November 2010, http://www.nbcnewyork.com/news/local-beat/Jurors-Deliver-Verdict-in-Guantanamo-Detainee-Trial-108785579.html.

[188] "Obama Backs Civilian Trials for Guantanamo Detainees," *Columbus Dispatch*, 8 January 2011, http://www.dispatchpolitics.com/live/content/national_world/stories/2011/01/08/copy/Obama-backs-civilian-trials-for-Guantanamo-detainees.html?sid=101; Carrie Johnson, "Military Trials to Resume for Guantanamo Detainees," http://www.npr.org/2011/01/24/133171238/White-House-To-Re-Launch-Military-Trials-For-Gitmo-Detainees.

British soldiers because his son and a pastor condemn the killings, claiming that the militia are better men than these acts would indicate. No such redemption emerges from the Spielbergian view of World War II, because the prisoners being summarily shot are Nazis. While we know such actions are wrong, we tend to reward artistic representations of retribution meted out, often by single heroes, against America's enemies.

But the truth is that we *are* better than this. In this war we have no equivalents to Andersonville or Elmira. The mistreatment or outright murder of prisoners that historians reported in World War II or Korea would not go unpunished now. Merely slapping a prisoner in Iraq, Afghanistan, or Guantanamo is likely to get a soldier court-martialed in the current war.[189] On the other hand in our previous conflicts, enemies alleged to have mistreated American or allied prisoners or otherwise engaged in violations of the laws of war received relatively swift justice in processes lasting from a few days to weeks in some cases. The leading war criminals in World War II were tried quickly. In the current war, most of the leading criminals are likely to wait for a decade or more for their trials – while their victims wait for basic justice - as wrangling continues over style of tribunal, rules of evidence, trial procedures, venue and the extent to which U.S. constitutional rights will be extended to illegal combatants. Meanwhile parties and politicians have sought to derive whatever domestic political advantage is possible from one side or the other of the issue.

We face an enemy in no way beholden to the customary laws of war. With few exceptions any American or Allied prisoners have been murdered. Yet our side, while certainly not perfect, has detained and cared for tens of thousands of prisoners. Senator Durbin's point of departure (see quote at the beginning of this chapter) was an FBI agent's report that he had seen a

---

[189] "Navy SEAL Found Not Guilty of Assaulting a Suspected Terrorist," 6 May 2010, Fox News, http://www.foxnews.com/us/2010/05/06/navy-seal-guilty-assaulting-suspected-terrorist/

prisoner chained in Guantanamo, who had allegedly spent all night in that position. Some prisoners, the agent had heard, might be left in such a position with the room too hot or too cold, and some were made to listen to rap music. The FBI agent did not say that he had seen himself all of this abuse, but was reporting the hearsay of others. Even if every alleged detail was true, such treatment would indeed be harsh; comparing it to the treatment that caused millions of deaths at the hands of the Nazis, the Soviets, or Pol Pot's thugs is ugly hyperbole of the sort that manifests itself in the safety of vitriolic U.S. domestic politics. Had the prisoners at Guantanamo or in the detention camps in Iraq or Afghanistan been treated like those in totalitarian prisons, a similar death rate would have resulted, or maybe a rate of death at least as high as that in Union camps during the Civil War. Yet, of the tens of thousands detained in this decade of war, only a handful have died in captivity.

If we have an international image problem because of Guantanamo or Abu Ghraib or any other detention center, it is one largely resulting from our own domestic political machinations, projected out into the world. We have condemned ourselves for our treatment of prisoners, particularly at Guantanamo, even though that treatment has been much more lenient in general than the standards used in our past, and then invited the world to condemn us as well.

DISASTERS AND BLUNDERS

Now that wars are televised live, and simple soldiers have access to the internet, any tactical action, no matter how small, can appear to an audience of potentially billions. Since the advent of the 24-hour news cycle, the world has seen the rise of "CNN Wars" where human suffering, or just the *potential* for human suffering, prompts some sort of international military intervention into the internal affairs of another country in response to a public outcry external to the targeted country. Often the interventions occur under cover of a vague UN Security Council resolution. Examples of these "CNN wars" that involved U.S. personnel include Somalia (1992), Haiti (1994), Bosnia (1995), Kosovo (1999), and Libya (2011).

Perhaps when the general slaughter in a war is so great, what would otherwise be a public relations disaster in calmer times gets lost in the casualty reports. In the War on Terror and in the "CNN Wars," with the rarity of heavy industrialized combat coupled with the opportunity to provide an almost immediate account of fighting, any tactical setback is a potential disaster.

When you read about the modern disasters of American foreign or military policy, particularly as portrayed by our journalists and political leaders, consider the following examples from our history.

CURRENT SITUATION

"Yet until the defeat in Vietnam, there was a sort of tragic acceptance of military error as inherent in war. Ours was once a largely rural population, inured to natural disaster and resigned to human shortcoming."

-   Victor Davis Hanson[190]

"That firefight [at Wanat], a debacle that cost nine American lives in July 2008, has become the new template for how not to win in Afghanistan. The calamity and its roots have been described in bitter, painstaking detail in an unreleased Army history, a devastating narrative..."

-   Tom Shanker, New York Times[191]

CIVIL WAR

Cold Harbor

On 31 May 1864, dissatisfied with the conduct of the war to that point, Radical Republicans met in Cleveland to nominate former Major General John C. Fremont as an alternative presidential candidate to run against the incumbent Abraham Lincoln. The next day, LTG Grant's Union forces closed in on the Confederate's Army of Northern Virginia near Cold Harbor. Grant was determined to attack and keep attacking in order to wear down the rebels in the hope of winning the war in that campaign season, in full knowledge of the political stakes in the 1864 presidential elections. As the armies prepared for battle, one Union general noticed that his soldiers, almost all volunteers, were sewing slips of papers onto their uniforms. The slips had their names and home addresses on them, in the expectation of the slaughter to come. On 3 June, the Union's main assault began against the entrenched Confederates. The fire was so intense that in the first 30 minutes, as many as 7000 Union soldiers fell. Grant ordered another assault

---

[190] Victor Davis Hanson, "In War: Resolution," *Claremont Review of Books*, Winter 2007, http://claremont.org/publications/crb/id.1500/article_detail.asp, accessed 24 April 2011.

[191] Tom Shanker, "Review of Battle Disaster Sways Afghan Strategy," *The New York Times On Msnbc.Com*, 3 October 2009, http://www.msnbc.msn.com/id/33150671/ns/world_news-the_new_york_times, accessed 21 April 2011.

that the rebels also crushed by withering fire. The order for a third assault was widely ignored by Grant's subordinate commanders. Neither Grant nor the Confederate commander, Robert E. Lee, would request a truce in the fighting until 7 June. By then, most of the Union soldiers wounded on 3 June had died, with the exception only of those closest to the two battle lines.[192]

Grant lost 12,000 men in the three days of Cold Harbor, 1-3 June 1864. Writing years later in his memoirs, "At Cold Harbor no advantage whatever was gained to compensate for the heavy loss we sustained."[193] Such actions confirmed the worst fears of the Radical Republicans and the Copperhead Democrats. The latter would declare Lincoln's war effort to be a failure, and would eventually nominate the dissident Union Major General McClellan to be their candidate.

The *Sultana*

"News of a terrible steamboat tragedy was relegated to the newspaper's back pages. In a nation desensitized to death, 1,700 more did not seem such an enormous tragedy that it does today."
- Stephen Ambrose, 1 May 2001. [194]

After the surrender of the Army of Northern Virginia at Appomattox on 9 April 1865, signaling the end of major hostilities, troops and prisoners began going home, even as residual fighting continued in the deeper South and West of the Confederate States. As recounted in the chapter on prisoners, the treatment afforded POWs on both sides in the Civil War was horrendous,

---

[192] Bowman 205-207.

[193] Ulysses S. Grant, *Personal Memoirs of U.S. Grant* (Kindle Edition by B&R Samizdat Express, downloaded 2010), locations 15903-15908. Hereafter "Grant."

[194] Stephen Ambrose, "Expedition Journal: Remembering *Sultana*, "*National Geographic News*, 1 May 2001, http://news.nationalgeographic.com/news/2001/05/0501_river5.html, accessed 18 April 2011.

with high death rates. Having survived these camps to head home must have seemed like a miracle to those liberated by the ending of the war.

The *Sultana* was one of the Mississippi riverboats carrying home Union soldiers recently released from Confederate POW camps. Although built to carry a maximum load of 376, Sultana was carrying more than 2300 as a result of a scheme whereby steamboat owners kicked money back to Union officers for overloading each trip upriver. On 27 April, three of the four boilers on the *Sultana* exploded. Of the more than 2300 onboard, more than 1700 perished either in the blast or from drowning. The sinking of the *Sultana* is the worst maritime accident in American history, and provided a sad exclamation point to the end of the sorry saga of the treatment of Civil War prisoners.[195]

WORLD WAR I: The Lost Battalion

"Major Charles W. Whittlesey's luckless outfit from the 77th Division (1st Battalion of the 308th Infantry Regiment), which is better remembered than the battle, became the chief castaway of a wretchedly coordinated battle line."

- S.L.A. Marshall, *World War I*[196]

In the last six weeks of World War I, the American Expeditionary Forces suffered 117,000 casualties in the Meuse-Argonne offensive, while causing the defending Germans to lose 100,000. The Argonne was a thick, hilly forest that was passable only by foot infantry, fighting each step of the way. Staffing and leadership failures hindered the American effort, leading to a widespread morale problem in the assaulting forces.

---

[195] Details taken from Ambrose, 21 May 2001.
[196] S.L.A. Marshall, *World War I* (New York: Mariner Books, 2001) 446.

On 2 October 1918, MAJ Whittlesey's unit of 600 men got separated in the rough terrain from the rest of his division. Cut off for five days of constant fighting, they became the famous "Lost Battalion." Despite running low on ammunition, water, and food, and suffering friendly fire from artillery batteries, they held their ground and refused to surrender. A two-division attack finally broke through to rescue them. Only 194 of the original 600 remained; the rest were killed, missing, or captured.

As the British historian, Max Hastings, once observed, "It is noteworthy how often in military history a deluge of decorations have been conferred on survivors to ease the pain of catastrophe."[197] A battalion got lost and was subsequently cut off from its sister units. Messages were garbled, locations misunderstood, and the result was "friendly fire" by supporting artillery units. Air units tried to locate the missing battalion in the first American attempt at aerial resupply, only to drop the supplies into enemy hands. Subsequent to this list of errors, five Medals of Honor were awarded to those involved in this small battle, in recognition of their courageous response to the mistakes they and others made. Two of those medals went posthumously to the airmen killed in the failed re-supply attempt, and represented half of the Medals of Honor awarded to airmen in World War I.[198] As so often happens in war, courage makes up for blunder. The courage was remembered, and the three surviving Medal of Honor winners - officers that had held the Lost Battalion together - became public heroes.

---

[197] Max Hastings, ed., *The Oxford Book of Military Anecdotes* (New York: Oxford University Press, 1985) 286.
[198] For details, see Marshall, 436, 442, 446. Also see "Charles Whittlesey: Commander of the Lost Battalion," *Doughboy Center: The Story of the American Expeditionary Forces*, http://www.worldwar1.com/dbc/whitt.htm, accessed 18 April 2011.

WORLD WAR II: Kasserine Pass

"Behold, we the American holy warriors have arrived....We have come to set you free."

- The script to be broadcast to Berber tribes in French North Africa when Allied landings commenced in November 42[199]

"I bless the day you urged Fredendall upon me, and cheerfully acknowledge that my earlier doubts of him were completely unfounded."

- LTG Eisenhower to GEN Marshall on MG Fredendall, who was a "Marshall man"[200]

As a global war with many theaters, World War II was replete with American military disasters among which one could include the surprise at Pearl Harbor, the amphibious assault on Tarawa, the training disaster at Slapton Sands, or the failure to plan for exiting the Normandy *bocage*. However, the best example for illustrating the poor state of the American military and its leadership at the very start of the war is the disaster at Kasserine Pass in Tunisia.

In Operation TORCH, a very new and untried American military force, acting in unison with British forces, began landing in Morocco and Algeria on 8 November 1942, eleven months after Pearl Harbor. The colonial forces of Vichy France were the first enemy the Americans faced. After a few days of fighting the French surrendered and then joined the Allied ranks. The main Axis enemies – the Germans and Italians – were farther east in Tunisia and Libya. The British 8th Army, under LTG Montgomery, had broken the Axis lines in the Second Battle of El Alamein on 5 November inside Egypt, and had

---

[199] Rick Atkinson, *An Army at Dawn: The War in North Africa, 1942-1943* (New York: Henry Holt and Company, Kindle version, 2002), location 844.
[200] Atkinson, location 5568.

begun to push the Axis forces west across Libya. The Germans and Italians were in danger of being hemmed in by the Sahara to the south, the Mediterranean to the north, and the two Allied forces advancing from east and west.

U.S. TROOPS SWARM ASHORE IN NORTH AFRICA

"And if our lines should form and break
Because of things you failed to make —
The extra tank or ship or plane
For which we waited all in vain,
And the supplies that never came —
Will you then come and take the blame?
For we, not you, will pay the cost
Of battles you, not we, have lost."

OLD GLORY LEADS MARCH ON ALGERIAN AIRFIELD

U.S. Information Poster for Operation TORCH[201]

---

[201] The National Archives, U.S. Troops Swarm Ashore in North Africa. Old Glory Leads March on Algerian Airfield, *ca. 1942 - ca. 1943*, ARC Identifier 534122 / Local

On 17 November, the Allied forces coming from Algeria first engaged Axis units in Tunisia. By 27 November, only 19 days after the initial landings, the Allies had closed to within 12 miles of Tunis, before bogging down. Presaging the logistical bounty that enabled the final Allied victory in all theaters, the Allies landed 427,000 troops and 42,000 vehicles over a front of almost 1000 miles in the first 12 weeks after the initial landings. The planning and organization, though, was abysmal, and only a fraction of troops and equipment had moved forward to confront the Axis forces in Tunisia.[202] Meanwhile, Axis forces retreated westward across Libya, and reinforcements were flown and shipped from Italy into Tunisia. By mid-February, the Axis forces had concentrated enough strength under Field Marshall Rommel that they launched a massive assault against the stalled Allied forces dug into the Atlas Mountains along the Tunisian-Algerian border. The heaviest blow fell on the U.S. II Corps, commanded by MG Fredendall, near Kasserine Pass.

Fredendall was a "Marshall man" who had been sent by the Chief of Staff, GEN Marshall, to command the first large body of American soldiers sent into battle. Fredendall, though, chose to place himself 70 miles behind the stagnated front lines, and busied himself with tunneling a command post into a mountain side, an odd activity to say the least for a leader of a force intended to eject the Axis from Tunisia. The battles in and near Kasserine Pass that began on 14 February were the first battles between the new American Army and the Axis veterans, and the Americans fared poorly for the first several days. American units disintegrated into confusion, abandoning their equipment as they fled miles to the rear.

American units and individual soldiers were green, and most of their tanks were inferior. Making matters worse, the Americans and their attached allies suffered from a jumbled command structure. Fredendall rarely left his

---

Identifier 179-WP-273, Item from Record Group 179: Records of the War Production Board, 1918 – 1947.

[202] Atkinson, location 5538.

command post, but nonetheless issued detailed orders for the disposition of platoons, sometimes using his own unintelligible personal code. One official history recorded that Fredendall's command was "a tangled skein of misunderstanding, duplication of effort, overlapping responsibility, and consequential muddle."[203] The command structure above II Corps was little better. During the Kasserine Pass battle, eight different overall tactical commanders were appointed in less than a week. "Never were so few commanded by so many from so far," a GI saying coming from the disorganized landings was still applicable in this first major battle.[204]

Suffering from his own form of micromanagement coming from Washington and London, the Allied commander, Eisenhower, had been told to spend more time at the Tunisian front when it bogged down in late 1942, and subsequently made one trip. By early February, as Eisenhower planned his second trip, contrary advice came from Marshall, who recommended less time at the front, and more reliance on reports from subordinates.[205] In the event, Eisenhower made his second trip just as the Kasserine Pass battle began. He spent 36 hours travelling in an armored staff car to pass a few hours with Fredendall on 13 February, ironically departing to return to Algeria just a few hours before the Axis attack began. Reviewing the results of Kasserine later, Eisenhower recorded that unit leadership was "thin," and that troop discipline was akin to a "disorderly mob." [206] Ultimately, Eisenhower was responsible for accepting the weak leaders foisted on him from Washington and for creating and maintaining the shifting, contorted command structure. His own leadership had been thin, which contributed in large measure to the mob that fled from the Axis attack. Not until 6 March did Eisenhower finally relieve the strangely detached Fredendall, after the

---

[203] Dear 644.

[204] Atkinson, locations 7904, 4069.

[205] Atkinson, location 6740-6743.

[206] Allan R. Millett and Peter Maslowski, *For the Common Defense: A Military History of the United States of America* (New York: The Free Press, 1994) 444.

fighting around Kasserine had died down, and sent Patton forward as the new II Corps commander to retrieve the situation.

2802.0000 Bombing, Results of Air Operations (.TO)

Bogged Down in North Africa, 1942[207]

By the time the front lines stabilized again, ten days after the initial attacks, the Americans had lost 6000 of the 30,000 men engaged, 183 tanks, 104 half-tracks, more than 200 artillery pieces, and 500 other vehicles.[208]

---

[207] The National Archives, **Bombing campaign. Europe & North Africa, *ca. 1942 - ca. 1945,*ARC Identifier 292586;** Item from Record Group 338: Records of U.S. Army Operational, Tactical, and Support Organizations (World War II and Thereafter), 1917 – 1999; NARA's Central Plains Region (Kansas City) (NREA), 400 West Pershing Road, Kansas City, MO, 64108.

[208] Atkinson, locations 7936-7937.

Censorship meant that the true extent of the Allied defeat was not known at the time, which allowed MG Fredendall to receive a heroes' welcome back in the States and a promotion to a third star.[209]

One could argue that the first several months of Operation TORCH represented a collective disaster. Many of the generals involved we now lionize as heroes of WWII, but it is doubtful they would have survived in today's media-saturated, hyper-politicized climate, including Eisenhower and possibly Marshall. The landings had been a mess, logistics were poorly planned and incompetently executed, and Eisenhower and his subordinates piecemealed their units into battle with little to no unit cohesion and without adequate artillery or air support. The battle of Kasserine Pass was the culminating point of these failures, but also demonstrated what American forces have learned throughout our history – dogged determination and perseverance can still overcome defects in planning and leadership.

KOREA: Kunu-Ri

"The reason for this [pessimism] is primarily because of the American lack of determination and their inability, up to the time of my visit, to stand and fight. Most Americans soon or later bring the conversation around to an expression of the view that the United Nations forces ought to quit Korea....I would judge the American morale as low, and in some units thoroughly bad...."

- A secret report from British General Leslie Mansergh reporting to British Chiefs of Staff in late 1950[210]

"In the pass at Kunu-ri 'the order came – "Every man for himself"'"
- Quoted in Max Hastings, *The Korean War*[211]

---

[209] Atkinson, location 8092.
[210] Hastings 173.

The Chinese intervention in the Korean War in November 1950 ranks as one of the worst intelligence failures in U.S. history. The UN forces under GEN MacArthur simply ignored the available evidence – engagements with units that were clearly not North Korean, and the capture of significant numbers of Chinese troops. MacArthur had convinced himself and his staff that the Chinese would not intervene as the UN forces approached the Chinese border along the Yalu River, and this was his consistent message back to the U.S. and allied governments.[212]

The strategic surprise of Chinese intervention occasioned operational and tactical disaster for the UN units involved as they fought a generally disorganized retreat southwards over terrain recently taken after the Inchon landings of September 1950. The worst unit disaster was the destruction of the U.S. 2nd Infantry Division in the mountain pass at Kunu-Ri.

Although the Chinese had been operating in force along the border for three weeks prior, on 25 November 1950 the Chinese launched major attacks throughout North Korea, causing a general collapse of the U.S. 8th Army and UN front in northwest Korea. On 30 November, the 2nd Infantry Division began their retreat along the constricted 6-mile-long road through Kunu-Ri. The Americans stuck to the road in the valley, ceding the high ground to the Communist Chinese forces that had the advantage of shooting down at the fleeing units. The American vehicles were trapped in a deadly traffic jam, as the Chinese maintained a relentless fire. In this one day, the division lost some 3000 of its men, and much of its transport equipment.

Weeks passed before the 2nd division was reconstituted and ready for battle again.[213] By 5 December, the 8th Army had lost 11,000 men and was in full retreat in the west of the Korean peninsula, while the Marines of the X Corps

---

[211] Hastings 144.

[212] Larry Schweikart and Michael Allen, *A Patriot's History of the United States From Columbus' Great Discovery to the War on Terror* (New York: Penguin, 2004) 643.

[213] Hastings 143-146.

were still retreating on the eastern side from the "Frozen Chosin" reservoir to the port city of Hungnam, where 200,000 troops and civilians were eventually evacuated.

A Cold Retreat from the Yalu[214]

AFGHANISTAN: Wanat

"Review of Battle Disaster Sways Afghan Strategy"
- *New York Times* headline on Wanat Battle[215]

The incidents described above involved the loss of hundreds or thousands of men and their associated equipment from errors in planning and organizing, or from mistakes as simple as land navigation through rough terrain or as complex as strategic miscalculation. These past events are unknown to or forgotten by most Americans. More familiar, of course, are reports out of Afghanistan, where modern media and communications technology make even the smallest engagement subject to fierce scrutiny. In such an

---

[214] The National Archives, **BITTER COLD, BITTER FIGHT: ca. 12/1950**, ARC Identifier **542210 / Local Identifier 342-AF-78460AC,** Still Picture Records Section, Special Media Archives Services Division, College Park, MD. Item from Record Group 342: Records of U.S. Air Force Commands, Activities, and Organizations, 1900 – 2003.
[215] Shanker.

environment, the threshold for "disaster" or "blunder" has been concomitantly lowered.

In July 2008, U.S. forces continued their long-standing tactics of moving into valleys along the Afghanistan-Pakistan border. Insurgents used the valleys as "rat lines" to move men and supplies deeper into Afghanistan to attack U.S. and allied forces. In one of those valleys, the Waygal, lies the village of Wanat. On 8 July 2008, 48 soldiers of the 2nd platoon of Chosen Company, 2nd Battalion of the 503d Infantry, 173d Airborne Brigade, accompanied by 24 Afghan soldiers, left their company's main camp to establish a Combat Outpost at Wanat, two weeks before their scheduled end-of-tour departure from Afghanistan. On 13 July, while the outpost was still being built, along with an associated Observation Post (OP), an insurgent force of 200 or more suddenly attacked. In the ensuing four-hour battle, the enemy threatened to overrun the OP, and reached the perimeter wire of the outpost. Several Americans were wounded or killed in attempts to relieve the OP, including the Platoon Leader, 1LT Jonathan Brostrom. At one point, only one man was left alive in the OP, wounded, while those in the main outpost tried to reinforce him. Despite being outnumbered, with their leader killed, and fighting from an outpost not yet fully fortified, the combined American and Afghan force held on during the four-hour fight, calling in artillery, helicopter, fighter jet, and bomber support, thereby breaking the back of the enemy assault and driving them off. Nine Americans and four Afghans were killed and another 27 Americans wounded.[216]

The New York Times called the battle a "disaster," a "debacle," a "calamity." Senator James Webb demanded an investigation. The Chairman of the Joint Chiefs addressed the battle in a news conference. The Army launched at least 4 different investigations involving four-star, three-star, and two-star generals, the Army Inspector General and the Army Criminal Investigation

---

[216] For an account of the Battle of Wanat, See Sebastian Junger, *War* (New York: Hachette Book Group, 2010, Kindle version) locations 3104-3175.

Command. The 248-page historical study of the battle, written by the Combat Studies Institute attached to the Command and General Staff College, became a political football. But the fact is that an American-Afghan force of 72 men entered enemy territory, was surprised by a force far superior in numbers, refused to abandon their fellow soldiers who were cut off, and whose lower-ranking enlisted leaders stepped up after their platoon leader's death to defend the perimeter and call in massive firepower to win the battle. The polemical Combat Studies Institute report concluded that Wanat was "as remarkable as any small-unit action in American military history."[217] The journalist Sebastian Junger, who was embedded with the 173d, called it "nothing short of a miracle" that Wanat was not overrun.[218]

The result at Wanat was not a miracle, but rather a direct result of the valor and training of the troops involved, consistent with the Army warrior ethos of "I will never accept defeat" and "I will never leave a fallen comrade." This should have been the stuff of legends.

CONCLUSION

"Again, what loses wars are not the inevitable mistakes, but the failure to correct them in time and the defeatism and depression (because errors occurred at all) that we allow to paralyze us."
- Victor Davis Hanson[219]

As Stephen Ambrose put it, a large loss of life in war due to blunder or malfeasance in the midst of much greater battlefield slaughter was not even worthy of front page news in the Civil War, in much the same way that the destruction of the 2nd Infantry Division was lost in the larger disaster of the UN retreat from the Yalu. In World War I, the blunder of the Lost Battalion

---

[217] Quoted in Shanker.
[218] Junger, location 3122.
[219] Hanson.

became heroic. At Kasserine Pass, censorship kept the bad news from having a political or strategic effect. In the Waygal Valley in Afghanistan, though, during an election year, 72 Americans and Afghans moved into contested terrain, and successfully fought off an enemy force three or four times larger, and the event suddenly was denoted a disaster, and became loaded with connotations for the future of the efforts of a 50-nation coalition. Higher headquarters, journalists and a senator launched multiple investigations; a staff college wrote a book-sized report about the engagement and the weighty lessons to be learned. Maybe we have simply lost our sense of proportion.

The North African campaigns exhibited poor planning, worse execution, enormous logistical inefficiencies, and poor generalship that wasted the lives of thousands of inexperienced soldiers. Most those generals from the European Theater that we now consider "Great Captains" played a part in the bloody saga of Tunisia – Marshall, Eisenhower, Patton, Bradley, Montgomery. All made grievous, costly errors. In Korea, the other great American general, MacArthur, made equally grievous errors in operational planning and intelligence analysis after Inchon that set up the disaster at Kunu-ri. By the journalistic standards of the War on Terror, all of these generals should have been sacked, and early on, which thankfully did not happen.

Disaster in American military history is not infrequent. American soldiers have been asked to rebound from disasters of planning or execution, to respond with bravery and innovation to compensate for a lack of foresight or ineptitude or just bad luck. The American soldiers have always responded, as they did again in the Global War on Terror with the same resilience of those that bounced back from Kasserine and Kunu-ri.

THE HOME FRONT

Coached as we are by Hollywood and the recollections of loved ones of the "Greatest Generation," we know that America pulled together in World War II to an unprecedented level. Less clear is the effort from World War I, perhaps because it was short in comparison to the later effort. Most Americans know that the federal Government exerted enormous control over most aspects of the economy, in the name of war production, an effort that touched all households in World War II through rationing of most consumer goods, food, and fuel. Most Americans also know that later war efforts in Korea and Vietnam did not require such efforts. Indeed, in those efforts, like the current war, the government sought to minimize the effect of war on domestic life.

This brief chapter will highlight some of the key differences between the two World Wars and the current war. These examples will set the stage for subsequent chapters on Presidential Lying, Generals in Politics, The Draft, Dissent, The Media, and Heroes.

CURRENT SITUATION

"You can romanticize [World War II] too much, I suppose.... There were "slackers" and draft dodgers and black marketers back then as there are now. But they were on the periphery of things then. Now they run things."

- Don Kaul, Washington correspondent, *Topeka Capital-Journal*, 19 October 2007[220]

---

[220] Donald Kaul, "WWII Homefront Was Better Than This," *The Topeka Capital-Journal*, 19 October 2007, at
http://cjonline.com/stories/101907/opi_209891903.shtml.

WORLD WAR I

"The citizen should begin to work now for the election of a Congressman who represents his views on the war issues. If he would preserve his liberties, his freedom of thought and speech and action he should not be intimidated by the threats of the war traders and their newspapers."

- Senator Robert La Follette, progressive Republican from Wisconsin, August 1917[221]

In World War I, the US government mobilized industry and society by extending federal control into most facets of the industrial economy. War production surged in keeping with the mobilization and the overseas deployment of truly large American forces, which were arriving in Europe at the rate of 10,000 per day by mid-1918.[222] Those American industrialists and financiers that profited most from the increase in war production were the same leaders that the Wilson Administration tapped to lead the industrial effort. The Council of National Defense, formed in late 1916 from members of President Wilson's Cabinet, appointed an Advisory Commission containing industrialists, railroad executives, retailers, and bankers. The President's son-in-law, William Gibbs McAdoo, serving as Treasury Secretary and himself from the railroad industry, was instrumental in picking the Commission. In mid-1918, this apparatus became the War Industries Board that coordinated purchases (generally without bidding), established prices and allocations of raw materials, and set industrial production priorities.[223]

---

[221] Quoted in "Pro-German papers Under Close Watch," *The New York Times*, 9 August 1917, at http://www.oldmagazinearticles.com/pdf/WW1_Press_control.pdf.
[222] "The Home Front (World War I)," at http://www.woodrowwilson.org/topics/topics_show.htm?doc_id=398814.
[223] See Murray N. Rothbard, "War Collectivism in World War I," The Ludwig von Mises Institute, 2005, at http://mises.org/resources/2024, 3-5.

Food was brought under governmental control through the creation of the US Food Administration, whose head was called the "food dictator."[224] Wilson turned to America's most famous engineer, Herbert Hoover, to lead the food effort. While overtly harkening successfully to America's sense of volunteerism, Hoover had coercive power and used it to set prices, particularly of wheat. By 1918, America's food exports had grown three-fold.

The government also sought societal mobilization, which required a level of governmental exhortation never before seen, directed by organs such as the Committee on Public Information and the Advertising Section of the Food Administration. Societal mobilization was largely successful in raising volunteers, selling Liberty Bonds to finance the war, promoting cooperation between business sectors and organized labor, and most importantly, reducing the need to resort to governmental coercion - only one percent of those eligible for conscription resisted.[225] The industrial mobilization also opened up jobs for women and African-Americans, causing a large migration of the latter to northern cities.

A darker side of this mobilization and consequent government control did exist. The Committee on Public Information was also known as the Creel Commission, and was entrusted with press censorship, although of a lighter touch than that experienced in World War II. Congress also authorized prosecution under the Espionage Acts of 1917 and 1918 for *"among other things, for any person to say anything with intent to obstruct the sale of war bonds; to utter, print, write, or publish any disloyal, profane, scurrilous, or abusive language intended to cause contempt or scorn for the form of government of the United States, the Constitution, the flag, or the uniform of the army or navy; to urge the curtailment of production of war materials with*

---

[224] The National Archives, "Teaching With Documents: Sow the Seeds of Victory! Posters From The Food Administration During World War I," http://www.archives.gov/education/lessons/sow-seeds/.
[225] "The United States Prepares for War", *Macrohistory and World Report*, http://www.fsmitha.com/h2/ch07-US2.htm.

the intent to hinder the war effort; or to utter any words supporting the cause of any country at war with the United States or opposing the cause of the United States."[226]

Left: An example of governmental exhortation that helped increase US food exports by three-fold.[227] Right: The motto of this poster was, "Save Her from the Hun – Buy Liberty Bonds"[228]

---

[226] "Sedition and Domestic Terrorism - The Espionage Acts Of 1917 And 1918," http://law.jrank.org/pages/2025/Sedition-Domestic-Terrorism-Espionage-Acts-1917-1918.html.

[227] National Archives and Records Administration, Records of the U. S. Food Administration
Record Group 4, ARC Identifier: 512498,
http://www.archives.gov/education/lessons/sow-seeds/.

[228] The National Archives; **Save Her From Hun-Buy Liberty Bonds. From a photograph posed for by Miss Francis Fairchild, a 1918 debutante of New York, in behalf of the Fourth Liberty Loan. Underwood and Underwood: 08/1918; ARC Identifier 533723 / Local Identifier 165-WW-458C (20);** Still Picture Records Section, Special Media Archives Services Division, College Park, MD; Item from Record Group 165: Records of the War Department General and Special Staffs, 1860 – 1952.

More than 2000 Americans would eventually be prosecuted under the act, including political figures like the perennial Socialist presidential candidate Eugene Debs. Pressure groups formed to engage in anti-German vigilantism. Some establishments renamed sauerkraut as "liberty cabbage" and hamburger as "Salisbury steak." Worse, federal and state governments took action against the public speaking of German and against German-language publications. German music and songs were banned in some areas.

WORLD WAR II

During the depths of the Great Depression, American political leaders sought scapegoats. Available for easy demonization were those business icons of the Roaring Twenties, many of whom were also leaders in the war production effort in 1917-1918. Such thinking began soon after the War. An example from popular culture was Daddy Warbucks, one of the main characters in the popular comic strip *Little Orphan Annie* that debuted in 1924; he had made his fortune as an industrialist during the War. War and Depression were pressed into a marriage of political convenience by the means of profiteering. In 1934, sixteen years after the end of World War I, the Senate Special Committee on Investigation of the Munitions Industry began two years of hearings on the alleged war profiteers, led by Senator Gerald Nye, a progressive Republican from North Dakota. The Nye hearings embedded in the popular mind that perhaps the great slaughter of the trenches was promoted by the same business class that had helped bring on the Depression. The Nye hearings might also be seen as a form of political payback, since the Roosevelt Democrats had been blaming a cozy Republican relationship with business in the 1920s for the Depression. The hearings allowed the connection to be made in the mind of the public that the governing Democrats of 1934 were the same party that had led the country into war in 1917 allegedly in collusion with the war profiteers – handy politics for hard times. In this line of thinking, the slackers, draft dodgers and black marketers didn't suddenly show up running the show in the 2000s, but had been firmly in place in America's first big industrial war effort. These investigations and the consequent popular pressure contributed to the passage of the Neutrality Acts of 1935, 1936, 1937, and 1939, ostensibly to keep the Roosevelt Democrats from committing the same foreign policy errors as the Wilson Democrats, but which certainly made US preparedness for World War II much, much more difficult.

War collectivism or war socialism came back strong with US entry into World War II. This is not surprising given the governmental experience in World War I and the fact that several members of President Roosevelt's "brain trust" behind the New Deal had once looked with admiration upon the apparent organizing skills of the collectivists working for Mussolini and Stalin.[229] Roosevelt himself had been Assistant Secretary of the Navy in World War I, and had seen America's first experiment with war collectivism from the inside. The Roosevelt Administration created a dizzying array of more than two dozen executive agencies to manage the war effort. In 1943, he created a super agency – the Office of War Mobilization – to oversee all of the other agencies.[230]

As in 1917, though, the powers of government were not enough, and the Roosevelt Administration turned to the much-maligned leaders of big business that it had done so much to demonize in the 1930s to fill in the gaps. Among many others, executives like Edward R. Stettinius Jr. of US Steel and William S. Knudsen of General Motors were called to Washington as major advisors or governmental executives. Knudsen received a direct commission as a Lieutenant General, and Stettinius finished the war as Secretary of State.

Against the wishes of his New Dealers, Roosevelt stopped antagonizing business, and allowed businessmen to make handsome profits through

---

[229] See Amity Shlaes, *The Forgotten Man: A New History of the Great Depression*, (New York: HarperCollins e-books, Kindle version, 2007).
[230] Dear 1187-1188

open-ended cost-plus contracts to encourage their full-fledged support, with stupendous results. Durable manufacturing output rose 38% between 1940 and 1945, even as productivity per worker-hour increased 21%. Unemployment had stood at 14.6% in 1940, despite eight years of New Deal efforts to revive the economy, but essentially disappeared during the military and industrial mobilization efforts.[231]

The social mobilization in World War II was much deeper than the shorter duration effort of the previous war. The Office of Price Administration controlled prices down to the shop level and issued ration cards to all consumers. In a preview of what burdensome government could achieve, the manual for meat rationing ran 40,000 words. The War Production Board allocated raw materials to industry based on military priorities, and banned all production of light trucks and automobiles until the war crisis was over. Some emphasis was placed on smaller companies to aid war production, but only a small amount of value went to these enterprises as big business dominated vital production.

While volunteerism was a common virtue, the Office of Information maintained a flow of information to boost morale and cooperation, including through its Hollywood office. This was particularly important to the seven bond drives that financed slightly more than 50% of the cost of the war.

---

[231] Dear 1180-1182.

An example of exhortation extolling the virtues of rationing and high taxes, while also suggesting that an individual's wages no longer belong entirely to the individual. The War Advertising Council would eventually morph into the Ad Council that continues to exhort Americans on behalf of government agencies more than 65 years after the end of the war.[232]

Some six million volunteers sold $157 billion in bonds.[233] The last bond drive was a near perfect marriage of useful but emotional information to financial necessity. This drive raised $24 billion in a few short months of 1945 at a time when the entire federal budget was just $56 billion. The principal

---

[232] From http://www.old-time.com/commercials/OTR/Home%20Front%20II.htm. See also http://www.adcouncil.org/default.aspx?id=68.
[233] Dear 1182.

means was the enigmatic flag raising photograph from the slaughter on Iwo Jima and the use of the three surviving flag raisers on a two-month barnstorming tour. The Iwo Jima pictures appeared in as many as one million shop windows, two hundred thousand factories and five thousand bulletin boards, thus welding the image into the American consciousness for generations to come.[234]

Examples of posters designed to promote Americanism and the war effort.[235] Compare this to the current negative reaction to any use of 9-11 imagery to promote social or political unity on behalf of the War on Terror.

As the Wilson Administration had discovered in 1917-1918, exhortation and volunteerism in World War II was not enough. As did its predecessor, the Roosevelt Administration resorted to a governmentally-influenced self-censorship of the generally supportive Press. Just as in World War I, soldiers' mail was censored to ensure no useful information would fall by chance into

---

[234] "An Enduring Image,"
http://www.pbs.org/memorialdayconcert/features/iwo_jima.html. See also Bradley, *Flags*.
[235] The National Archives, **ARC Identifier 514327 / Local Identifier 44-PA-833,** Still Picture Records Section, Special Media Archives Services Division, College Park, MD, Item from Record Group 44: Records of the Office of Government Reports, 1932 – 1947; and **ARC Identifier 513637 / Local Identifier 44-PA-191** Still Picture Records Section, Special Media Archives Services Division, College Park, MD, Item from Record Group 44: Records of the Office of Government Reports, 1932 – 1947.

enemy hands. A few newspapers were closed, including that of Roosevelt's populist critic Charles Coughlin. Most notorious was Roosevelt's policy on internment of suspected immigrant populations – some 10,000 Germans and Italians and more than 120,000 Japanese were sent to camps.[236]

Another example of uplifting Americanism from a time when such messages were welcomed.[237]

---

[236] Dear 912-13, 1184.

[237] The National Archives, **ARC Identifier 515762 / Local Identifier 44-PA-2067,** Still Picture Records Section, Special Media Archives Services Division, College Park, MD, Item from Record Group 44: Records of the Office of Government Reports, 1932 – 1947.

THE GLOBAL WAR ON TERROR

"I was just a boy then but I remember collecting tin-foil for the war effort, carting my wagon around for paper drives, buying stamps to put in a book until I had enough for a war bond....Contrast that total effort to our feeble commitment to the Iraq war, which the Commander-in-Chief calls a "clash of civilizations." No draft, no rationing, no war bond drives, no nothing. We've been told that we can best support our boys by buying things. What a contemptible notion."

> - Don Kaul, Washington correspondent, *Topeka Capital-Journal*, 19 October 2007[238]

"Under the Patriot Act, Muslims, innocent of any crime, were picked up, often physically abused, and held incommunicado indefinitely."

> - Former Vice President Al Gore, 26 May 2004[239]

Since 2001, the US government has not asked Americans to sacrifice, has neither called for volunteers to enlist nor instituted a draft, has not instituted war-related price controls or commodity rationing, has not interned suspected populations of Arabs or Moslems, and has not censored the press or soldiers' mail. Still, in the first eight years of the war, President George W. Bush was regularly called a Hitler or a Fascist seeking to install a police state because of the comparatively mild provisions of the war time Patriot Act, which had passed overwhelmingly six weeks after the 9-11 attacks by Congress in October 2001 (357-66 in the House, and 98-1 in the Senate), renewed in March 2006, including with the vote of then-Senator Obama

---

[238] Donald Kaul, "WWII Homefront Was Better Than This," *The Topeka Capital-Journal*, 19 October 2007, at http://cjonline.com/stories/101907/opi_209891903.shtml.

[239] "Remarks by Al Gore," 26 May 2004, http://www.moveon.org/pac/gore-rumsfeld-transcript.html. The former Vice President does not clarify who these Arabs or Muslims were, or in what numbers, or in what U.S. jurisdictions these abuses allegedly happened.

(part of an 89-10 majority in the Senate; the House vote was 280-138), and then renewed again in May 2011, with the key support of the Obama administration (the House vote was 250-153; the Senate was 72-23; most of the "No" votes in both Houses came from the President's party) .

In the absence of any sort of national mobilization, the current war has become a vicious game of seeking cheap domestic political advantage. When General David Petraeus appeared before Congress in 2007 to explain the early days of the Iraqi Surge, he was attacked by MoveOn.org, a major financier of Democrat campaigns, in a notorious ad as "Betray Us." No Democrat politician of note returned MoveOn.org contributions, nor did they make vociferous denunciations of their financial benefactor's defamation of the general leading the main war effort. Perhaps even worse, leaders of the Democrat majority in Congress questioned the general's integrity throughout the Iraqi Surge operation. In April 2007, when the Surge was only two months old, Senate Majority Leader Harry Reid said of Petraeus, "I don't believe him, because it [the success of the Surge] is not happening. All you have to do is look at the facts."[240] In the Senate hearings of September 2007, Senator Hillary Clinton told General Petraeus that his presentation of the preliminary results of the Surge required "a willing suspension of disbelief," thus all but calling him a liar.[241] Later in September 2007 when Republicans in the Senate introduced a measure defending the honor and integrity of General Petraeus, twenty-five Democrats voted against the measure, including Senators Reid and Clinton; Senator Obama chose not to vote. [242]

---

[240] Alexander Bolton, "Gen. Petraeus' Nomination Puts Some Democrats in Awkward Spot," *The Hill*, 29 June 2010, http://thehill.com/homenews/administration/106045-petraeus-nomination-puts-some-dems-in-awkward-spot.

[241] Eli Lake, "Clinton Spars With Petraeus on Credibility," *New York Sun*, 12 September 2007, http://www.nysun.com/national/clinton-spars-with-petraeus-on-credibility/62426/.

[242] See http://www.senate.gov/legislative/LIS/roll_call_lists/roll_call_vote_cfm.cfm?congress=110&session=1&vote=00344.

In an act of supreme irony, in June 2010, now-President Obama appointed General Petraeus to command directly the US and international effort in Afghanistan, requiring him to work closely with the State Department, which reported to now-Secretary of State Hillary Clinton. The colloquial name of this phase of the international operation was the "Afghan Surge."

While there has been no mobilization of manpower or industry, and no attempt at social mobilization in support of the war effort, volunteers have nonetheless quietly worked in USO facilities, or as greeters and "huggers" in airports for returning troops. Ladies Auxiliary clubs knit scarves and pack "goody boxes" addressed to "any soldier" and then send them to the war theaters. When chartered aircraft return from the war zones, very often the ground crews at civilian airports create an arc of water from fire hoses for the airplanes to pass through. In small towns, when the remains of soldiers return home for burial, firemen and policemen, and passing citizens will line the streets or country roads while the hearse passes. Early in the Iraq campaign, the cafeteria menus in the three restaurants serving the House of Representatives changed the name of "French Fries" to "Freedom Fries" harkening back to the days of Liberty Cabbage in a backhanded swipe at French reticence to back military operations against their former client, Saddam Hussein. Any use of photographs from 9-11 or from battles in Iraq or Afghanistan to promote higher morale among the general public or the troops has been considered by the broader media, Hollywood, and the American intellectual elite as an unacceptable politicizing of a national tragedy and of war itself. Contrast this with the frequent symbolism of Pearl Harbor and the flag raising on Iwo Jima during World War II.

A snide view of the political debate about the Iraq Surge.[243]

CONCLUSION

The American history of the two World Wars that most public school children learned as late as the 1970s marveled at American resilience in face of adversity, at the incredible industrial output, at the seemingly necessary governmental controls and rationing. The images still come to us in the form of the old black-and-white films of the World War II generation, like the character of George Bailey of fictitious Bedford Falls, in *It's a Wonderful Life*. Bailey may have been unable to serve because of a childhood injury, but nonetheless helped organize his small town's contribution to the domestic

---

[243] Michelle Malkin, "Nancy Pelosi brings out the White Flag again: Iraq withdrawal returns to the House floor," 8 November 2007, http://michellemalkin.com/2007/11/08/nancy-pelosi-brings-out-the-white-flag-again-iraq-withdrawal-returns-to-the-house-floor/.

war effort. We see Rosie the Riveter in other images alongside those of pining mothers with stars posted in their windows. We've heard the stories from our parents and grandparents, perhaps as they swapped proud reminiscences with others of their own generation about the hard times and how they made it through. Where we have trouble is seeing ourselves willing to make similar sacrifices, or indeed much of any kind of personal sacrifice in today's conflicts. Few among us choose to serve or choose to volunteer to help those who serve. On the other hand, our leaders have not called us to service and sacrifice. Mostly, like the journalist Don Kaul quoted above, we fondly remember the past while sitting around comfortably complaining about the present.

GENERALS IN POLITICS

Modern American military tradition is for soldiers, officers especially, to maintain political neutrality, although earlier in our Republic this was not the case. Generals nowadays mostly engage in politics after retirement, although some leave the service noisily after policy disagreements. In the 2000s, American media accounts made much of a handful of retired generals who openly opposed either the Iraq war or the method of prosecution of the war, as if such opposition represented something new and radical in American politics during wartime. The strict political neutrality expected of officers today was not always the norm, as our history serves up several prominent examples that make the generals' public opposition during the Bush 43 administration nothing unusual.

CURRENT SITUATION

"The consequence of the military's quiescence was that a fundamentally flawed plan was executed for an invented war."

- Lieutenant General (retired) Gregory Newbold, former Director of Operations for the Joint Staff of the Joint Chiefs of Staff, 2006.[244]

HISTORICAL EXAMPLES

Lieutenant General Winfield Scott

Commissioned in 1808, Scott was a hero of the War of 1812, and had commanded US troops in several campaigns against American Indians. Named general-in-chief of the Army in 1841, he would again become a hero for his actions in the Mexican War, more than three decades after first

---

[244] Public Broadcasting System, "NewsHour with Jim Lehrer: Generals Speak Out On Iraq," 13 April 2006, http://www.pbs.org/newshour/bb/military/jan-june06/iraq_4-13.html.

winning public acclaim. In 1852, the Whig Party nominated Scott as their presidential candidate instead of their incumbent president, Millard Fillmore. Scott ran and lost, even as he maintained his position as general-in-chief. Scott finally retired in 1861, after devising the Anaconda Plan for dealing with the Confederacy.[245]

Major General John C. Fremont

John C. Fremont was the Army officer and pioneer that led the California revolt against the Mexican government in 1846-1847, and then led California into the Union as a Free State. In 1856, the new Republican Party chose then-Senator Fremont to be its first Presidential candidate, an ultimately unsuccessful effort. In 1861, President Lincoln commissioned Fremont as a Major General and sent him to the volatile border state of Missouri, where he quickly became a liability in the political calculation of keeping Missouri in the Union. Assigned to other duties, including a Corps command in Virginia, Fremont proved a failure and resigned in 1862. In 1864, radical Republicans dissatisfied with Lincoln's management of the war and desirous of much more punitive measures against the South put Fremont's name into contention to stand against the re-election of Lincoln. As Fremont attracted little following among the Republicans, his candidacy quickly ended in September 1864. [246]

Major General George B. McClellan

A more serious threat to Lincoln's re-election came from Major General George B. McClellan, running as the Democrat nominee. By 1864, Lincoln had replaced the leader of the Army of the Potomac five times. Worse, three bloody years into the war, casualties were soaring in mid-1864 as a result of

---

[245] Bowman 373.

[246] Henry Ketcham, *The Life of Abraham Lincoln* (New York: A.L. Burt, Kindle version, 1901), locations 2180-2183. See also Bowman 335-336.

the Union campaigns of attrition against Confederate forces along several fronts. The northern Democrats, or Copperheads, may have been opposed to secession, but they were not pro-Lincoln, blaming him for the war, the heavy human losses in the war, the bloody draft riots of 1863, and for other acts that had critics denouncing Lincoln as a king and a dictator. The Copperhead platform called for an immediate end to fighting, and ending the war through a negotiated peace. They went to the extraordinary length of nominating a widely-respected serving general, McClellan, as the man to oppose the sitting president and to implement a plan radically opposite to Lincoln's.[247]

MG George B. McClellan[248]

Worse for Lincoln, McClellan knew from the inside how Lincoln chose to manage the war. McClellan had been Lincoln's general-in-chief, and then had led the Army of the Potomac, the main Union force, early in the war. He clashed with Lincoln over the pace of the Union war effort, and the president

---

[247] Bowman 357-358.

[248] National Archives Digital Photographs on-line, **ARC Identifier 528744 / Local Identifier 111-B-4624,** Still Picture Records Section, Special Media Archives Services Division, College Park, MD, Item from Record Group 111: Records of the Office of the Chief Signal Officer, 1860 – 1985.

removed him as commander but retained him on active duty. The general along with other critics inside and outside of government would refer to Lincoln as a baboon or gorilla.[249] Like Winfield Scott, McClellan continued serving as a general while campaigning for president.

Lincoln considered that the impression of Northern unity was supremely important, both domestically and internationally. To achieve this impression, Lincoln tried to buy off McClellan with the offer of the highest ranking position in the US Army, as well as promoting McClellan's father-in-law to Major General, and promising to appoint other Democrats to high office.[250] Such an offer would be illegal today, and McClellan rejected the offer, but was nonetheless soundly defeated in the Electoral College. The general resigned his commission on election day, and left for an extended tour of Europe.

Major General Smedley Butler, U.S. Marine Corps

"I helped in the raping of half a dozen Central American republics for the benefit of Wall Street....In short I was a racketeer for capitalism."
-   Major General Smedley Butler, 1935[251]

The son and grandson of congressmen, Major General Smedley Butler came from a blue-blooded Philadelphia family whose connections secured him a commission in the Marines. His courage and resilience made him a legend in the Marines in an era when they landed frequently in the Caribbean Basin and in China. Without a college education, Butler rose through the ranks through bold action. When on leaves of absence, he successfully ran a coal mine and reorganized the Philadelphia police department.

---

[249] Critics of President George W. Bush also portrayed him frequently as a chimp.
[250] Ketcham, locations 2269-2274.
[251] Quoted in Max Boot, *The Savage Wars of Peace: Small Wars and the Rise of American Power* (New York: Basic Books, 2002) 269.

After successfully defending the US legation in Shanghai and Peking during the rise of Chiang Kai-shek, Butler got into serious trouble when he made public remarks insulting the Italian dictator, Mussolini. At the time, the dictator was still seen as an innovative leader by more than a few among the American intelligentsia, particularly on the Left.[252] The Hoover administration apologized to Mussolini, and Butler's military career ended in 1931. In 1932, he ran unsuccessfully for the Senate in Pennsylvania as a Republican. He was then recruited by a group of Wall Street executives to be the military leader of a potential coup against FDR and his anti-business New Deal. In an ironic twist for a well-connected man of privileged upbringing who exhibited for most of his adult life a liking for combat and was clearly thought to be rightwing in his politics by the Wall Street plotters, Butler spent the last years of his life as a leftwing isolationist opposed to all use of the American military outside of the continental U.S., even as the Axis menace became unmistakable.[253]

General Douglas MacArthur

"'When we lose the next war and an American boy is writhing in pain in the mud with a Japanese bayonet in his belly, I want the last words that he spits out in the form of a curse to be not against Douglas MacArthur but against Franklin Roosevelt.' FDR was enraged, and he said, 'Never speak to the President of the United States that way.' And MacArthur offered to resign, but Roosevelt brightened and said, 'No, no, Douglas, we must get together on this.'"[254]

---

[252] For the influence of Mussolini on the New Dealers of the American Left, see Shlaes, locations 165-171, 854-858, 1951-1953, 3479-3482.

[253] For an excellent synopsis of Butler's life and exploits, see Boot 142-148, 161-165, 264-270.

[254] Quoted by Robert Dallek in Public Broadcasting System, enhanced transcript of the film, "*The American Experience: MacArthur*," http://www.pbs.org/wgbh/amex/macarthur/filmmore/transcript/transcript1.html.

- Robert Dallek, *The American Experience: MacArthur*

The 1930s was the decade of Depression, when politicians cultivated the notion that in addition to causing the economic calamity, businessmen had also caused or exacerbated the First World War to increase their profits. Meanwhile, direct threats to the U.S. seemed geographically and politically distant, even on the eve of Pearl Harbor. Consequently, military spending languished. Worse, during the Depression the American Army was used in 1932 against World War I veterans composing the "Bonus Marchers," and then was forced to support social projects like the Civilian Conservation Corps under the New Deal. Liberal columnist Drew Pearson would denounce MacArthur, the Army Chief of Staff, as a potential dictator for the treatment of the Bonus Marchers. Upon coming to office less than a year after the Bonus March, FDR considered MacArthur to be the most dangerous man in America. For the next twenty years, MacArthur would be both a political and military figure.

After his stint as Army Chief of Staff, FDR sent MacArthur to the Philippines as its principal military advisor, at least partly to keep him from becoming a rival candidate in 1936.[255] In 1937, for fear of antagonizing the Japanese, FDR scaled back support to the Philippine military mission, and cancelled the outspoken MacArthur's assignment, provoking the general to retire, while nonetheless remaining as a military adviser, but on the Philippine payroll. In 1941, when FDR began reaching out to his opponents in the name of national unity, he recalled MacArthur to active duty.

MacArthur's forces were caught off guard by the Japanese attacks on 8 December in the Philippines. Despite this, he was not fired, which was the fate suffered by the commanding officers at Pearl Harbor. Some historians

---

[255] For FDR's views on MacArthur and his actions with respect to MacArthur, see PBS, *"The American Experience: MacArthur."*

allege this is partly because he was so well connected with the Republican opposition to FDR, but he was also engaged in a desperate fight. MacArthur's actions in the Philippines and elsewhere in the Pacific need not be recounted here, except to say that he became quite popular in a country looking for anything heroic in the weeks of almost continual defeats in December 1941 and early 1942.

In 1944, a presidential election year, when MacArthur was in constant inter-service conflict over division of resources between his Southwest Pacific Theater and the campaigns under the command of Admiral Nimitz, a Republican congressman approached MacArthur about running against FDR. [256] When this became public, MacArthur withdrew himself from contention, but not before using the threat of his campaigning against FDR to obtain resources for his desired return to the Philippines. In fact, the president traveled to Hawaii the day after the 1944 Democrat convention to meet the general half-way. At the meeting, MacArthur ensured that FDR understood that if his return to the Philippines was by-passed in favor of Nimitz's preferred route to Formosa (Taiwan today), then the elections would be affected. FDR gave sufficient assurance that MacArthur would get more resources in return for some good publicity from the general's press releases on the course of the war. [257]

MacArthur remained a political concern of FDR throughout FDR's tenure in office, but the President managed the general to very good effect. MacArthur's relationship with President Truman was worse, and came to a bad end. From the beginning, Truman thought MacArthur "a stuffed shirt" and a "Prima Donna." [258] In 1948, MacArthur was declaring that the occupation of Japan should end soon at the same time that Truman was considering turning Japan into a forward base in the Cold War. Newspapers

---

[256] PBS, "*The American Experience: MacArthur.*"

[257] Ronald H. Spector, *Eagle Against The Sun: The American War With Japan* (New York: The Free Press, 1985) 417-418.

[258] PBS, "*The American Experience: MacArthur.*"

and Republicans again floated the general's name for president, and MacArthur issued a public message from Tokyo that he would serve if called but would not actively campaign. His poor showing in the Wisconsin primary (his father's home state) convinced him to withdraw again, but this did nothing for his standing with Truman.

MacArthur is, of course, best remembered for his frequent public criticism of Truman's policies on waging the Korean War. Whereas the general was softer than Truman on Japanese occupation, he wanted to wage a much more aggressive campaign than Truman did in Korea. Finally, and historically, Truman famously fired MacArthur in 1951, saying in the process, "The son of a bitch isn't going to resign on me. He's going to be fired."[259] His firing was not the end. MacArthur returned to a ticker tape parade in Manhattan and an address to a joint session of Congress, all the while ripping the president's policies as tantamount to appeasement. His speaking tour would go on for over a year.

MacArthur was once again touted as a Republican candidate for president in 1952 amidst a rising tide of discontent over the stalemated Korean War. And as before, he fared poorly in the primaries, and had to watch the Republican nomination go to his former "clerk," General Dwight David Eisenhower. MacArthur, a thorn in the side of leftists and Democrats for twenty years, was finally humbled and faded into history.

General Dwight David Eisenhower

The example of MacArthur is the best-known and most-used example of political generals, perhaps because until recently it was within the living memory of most Americans. In 1952, though, the presidential campaign featured two Generals of the Army – MacArthur and Eisenhower. The former essentially began his campaign upon his firing in Korea in early 1951. The

---

[259] PBS, *"The American Experience: MacArthur."*

latter retired from his post as the first Supreme Allied Commander – Europe on 31 May 1952, a post to which Truman had appointed him. Ike entered the presidential race shortly thereafter campaigning against "Korea, Communism, and Corruption," a somewhat startling indictment against his recent commander-in-chief and the Democrat Party as whole. FDR had considered MacArthur the most dangerous man in America because MacArthur so diligently sought publicity, and was overtly political in his service. Eisenhower, on the other hand, served apolitically, was recruited by both parties for the 1948 race, and only became overtly political after his retirement, thus setting the standards generally followed today by generals and admirals.

General Wesley Clark

Like Smedley Butler before him, General Wesley Clark had difficulty deciding his party affiliation. Clark said that he would have been a Republican if only Karl Rove, Deputy Chief of Staff for the Bush White House, had returned his phone calls.[260] That political slight evidently drove Clark to become not only a Democrat, but a Democrat candidate for president in 2004, despite being shabbily treated by the Democrat administration of President Clinton when they removed him early from command of NATO after the Kosovo intervention in 1999. Like Butler who seemed to relish the interventions in which he participated only to turn against such interventions later in life, Clark was on record as supporting the Iraq War, only to proclaim later that he had always been consistently opposed to the war.[261] Although a useful

---

[260] Matthew Continetti, "Clark Never Called Karl," *The Weekly Standard*, 22 September 2003, http://www.weeklystandard.com/Content/Public/Articles/000/000/003/152tuawi.asp.

[261] See the various quotes from Clark supporting the war before Congress in September 2002 and as a CNN analyst in February 2003 at "Archives of the Progressive Review: Wesley Clark; Recovered History: Clark Pro-war Ante-bellum, Anti-war Post-bellum," http://prorev.com/clark.htm. For an example of his contrary statements on having consistently opposed the war, see William Saletan, "Dear

candidate to bash the sitting president for everything from strategy to tactics, Clark elicited no great public support for his candidacy.

THE GLOBAL WAR ON TERROR: Iraq and Afghanistan

"V CORPS HEADQUARTERS, near the Kuwait-Iraq border, March 31— Long-simmering tensions between Defense Secretary Donald H. Rumsfeld and Army commanders have erupted in a series of complaints from officers on the Iraqi battlefield that the Pentagon has not sent enough troops to wage the war as they want to fight it."

- Bernard Wienraub, *New York Times*, 1 April 2003, referring to the ground war then on-going, which would end sooner than expected a few weeks later.[262]

"Last fall, during the question-and-answer session following a speech he gave in London, McChrystal dismissed the counterterrorism strategy being advocated by Vice President Joe Biden as "shortsighted," saying it would lead to a state of "Chaos-istan"... unable to help themselves, he and his staff imagine the general dismissing the vice president with a good one-liner.
'Are you asking about Vice President Biden?' McChrystal says with a laugh. 'Who's that?'
'Biden?" suggests a top adviser. "Did you say: Bite Me?'"

- Quoted by Michael Hastings, June 2010[263]

John: Why is Wesley Clark Getting John Kerry's Role?" *Slate*, 23 September 2003, http://www.slate.com/id/2088811.
[262] Bernard Weinraub with Thom Shanker, "A NATION AT WAR: UNDER FIRE; Rumsfeld's Design for War Criticized on the Battlefield," *The New York Times*, 1 April 2003, http://www.nytimes.com/2003/04/01/world/nation-war-under-fire-rumsfeld-s-design-for-war-criticized-battlefield.html?pagewanted=1.
[263] Michael Hastings, "The Runaway General," *Rolling Stone*, 22 June 2010, http://www.rollingstone.com/politics/news/17390/119236.

In the Bush administration, Army Chief of Staff General Eric Shinseki (2004), Chairman of the Joint Chiefs of Staff General Peter Pace (2007), and CENTCOM Commander Admiral William J. Falon (2008) were all allegedly retired early or were surprisingly not reappointed to their positions. To political critics of the Bush administration, these officers were fired for their dissenting views. Vaguely reminiscent of MacArthur's appearance before Congress in 1951, the newly Democrat-controlled Congress held hearings in January 2007 in which a panel of retired senior generals were invited to prejudge the failure of President Bush's days-old announcement of the Iraq Surge.[264] This was clearly an attempt to give dissident generals, supposedly ignored by the Bush Administration, an open platform to speak for themselves and give voice to those on active duty who, also allegedly, were keeping their opposition to Bush policies quiet in keeping with the modern tradition.

In the Obama administration, the commanding general in Afghanistan, General David McKiernan was fired in early 2009, after less than a year in command. No specific reasons were noted for the dismissal of McKiernan, the first such event since MacArthur's firing in Korea, other than the desire of the new administration for a new plan and new leadership. In 2010, the new Afghanistan commander, General Stanley McChrystal requested retirement when his insulting remarks about the Obama White House and Vice President Biden were published. Handpicked by President Obama to succeed McKiernan, McChrystal (who had publicly acknowledged voting for Obama) would clearly have been fired had he not resigned.

The Secretary of Defense serves alongside the president as the "National Command Authority" to ensure civilian control of the military. In all the cases above except for GEN Shinseki, the Secretary of Defense involved in the

---

[264] John Holusha, "Retired Generals Criticize Bush's Plan for Iraq," *The New York Times*, 18 January 2007, http://www.nytimes.com/2007/01/18/world/middleeast/18cnd-general.html?_r=2.

decisions not to re-appoint, the firings, and the early retirements, was Robert Gates, under both Bush and Obama. Also of note is that the Democrat-controlled Congress under President Obama in 2009-2011 did not give any forum to dissident generals to criticize the new president's policies. In June 2011, President Obama announced the beginning of withdrawals from Afghanistan at a pace significantly faster than his highest-ranking generals had recommended, but no hearings ensued. As the blogger, Glenn Reynolds, a law professor, noted, "Under a Republican President, it's *listen to the generals*. Under a Democratic President, it's all about *civilian control of the military*."[265] (emphasis original) The result is the same – the four different commanders in Afghanistan in little more than 26 months represent a turbulence in the top leadership ranks that one could fairly argue the American military has not experienced since the Civil War.

CONCLUSION

War or even the smallest military campaign is an inherently political act. Both generals and politicians will be involved. Given this situation, to paraphrase Trotsky's famous comment on war, "generals may not be interested in politics, but politics is interested in generals." The question is how to maintain public confidence in the generals who must be seen as serving the national needs set forth by the constitutional officials of the government, and not serving party or personal goals.

---

[265] Glenn Reynolds, *Instapundit*, 22 June 2010, http://pajamasmedia.com/instapundit/101631/.

THE DRAFT

The issue of the Draft – forced conscription of Americans to be soldiers – comes and goes in our history. Given the founding of the country by states jealous of their own prerogatives and perceived constitutional rights, the means of raising troops for American conflicts from the Revolution until the Civil War was through the use of state militias called out by their governors, and manned mainly by volunteers.

With the need for mass armies in the Civil War and both world wars, the Federal government resorted to forced service, which also coincided with emerging political views on social mobilization in industrial societies. With the advent of the Cold War and the resulting maintenance of large standing forces in Europe and Korea, America continued the Draft in peacetime to maintain the forces required. In 1973, amidst the general unpopularity of the Vietnam War, the Draft ended and forces of above 2 million were thereafter maintained through recruitment of volunteers until the end of the Cold War in the early 1990s. Active duty forces of 1.4 million have since been maintained through volunteerism, even during the last ten years of warfare.

However, periodically since 1973, politicians generally of the Left, the same side of the political spectrum that most pressured to end the Draft in the early 1970s, have mooted the idea of returning to some sort of Draft, or "universal national service," not because of any military necessity, but rather from a desire to re-capture some of the magic they see in the social mobilizations achieved particularly in the world wars. This time, though, the conscripted manpower would be applied to perceived needs of social justice or social equity.

CURRENT SITUATION

"You've got stop-loss policies, so people can't get out when they were supposed to. You've got a backdoor draft right now."

- Senator John Kerry, 2nd Presidential Debate, 8 October 2004[266]

CIVIL WAR

"A more complicated, defective, and impracticable law could scarcely have been framed..."

- Major General Henry W. Halleck, letter to Major General William T. Sherman, October 1963, referencing the Union's Conscription Act.[267]

President Lincoln originally called for volunteers – 75,000 – to put down the secession of the Confederacy. The northern states were to raise these volunteers from among their citizens, and each did so, with states, cities, towns, and even individuals raising and equipping units under the old colonial concept that all able-bodied men were members of their state militia, subject to call-up.[268] When this proved insufficient as the "butcher's bill" of battle in 1861 and 1862 rose to unthinkable numbers, the Union had to resort to conscription. After northern states failed to provide sufficiently for a new levy of militia in July 1962, President Lincoln announced on 4 August 1962 a mandatory call-up of 300,000 state militia for 9-months, to be managed by the states. Any State failing to comply with its quota would see its citizens subjected for the first time ever to a Federal draft. The immediate negative political response from the Northern states led to the indefinite

---

[266] This would be a consistent Democrat campaign theme of the 2004 campaign, where internet rumors abounded that the Bush administration was about to re-start the draft. See "The 2004 Campaign: The 2nd Presidential Debate; The Presidential Candidates' 2nd Debate: 'These Are the Differences,'" *The New York Times*, 9 October 2004, http://query.nytimes.com/gst/fullpage.html?res=9B06E1D6123BF93AA35753C1A96 29C8B63&sec=&spon=&pagewanted=5.

[267] Millett 209.

[268] Weigley 203.

suspension of the president's act, although volunteers and state-provided militia eventually exceeded 500,000 under the July and August call-ups.[269]

With the slaughters in the late 1862 battles – Antietam, Chancellorsville, and Fredericksburg among them – reaching ever higher totals, even more troops were needed. The Enrollment Act of 3 March 1863 (or Conscription Act) proclaimed a Federal draft of all males between twenty and forty-five years of age to be managed by the Federal government – an extension of Federal power at the expense of the historically understood prerogatives of the states that the Lincoln administration asserted under the Article I Section 8 constitutional provision "to raise and support armies."[270] The law included provisions for substitution where a draftee could pay someone else to serve in his place, and "commutation" whereby a draftee could buy his way out of the draft. Worse politically, Army provost marshals were set to enforce the draft by going home to home to verify the number of draft-age men, which came across as an unacceptable Federal intrusion into the homes of Union citizens.[271] When registrations for the Federal draft began on 13 July, anti-draft riots broke out in several northern cities, most notably New York. Many of the rioters in New York were Irish immigrants. They attacked wealthy neighborhoods and the mayor's house, burned the newspaper offices of Horace Greeley (a leading abolitionist), and killed African-Americans and a Union colonel. The State governments and Federal troops responded with force, killing or wounding more than 1000 in New York alone making this the worst race riot in American history.[272]

In total, the Union government only examined 522,197 men for conscription, and exempted 315,509 of those called, mostly for physical reasons. Of the remainder, more than 86,000 "commuted" and 118,000 hired substitutes. Of the more than 1 million men that re-enlisted or were first-time enlistees in

---

[269] Weigley 206-208.
[270] Millett 207.
[271] Weigley 208-209.
[272] Bowman 162.

the Union Army in 1864-1865, only 46,347 were conscripts. Another 161,000 Union citizens refused to report to their local boards when summoned.[273] While the Civil War provided a precedent for a Federal Draft, which itself provoked some of the worst riots in American history, the actual manpower provided by the Draft was insignificant to the final Union victory.

WORLD WAR I

Troop requirements for the slaughter in the trenches were clearly going to exceed the number of willing volunteers. Yet, the Draft was not a popular tool. In late 1915, the pacifist Secretary of War Baker forbad the circulation to the Army staff of a paper advocating conscription. President Wilson resisted calls for conscription until February 1917, after he had won re-election using "He kept us out of war" as his campaign slogan.[274] He ordered Secretary Baker in February to prepare plans for a Draft, but as late as April, after America declared war, the president was still not convinced of the need for mass American armies. The Selective Service Act of 18 May 1917 was so unpopular with some members of Wilson's Democrats, particularly from rural states, that the bill was managed through the House by the minority Republican leadership.

Whereas the Draft supplied only 6% of the total Union Army in the Civil War, 67% of the 4.7 million Americans under arms in all services in World War I were draftees.[275] About 2000 draft resisters and war opponents were prosecuted and sent to prison under the Espionage Acts of 1917 and 1918.[276] The law did not provide for the category of "Conscientious Objector" but only 1697 draftees claimed such objection. At one point or another in the

---

[273] Millett 207, 209-210.
[274] Weigley 342-342.
[275] CRS 2. Weigley 357.
[276] "Sedition and Domestic Terrorism - The Espionage Acts Of 1917 And 1918," http://law.jrank.org/pages/2025/Sedition-Domestic-Terrorism-Espionage-Acts-1917-1918.html.

conflict, though, 337,649 men were classified as deserters.[277] The overwhelming majority of those called simply complied and served. Unlike America's previous experience with large scale conscription, no mass riots occurred, despite the large German and Irish immigrant communities that were anti-British in sentiment.

World War II

"On this day more than sixteen million young Americans are reviving the three-hundred-year-old American custom of the muster. They are obeying that first duty of free citizenship by which, from the earliest colonial times, every able-bodied citizen was subject to the call for service in the national defense."

- President Roosevelt, radio address, 16 October 1940, Selective Service Registration Day.[278]

As a response to the Great Depression, one of FDR's first acts in his New Deal of 1933 was the creation of the voluntary Civilian Conservation Corps (CCC) to help reduce the effects of mass unemployment. FDR involved the Army in the CCC's administration over the protests of the Army Chief of Staff, General MacArthur. The Army deployed 3600 officers and 13,000 soldiers to support the CCC. However, peak enrollment never exceeded 500,000 at a time when as many as 13 million Americans were unemployed (24.9% of the labor force). At its peak, the CCC provided relief to less than 5% of those unemployed. Some 3 million Americans passed through CCC camps in the program's nine years, providing the Regular Army with exposure to running camps for civilians, and civilians with some exposure to the military, both of

---

[277] For the number of objectors and deserters, see Marshall 314.

[278] From http://www.ibiblio.org/pha/7-2-188/188-20.html, 71.The recording can be found at The National Archives, "Sound Recordings: Voices of World War II 1937-1945," http://www.archives.gov/research/ww2/sound-recordings.html.

which would be of some use in the next mass conscription in World War II.[279] More importantly, despite not being effective as a means of alleviating unemployment, the CCC program continues to hold a fascination until present times for those seeking mass mobilization of American youth.

As in World War I, calls began for conscription well before America's entry into World War II. Fearful of reaction by the isolationists in a presidential election year, neither FDR nor the War Department would sponsor a conscription act even as Europe and Asia sank into war. Those believing in preparedness sought leaders in Congress to force the issue, convincing Democrat Senator Edward R. Burke of Nebraska and Republican Representative James W. Wadsworth of New York to introduce bills for a limited conscription. The bill passed on 16 September 1940 providing for the nation's first peacetime conscription, but only in limited numbers (about 800,000) for a one year term and only for service in the Western Hemisphere and in US possessions.[280] Men ages 21 to 35 had to register with local draft boards, later lowered to men aged 18 years. In August 1941, renewal of the bill passed the House by 203 to 202, a very narrow margin given the continued threat of war.[281]

More than 36 million men registered for the Draft. Five million received deferments for work related to the war effort, including 2 million deemed critical to the tobacco industry.[282] In total, more than 16 million served in uniform; of these, more than 10 million were conscripts, which meant wide

---

[279] Brigadier General John S. Brown, "Defending the Homeland: An Historical Perspective," *Joint Forces Quarterly*, no. 31, Summer 2002, pp10-16, reprinted in *Warfighting*, Book 2, 14th edition (Maxwell Air Force Base: Air University Press, 2003) 496.

[280] In his 16 October speech, FDR mentioned that 800,000 would be trained in the first year, with one million per year thereafter. However, the 1940 Act required renewal after only one year.

[281] Dear 1179; Weigley 425-427, 434-435.

[282] Millett 428-429.

inclusion of all classes, faiths, and ethnicities.[283] As in the previous war, the vast majority of American men complied, including FDR's four sons and the sons of most prominent business and political leaders. Conscientious Objectors numbered about 100,000 or 0.0029% of those eligible. About 6000 were jailed. For those objecting, some served in non-combat roles in the services. Others chose Civilian Public Service, but did their service in military-style camps in the U.S. (probably like those that once composed the Civilian Conservation Corps).[284]

POST-WORLD WAR II AND KOREA

"It must be remembered that many thousands of the Americans joined the Army for the purpose of getting a cheap education after their service and that they, at no time, expected to fight."

- British General Leslie Mansergh, secret report to the British Chiefs of Staff, late 1950[285]

"...to develop skills that could be used in civilian life, to raise the physical standards of the nation's manpower, to lower the illiteracy rate, to develop citizenship responsibilities, and to foster the moral and spiritual welfare of our young people."

- President Truman on his proposal for 6 months of universal military training which had heavyweight support from leading college educators.[286]

As World War II ended, the demobilization began. The Army and Army Air Forces went from a peak of 8.2 million down to just over a million in two years, as the total serving declined from over 12 million in 1945 to 1.46

---

[283] CRS 2; Millet 428.
[284] Dear 262.
[285] Hastings 173.
[286] Weigley 498.

million by 1950.[287] As the clear political priority was to bring the troops home, Congress allowed the Selective Service Act of 1940 to expire on 31 March 1947.

Meanwhile, the Truman administration had become enamored with the possible social benefits of large scale mobilization of America's youth. The administration generated various ideas built around the concept of "universal military training." With the war won, Congress and the public remained skeptical of the need and the cost of mobilization. To address the political issues, the administration's proposals kept changing, watering down the purely military aspects until the required service was to be little more than camps run by a civilian commission to teach citizenship for a period of six months. Congress disagreed that military-style camps were the best means to teach citizenship skills. However, with tensions building with the Soviet Union, Congress did pass a new Selective Service Act in 1948, to run for only two years. This draft brought in only 300,000 before the outbreak of the Korean War. The Act was fortuitously extended on the eve of the surprise North Korean invasion.[288]

The Korean War was fought with a largely draftee military. With only 5.7 million serving in the War, though, the draft was not all-inclusive. Being drafted did become "selective" as the name of the law implied. Inevitably this led to charges that the draft was administered unfairly. In June 1951, Congress again extended the Selective Service Act, and amended it to approve the concept of universal military training, which was never put into effect. Several National Guard divisions and smaller units were called into service, as were large numbers of inactive Reservists who were sent into combat as individual replacements.[289] Some questioned why a Draft was

---

[287] Weigley 486. Also see U.S. Census Bureau, "Twentieth Century Statistics," *Statistical Abstract of the United States: 1999*, 22.
[288] See Weigley 496-500.
[289] CRS 2; Weigley 508-510.

needed at all, when the entire Reserve and National Guard forces were still available for use.

VIETNAM

"During World War II, men were impatient with the slowness of the draft and enlisted by the millions. Today there would be no combat force without the draft....In other words, it takes an act of Congress, unevenly and occasionally illegally administered, to get an adequate number of bullet stoppers on the Asian mainland...The present situation has become frighteningly clear. The price for mere continuation of the fighting, let alone further escalation of the war, is the total destruction of Democracy here at home."

> \- Professor Roy G. Francis, commencement address, Harford High School, Hartford, Wisconsin, 3 June 1970.[290]

The Korean era set the stage for most of the subsequent debate over the Draft: the desire on the part of some for collective mobilization of American youth; the difficulties if not impracticalities of coercing an entire age cohort into camps in the absence of a widely accepted societal need; the unavoidable perception of unfairness in any Draft that was not truly inclusive of the vast majority; the controversies inherent in any selective use of Reserve and National Guard forces.

In the midst of Vietnam, the Secretary of Defense resorted to some social engineering via the Draft. Like others in his party, McNamara was enamored of the idea of the Draft as a social leveler and also as a tool to raise up the lowliest in society. His thinking was close in intent to the spirit of the Depression-era CCC and the Truman administration's desires for citizenship camps after World War II. The program was called Project 100,000, or more

---

[290] John Clark Pratt, *Vietnam Voices: Perspectives on the War Years, 1941-1982* (New York: Penguin Books, 1984) 452-453.

derisively, "McNamara's Morons." The project used the Draft to induct initially 40,000 in 1966 and then 100,000 per year thereafter of those previously rejected by local Draft Boards as unfit to serve, with the goal of providing them with education and training that otherwise might not be available to them. One advocate, Daniel Patrick Moynihan, described the military as perhaps the "the only reasonable hope for America's disadvantaged poor – white and black alike." Other advocates called the Project a "civil rights" program, since about 41% inducted in the program were African-American; however, since many of the African-Americans in Project 100,000 were assigned to combat specialties and sent into combat, the program was also denounced as racist.[291]

At least the combat in Korea had ended in three bloody years. As the combat stretched on in Vietnam, the Draft issues described above became critical domestic political issues. A new popular narrative grew up that the Draft was biased by race and class; that African-Americans and the poor died in disproportionate numbers. Project 100,000 seemed to lend credibility to such views. The writer James Fallows described observing at his own induction physical in 1969 the "white proles of Boston" being sent through the examinations "like so many cattle off to slaughter."[292] This belief became so ingrained that it has become immune to contrary evidence. About half of the field forces serving in Vietnam were draftees, the rest volunteers, and only about a third of the battle deaths came from draftees.[293] The Congressional Research Service records that African-Americans were 12.4 % of the fatalities in Vietnam, slightly higher than their proportion of the

---

[291] Sol Stern, "When the Black GI Comes Back from Vietnam," *New York Times Magazine*, 24 March 1968, at http://www.aavw.org/protest/draft_100000_abstract14.html. See also Myra MacPherson, "McNamara's 'Moron Corps,'" *Salon*, 29 May 2002, http://dir.salon.com/story/news/feature/2002/05/29/mcnamara/.

[292] James Fallows, "What Did You Do in The Class War, Daddy?" *Washington Monthly*, October 1975, reprinted at http://www.washingtonmonthly.com/features/2009/0911.fallows.html.

[293] Millett 587.

national population.[294] Using zip codes from the wealthiest neighborhoods in the U.S. as a proxy, three researchers in the early 1990s established that the percentage of Vietnam casualties suffered by the wealthiest was only slightly lower than their percentage of the total population.[295] Indeed, about 34% of enlisted draftees at the height of the war in 1968 came from middle class families, who also provided many of the combat officers.[296]

In 1971, the Nixon administration announced the end of the Draft, which came in 1973. The Vietnam-era Draft and its repercussions continued to impact American politics for another 30 years, first in the campaigns of Bill Clinton, for having successfully manipulated the system to avoid the draft and military service altogether, and then the campaigns of Dan Qualye and George W. Bush for their service in the Army and Air National Guard respectively, widely seen as simply another means of avoiding service in Vietnam. The ingrained perception that the majority of the military are poor and non-white continues to this day.[297]

1980s-1990s

"Unless the pattern changes, we will very soon reach the point at which almost no educated white people...will have had any first-hand exposure to the military."

"Theoretically, many of today's soldiers might be planning to go to college once they finish their hitch. Some do – but most join the Army in the first

---

[294] CRS 6. African-American combat deaths in Iraq and Afghanistan have been less than 10% of the total. See CRS 14, 17.

[295] See Arnold Barnett, Timothy Stanley and Michael Shore," America's Vietnam Casualties: Victims of a Class War?" *Operations Research*, Vol. 40, No. 5, Sep. - Oct., 1992, pp. 856-866.

[296] Millett 587.

[297] See below for remarks made in 2006 by Senator Kerry and Representative Rangel.

place precisely because they do not have the money or opportunity to go to college and have no bright employment prospects in sight."

- James Fallows, 1981[298]

A Democrat administration brought the peacetime Draft to the nation in 1940, and with the exception of the brief period in 1947-1948, America had the Draft until a Republican administration ended it in 1973. In the latter years of Vietnam, as the Democrat Party lurched to the Left after their electoral defeat of 1968, the Draft became one more rallying cry for those opposed to the war. With the end of the Draft in 1973, the armed services became staffed entirely with volunteers. Yet, President Carter, another Democrat, reinstituted mandatory registration with the Selective Service for all males upon turning 18.[299] In 1981, James Fallows, the former chief speechwriter for President Carter, published an award-winning book on defense issues that called for the return to the Draft, even though Fallows himself resisted the Draft in his own youth.

The terms of the debate over military use of the Draft have changed little since Fallows' arguments in 1981. Fallows feared the creation of an "army of the poor" because only the dregs of American society were enlisting – some 41% of enlistees in 1979 were high school dropouts, presumably incapable of operating increasingly sophisticated equipment. Moreover, Fallows argued that the trends would lead to an Army were more than half of all the lower ranks would be black or Hispanic by the mid-1980s. He also noted that perhaps the main impediment to better recruitment was the lack of respect

---

[298] James Fallows, *National Defense* (New York: Vintage Books, 1981), which won the American Book Award. First quote from p. xvi; second from p. 127.

[299] The Carter administration undertook a comprehensive review of the concept of "national service," called "The President's Reorganization Project," in 1980, including the option of returning to a coercive draft. See "Appendix C: National Service Models and Proposals," *Citizenship and National Service: A Blue Print for Civic Enterprise*, Democrat Leadership Council, 1 May 1988, http://www.dlc.org/ndol_ci.cfm?contentid=250411&kaid=115&subid=145.

for those in uniform (ironically given that he was an ideological fellow traveler of the anti-war movement that had done so much to inculcate a disdain for all things military in the Vietnam era). Consequently, the armed forces would no longer be representative of society at large, a social defect that only a return to the Draft could remedy. [300] Such inclusiveness would also ensure appropriate political calculations, since Fallows observed that few of the Congressmen and Senators of the Vietnam generation then in office (in 1981) had ever served in Vietnam or on active duty. "Ultimately a nation must pay a price for using troops in war," Fallows wrote, "and it will be more attentive to the price from the start if all its members think they must pay."[301] Fallows favored a generalized system of national service with both civilian and military components, but was willing to adopt a fairly administered military Draft as a suitable substitute.

The ink was barely dry on Fallows' book award when the dire situation he described began to radically change. Only 33% of the enlistees in 1980 were dropouts. In 1982, this fell to 15%. The journalist Stanley Karnow, writing in 1983, had recorded many of the same horrendous statistics of the early All Volunteer Force, only to note that recruiters had "surprising success" from the white suburbs and among the middle classes in the early 1980s. Part of the turnaround was no doubt due to the sharp recession of 1980-1982, but much of it was also, as Karnow noted, due to a new respectability of military service.[302] As noted elsewhere in this book, though, the national debate over defense reforms in the 1980s was heavily predicated on the belief that American troops were of poor quality and insufficiently representative of American society until those same troops won the astounding, and generally unexpected, victory in the Gulf War.

---

[300] Fallows, *National Defense*, 123-129. Note the inherent bias that assumed that most blacks and Hispanics were poor and that Hispanics are uniformly non-white.
[301] Fallows, *National Defense*, 136.
[302] Stanley Karnow, *Vietnam: A History* (New York: The Viking Press, 1983) 25. Hereafter "Karnow."

Respectability for military service may have been restored in the Reagan Era, and the victory won in the Gulf War, but the idea of some sort of Draft to provide for higher quality inductees for all ranks, to provide for racial and class equity, and to provide a brake on military adventurism continued into and throughout the 1990s, as did the idea of a generalized system of national service that offered civilian alternatives to military service, perhaps with the simple intent of achieving greater social cohesion. Calls for some sort of national service continued throughout the late 1980s and 1990s, mostly coming from the Left of American politics, often from the Democrat Leadership Council, a consistent supporter of former draft resister, President Clinton.[303]

GLOBAL WAR ON TERROR: Iraq and Afghanistan

"President Bush and his administration have declared a war against terrorism that may soon involve sending thousands of American troops into combat in Iraq. I voted against the Congressional resolution giving the president authority to carry out this war....But as a combat veteran of the Korean conflict, I believe that if we are going to send our children to war, the governing principle must be that of shared sacrifice."

- Representative Charles B. Rangel (D-New York), 31 December 2002, calling for a return to the Draft[304]

---

[303] See for examples: *Citizenship and National Service: A Blue Print for Civic Enterprise*, Democrat Leadership Council, 1 May 1988, which called for a widespread voluntary program tied to student aid; By early 1997, the suggestion had changed to mandatory service, preferably through a high school requirement for graduation, "Talking Points: National and Community Service," Democrat Leadership Council, 24 April 1997. By 1999, "nationalize" and "universal" had crept into the Council's publications, with future college financial aid tied to some sort of required service. For all of these documents and others, go to http://www.dlc.org/ndol_sub.cfm?pagenum=3&kaid=115&subid=145.
[304] Charles B. Rangel, "Bring Back the Draft," The New York Times, 31 December 2002. http://www.nytimes.com/2002/12/31/opinion/bring-back-the-draft.html.

"Why isn't there an alarm that we've been perpetrating this war? Why is that? Well, more than a third of our soldiers have been sent back to the front lines multiple times. Some of the same soldiers sent back five and six times to the same war. Why is that? **Well, it's a way for the politicians to isolate on the poorest and the most isolated group of soldiers they can get and protect themselves from our society.**... *I think we have to raise the stakes on this to decide whether we get out or keep going. And the only way I can see to do that is to return the draft.* **Maybe if the sons and daughters of more Americans families, like those of our politicians, were either being killed in combat or facing the stresses of endless repeat deployment,** *our policymakers would start questioning why we're still there and come up with a different way to deal with insurgent warfare in the 21st century."* (emphasis added)

- Dylan Ratigan, MSNBC host, 1 July 2010[305]

During the fall of 2004, as the presidential elections heated up, rumors began that the Bush administration had plans to re-instate the Draft to deal with the military demands of the Iraq and Afghan campaigns. As candidate for Vice President, Senator John Edwards (D-North Carolina), told an audience on 16 September 2004 that if the Democrats won, there would be no return to the draft. In the same month, an anonymous email went viral on the internet alleging that the Bush administration was pushing legislation pending in the House and Senate to reinstate the Draft. In other campaign stops, the presidential candidate, Senator John Kerry (D-Massachusetts) criticized the Bush administration for use of the Reserves, National Guard, and the "stop-loss" provision of enlistment contracts to maintain troops on

---

[305] Kyle Drennen, "MSNBC's Ratigan: American's Don't 'Give A Damn' About Iraq and Afghan Wars; Calls for Draft", Newsbusters, 1 July 2010, http://newsbusters.org/blogs/kyle-drennen/2010/07/01/msnbcs-ratigan-americans-dont-give-damn-about-iraq-and-afghan-wars-cal.

active duty, and went so far as to claim the administration was secretly preparing for Draft boards.[306]

The only legislation to re-instate the Draft pending in Congress at this point in the campaign was a bill introduced in the House by Representative Rangel, co-sponsored by fourteen other Democrats, and in the Senate by Senator Earnest "Fritz" Hollings, (D-South Carolina). As the second presidential debate neared, the House Republican leadership brought up the Rangel bill for a vote on 5 October 2004 to suspend debate and proceed to passage, perhaps in response to the Democrat campaign tactics. The bill failed by a vote of 402-2, with even Rangel and all but one of his co-sponsors voting against it.[307] In the presidential debate four nights later, President Bush mentioned the Draft rumors, and Senator Kerry referred to the use of "stop-loss" as a "backdoor draft."

This political theater demonstrated that the Draft was still a politically-charged issue with little popular support. Representative Rangel acknowledged that the reason behind his bill was to create controversy and debate about the Bush administration's actions in Iraq. Rangel introduced the bill originally in 2003 and thereafter in 2006, 2007, and 2010, (presumably the 2010 bill was to protest the Obama administration's recently expanded war in Afghanistan).[308] Senator Hollings introduced bills in the Senate to reinstate the Draft four times before his retirement in 2005, in order to "better share the burden of the nation's defense and bolster U.S. troop strength."[309]

---

[306] See Associated Press, "Edwards: No Draft With Dems in Charge," Fox News, 16 September 2004, http://www.foxnews.com/story/0,2933,132559,00.html; and Trace Gallagher and David Miller, "Draft Scare Ignites Cyberspace," Fox News, 30 September 2004, http://www.foxnews.com/story/0,2933,134153,00.html.
[307] "House Opposes Military Draft Bill," Fox News, 6 October 2004, http://www.foxnews.com/story/0,2933,134546,00.html.
[308] Fox News, 6 October 2004.
[309] See http://www.fritzhollings.com/record.htm.

The well-worn belief in the inferiority of those volunteering for the armed services made another come-back a few days before the off-year elections of 2006. At a political rally at a California college on 31 October 2006, Senator John Kerry (D-Massachusetts) said, "Education -- if you make the most of it and you study hard and you do your homework, and you make an effort to be smart, you can do well. If you don't, you get stuck in Iraq."[310] Coming as it did on the eve of elections set to return the Democrats to control of Congress, criticism immediately flowed from all sides, and Senator Kerry quickly backtracked, arguing that this was a joke poorly delivered. Nonetheless, once the elections were over, Democrat Representative Charles Rangel of New York would say just a few weeks later, "If a young fellow has an option of having a decent career, or joining the Army to fight in Iraq, you can bet your life that he would not be in Iraq... No bright young individual wants to fight just because of a bonus and just because of educational benefits. And most all of them come from communities of very, very high unemployment." Representative Rangel was responding to a Heritage Foundation study that showed, contrary to the reigning perceptions, that 97% of enlistees were high school graduates compared to only 80% of the American population, and read at a full grade level higher than the average American adult.[311]

---

[310] Rick Klein, "Kerry's 'Stuck in Iraq' Remark Ignites Firefight with Bush, GOP," *The Boston Globe*, 1 November 2006, http://www.boston.com/news/nation/washington/articles/2006/11/01/kerrys_stuck_in_iraq_remark_ignites_firefight_with_bush_gop/.
[311] Josh Gerstein, "Rangel Adopts the Logic of Kerry's 'Joke,'" *The New York Sun*, 27 November 2006, http://www.nysun.com/national/rangel-adopts-the-logic-of-kerrys-joke/44138/.

In a photo distributed widely on the internet, Minnesota Army National Guardsmen respond to negative views of the intellectual quality of American volunteer soldiers.[312]

Fear of re-instating the Draft may have been an ineffective campaign tool for the Left in the 2004 elections, but that did not stop calls for some form of national service, despite criticism of such proposals as "paid volunteerism" or "welfare for yuppies" or "coerced volunteerism."[313] Quite aside from any military necessities of the current war, such calls followed the consistent theme of the previous decades – the need for a broader ethnic and social representation in the military, the need to re-connect all citizens with a sense of obligation to their country in order to promote social cohesion, and the need to focus on solving really urgent and seemingly intractable problems like illiteracy, homelessness, environmental degradation, elder care, or just the unwillingness of many Americans to vote (despite the many existing governmental programs already focused on these same issues).

---

[312] Bob Von Sternberg, "Minnesota Unit Behind 'Irak' Sign," *Star Tribune*, 2 November 2006, http://www.startribune.com/politics/11757706.html.
[313] Transcript, "United We Serve: National Service and the Future of Citizenship," The Brookings Institution seminar, 30 July 2003, http://www.brookings.edu/events/2003/0730governance.aspx, p 24.

A frequent analogy used was the hope that one day, through a new form of national service, a cab driver could swap stories with any passenger about where each had "done their service" just like in the aftermath of World War II. Proponents still come predominately from the Left, and still disagree over whether the goal of "universal national service" to meet the "cab driver test" would be voluntary or mandatory. In 2006, Representative Rahm Emanuel (D-Illinois), a former top Clinton advisor and Chair of the Democrat National Campaign Committee, and Bruce Reed, another Clinton adviser, published a plan to require 90 days of mandatory national service for civil defense training. [314] In 2007, *Time* magazine's Richard Stengel argued for a widespread voluntary program whereas political scientist Larry Sabato argued for a constitutional amendment requiring national service. [315] In the days after the Obama victory in 2008, the incoming administration's transition website announced on 7 November 2008 ongoing planning to require all middle and high school students to work 50 hours per year, and all college students to work 100 hours per year. By the end of the same day, the requirement had been changed to a mere goal. [316]

Paradoxically, in these same years volunteerism in the United States reached a post-Vietnam high, a fact acknowledged even by the proponents of required national service – some 27% of Americans volunteer some of their time, or 81 million Americans out of 300 million. This comes at a time,

---

[314] See Rahm Emanuel and Bruce Reed, *The Plan: Big Ideas for America* (New York: Perseus Books, 2006).

[315] Richard Stengel, "The Case for National Service, *Time*, 30 August 2007, http://www.time.com/time/specials/2007/article/0,28804,1657256_1657317_1657570,00.html; Larry J. Sabato, *A More Perfect Constitution: 23 Proposals to Revitalize our Constitution and Make America a Fairer Country* (NY: Walker and Company, 2007).

[316] See the links embedded at AllahPundit, "Flashback audio: Senator Obama talks about mandatory national service," http://hotair.com/archives/2009/08/13/flashback-audio-senator-obama-talks-about-mandatory-national-service/comment-page-1/#comments.

though, when confidence in government and its institutions is low.[317] However, as one universal service advocate put it, "Unless the decline of the American political institutions are [sic] reversed, our problem, our conflicts, will not be adequately addressed no matter how many bird-watching groups and church picnics we can attend. Self-government is not just a social venture; it's a political adventure."[318] The problem for such advocates is not lack of volunteerism, but rather a lack of volunteering in the right way on a set of governmentally-directed tasks designed to restore a faith in governmental efficacy. Left unsaid in this line of argument is how a few million additional draftees will solve societal problems – literacy, environmental degradation, homelessness, elder care, etc. - at which hundreds of billions of dollars per year in social programs are already directed, and in which hundreds of thousands of public employees are already professionally engaged.[319] Moreover, none of these proposals for required or coercive national service are directed at greatly enhancing the size or the power of America's armed forces to win the Global War on Terror; rather the focus is almost entirely domestic.

---

[317] See Stengel. This volunteerism is no doubt in addition to the more than 2 million volunteers currently serving in uniform in the active and reserve components in war time, or the millions serving as policemen, firemen, and emergency medical technicians, all of whom are volunteers for the most dangerous public service jobs.

[318] Kayla Drogosz, quoted in Transcript, "United We Serve," 29.

[319] Five states have more than 200 public employees per 100,000 in population engaged in the delivery of public welfare benefits. Another five have more than 145 bureaucrats per 100,000 in population. Thus it is hard to argue that government is not addressing any of the social problems that animate proponents of national service. That these problems endure despite the enormous quanta of tax dollars and bureaucrats deployed probably undergirds the public's low esteem of government competence. See Mark Tapscott, "By The Numbers: How Many Local Government Public Welfare Bureaucrats Are There?" *Washington Examiner*, 18 August 2010, http://www.washingtonexaminer.com/opinion/blogs/beltway-confidential/by-the-numbers-how-many-local-government-public-welfare-bureaucrats-are-there-101028144.html.

CONCLUSION

We have now spent almost ten years at war with an all-volunteer military. New recruits keep coming, and re-enlistment rates of veterans continue to be high, despite occasional missed goals in one service or another, or in the Reserves or National Guards. This is true despite rising end-strength requirements in the Marines and Army which have borne the bulk of the fighting and dying.

As shown above, the Draft continues to be a contentious political issue, as it has throughout American history. Nonetheless, the idea of a Draft continues to have a powerful attraction, particularly for the American Left, coalesced broadly into the Democrat Party, whose main purpose for a Draft is equity or fairness, rather than military strength. Many, though, also have the same social engineering instincts that once animated Secretary NcNamara. These proponents often take their inspiration from the early 20th century philosopher William James' essay on "The Moral Equivalent of War." This essay was anti-military, but recognized a social benefit in mass mobilization to "inflame the civic temper." As James put the case,

> "...I will now confess my own utopia. I devoutly believe in the reign of peace and in the gradual advent of some sort of socialistic equilibrium..... We must make new energies and hardihoods continue the manliness to which the military mind so faithfully clings. Martial virtues must be the enduring cement; intrepidity, contempt of softness, surrender of private interest, obedience to command, must still remain the rock upon which states are built..."

James hoped that through such conscription "of the whole youthful population" into non-military activities, citizens would come to regard such activities as the equivalent of a "blood tax."[320]

The major challenge facing such proponents, aside from any conflicting views of the coming utopia, is that the side of the political spectrum so strong in the current advocacy of a new form of national or universal service is the same side that was so deeply involved in the demise of the Draft forty years ago. As the case of James Fallows and the Democrat Leadership Council demonstrates, within a few short years of ending the Draft in 1973, the Left again became enamored with the possibilities of mass mobilization, and had to face the incongruity, if not the outright hypocrisy of its views. To the Vietnam Draft resisters, the Draft helped perpetuate an "immoral war," and was biased by class and race, and thus needed to be resisted on those grounds. From such premises, it is only a short distance to arguing that resistance to the Draft in the Vietnam era was actually itself really a form of public service to the nation.[321] Any future draft would be, of course, fairly administered the advocates assure us, and would thus provide a brake on foreign intervention by including the children of the wealthy and of the political class. Such thinking holds out the promise for the best of all possible worlds – coerced mobilization (William James' "blood-tax") without militarism. Nonetheless, the incongruity and hypocrisy remain. At least in 1975, James Fallows admitted "the beginning of the sense of shame."[322]

Meanwhile, America still has a war to win.

---

[320] William James, "The Moral Equivalent of War," 1906, at http://www.constitution.org/wj/meow.htm .

[321] See the remarks of E.J. Dionne, quoted in Transcript, "United We Serve," p 3, who likened participation in the anti-war Student National Coordinating Committee to a "form of national service."

[322] Fallows, "Class War."

PRESIDENTIAL LYING

Accusations of presidential lying about war are nothing new to the American experience. They are closely associated with the similar phenomena concerning presidential conspiracies to bring about war, generally on behalf of some special interest, whether Big Fruit in the case of interventions in Central America, Big Rubber in Vietnam, or Big Oil in the Middle East. However mendacious such allegations themselves are, they can be quite effective politically.

CURRENT SITUATION

"Let us be crystal clear. Let there be no illusions as it relates to Iraq....George Bush lied to the American public. He lied to the world."

- Terry McAuliffe, Democrat National Committee Chairman, September 2004[323]

THE MEXICAN WAR, 1846-1848

"Some if not all the gentlemen on the other side of the House who have addressed the committee within the last two days have spoken rather complainingly, if I have rightly understood them, of the vote given a week or ten days ago declaring that the war with Mexico was unnecessarily and unconstitutionally commenced by the President...I am one of those who joined in that vote; and I did so under my best impression of the truth of the case. How I got this impression, and how it may possibly be remedied, I will now try to show. When the war began, it was my opinion that all those who because of knowing too little, or because of knowing too much, could not conscientiously oppose the conduct of the President in the beginning of it should nevertheless, as good citizens and patriots, remain silent on that

---

[323] Associated Press, "Kerry Stops Short of Using L-word," Fox News, 24 September 2004, http://www.foxnews.com/story/0,2933,133451,00.html.

point, at least till the war should be ended... I carefully examined the President's messages, to ascertain what he himself had said and proved upon the point-- The result of this examination was to make the impression, that taking for true, all the President states as facts, he falls far short of proving his justification; and that the President would have gone farther with his proof, if it had not been for the small matter, that the **truth** *would not permit him.*"(emphasis in the original)

- Abraham Lincoln, Speech before the U.S. House of Representatives, 12 January 1848[324]

On 13 May 1846, Congress declared war on Mexico. The Senate voted 40-2 in favor, and the House vote was 174-14. The vote in favor of the war was thus overwhelming. However, those opposed more to President Polk, a Democrat, than to the war, sought ways to oppose the President without necessarily being seen as opposing the war. Attempting to have it both ways, sixty-seven of the opposition Whigs, most of whom voted to declare war, voted against military mobilization and against increased appropriations for the war.

The war began over the disputed boundary between the recently annexed Texas Republic and Mexico. Both the U.S. and Mexico claimed the land between the Nueces and Rio Grande rivers. Both countries sent troops into the disputed zone, which ended in a military skirmish in April 1846, which served as the cause for the declaration of war. Opposition to the war included those who thought the war a pretext to gain new territory for the expansion of slavery, and those who opposed the president's use of force in disputed territories without consultation with Congress, or without the express authorization of Congress.

---

[324]Abraham Lincoln to Congress, January 12, 1848, Abraham Lincoln Papers at the Library of Congress. Transcribed and Annotated by the Lincoln Studies Center, Knox College. Galesburg, Illinois, http://memory.loc.gov/cgi-bin/query/r?ammem/mal:@field(DOCID+@lit(d0007400)).

Elected in 1846 after the war commenced, and arriving in Washington 18 months after war was declared, Representative Abraham Lincoln challenged the basis, as expressed by President Polk, for the war in speeches on the floor of the House as well as in private letters. Within days of taking up his seat in Congress, Lincoln addressed the House in lawyerly fashion, citing the claims in the President's speeches to justify military action and the eventual request for a declaration of war. Lincoln demanded to know, in his famous "Spot Resolutions," the exact spot where such events occurred, and whether those spots could clearly be claimed as U.S. territory. This was a theme to which Lincoln returned in the speech quoted above. Note that Lincoln quite clearly states that President Polk could not justify the war because "the **truth** would not permit him" (emphasis in the original).

In essence, Lincoln eloquently called the president a liar. Despite his opposition to Polk's actions in the 1840s, Lincoln himself would later expand the war powers of the presidency quite beyond those claimed by Polk, and after solemnly promising for years that as president he would not act against the institution of slavery where it existed, he did precisely that when Union victories in the Civil War gave him the opportunity.[325] While Lincoln's opposition to Polk may have had a strong element of principle and constitutional interpretation as its basis, one cannot escape the conclusion based on Lincoln's later actions as president that Lincoln was not above playing simple partisan politics.[326]

---

[325] National Archives, "Teaching with Documents: Lincoln's Spot Resolutions," http://www.archives.gov/education/lessons/lincoln-resolutions/.

[326] As an example, in private letters from this period, Lincoln would refer pejoratively to his Democrat opponents in the House as "locofocos." See Letter from Abraham Lincoln to William H. Herndon, 1 February 1848, in Jennifer Erbach, "Lincoln, Patriotism and Protest," Document Packet #1, Lincoln and the Mexican War, http://dig.lib.niu.edu/mexicanwar/lesson6-packet1.html.

WORLD WAR I

"The example of America must be the example, not merely of peace because it will not fight, but of peace because it is the healing and elevating influence of the world, and strife is not. There is such a thing as a man being too proud to fight. There is such a thing as a nation being so right that it does not need to convince others by force that it is right."

> - Woodrow Wilson, Address in Philadelphia, 10 May 1915[327]

"HE KEPT US OUT OF WAR!"

> - Campaign Slogan for Wilson's re-election in November 1916, when he narrowly defeated Supreme Court Justice Charles Evans Hughes, 277 electoral votes to 254

"It is a fearful thing to lead this great peaceful people into war, into the most terrible and disastrous of all wars, civilization itself seeming to be in the balance. But the right is more precious than peace, and we shall fight for the things we have always carried closest to our hearts."

> - Woodrow Wilson, Address to Congress, 2 April 1917, calling for war on Germany, five months after winning re-election on his peace platform[328]

During World War I, the U.S. did not suffer a direct attack on its homeland, nor was an imminent attack threatened. Several hundred of our citizens did die as passengers on ships that German U-boats sank in the Atlantic, as when 123 Americans died in the *Lusitania* sinking of 7 May 1915. As a nation with tens of millions of recent European immigrants, emotions often ran high

---

[327] Columbia World of Quotations, Columbia University Press, 1996, http://quotes.dictionary.com/The_example_of_America_must_be_the_example.
[328] Columbia World of Quotations, http://quotes.dictionary.com/It_is_a_fearful_thing_to_lead_this.

between those tracing their lineage back to countries on one side or the other of the European war.

Wilson was a man of contrast, saying or promising one thing, then doing something apparently the opposite. While running for President in 1912 against incumbent President Taft and against former President Roosevelt, one of the key issues was the growth of federal government power to regulate social and economic activities. In the midst of the campaign at the New York Press Club on 9 Sept 1912, Wilson would say, "The history of liberty is resistance. The history of liberty is a history of the limitation of governmental power, not the increase of it."[329] Perhaps he was appealing to those who opposed Roosevelt's Bull Moose progressives who sought greater federal regulatory power. In any event, contrary to his campaign rhetoric Wilson instigated a massive expansion of federal power through the creation of the Federal Reserve, the institution of the income tax, the Espionage Act of 1917, the Sedition Act of 1918, and Prohibition, amongst other initiatives. As a candidate in 1912, Wilson felt that he should atone for the political and military blunders and aggressiveness of his predecessors in foreign affairs, but nevertheless sent troops to Haiti, the Dominican Republic, Nicaragua, and twice to Mexico. He proposed his famous 14 points as a plan for ending World War I, and then abandoned or watered down many of them in the Versailles negotiations.

In a tight re-election race, Wilson campaigned on the fact that he had kept America out of the bloody European war. Re-elected in November 1916 and inaugurated for a second term in early March 1917, two events occurred that gave Wilson an excuse for reversing the position on which he had so recently based his campaign. In February 1917, Germany re-instituted unrestricted submarine warfare, which meant that they would sink any ship thought to be carrying supplies to Britain or France. This endangered American passengers who continued to travel on such ships despite the war.

---

[329] Jewell 224.

The second event was the Zimmermamn telegram, sent in January 1917 from Berlin to the German minister in Mexico. The telegram instructed the minister to offer US territory to Mexico if Mexico entered the war on Germany's side if the US entered the war against Germany.[330] The British intercepted and decoded the message, releasing it to President Wilson on 24 February 1917. Still, the U.S. suffered neither direct attack nor any fundamental change to its strategic position. Nonetheless, on 2 April, President Wilson asked Congress to declare war against Germany. Therefore, in the vernacular of the 2000s, this was a "war of choice," not of necessity. In fact, the U.S. entered the war as an "associated power," not as a formal ally of Britain or France, at least in part to maintain Wilson's pretense that America was a different category of belligerent.

Did Wilson pay a price for his about-face on the war? The war was over quickly before the initial patriotic fervor, goaded on by the Creel Commission while dissent was stifled by the Espionage and Sedition Acts, had time to morph into the cynicism and rancor seen in the Civil War or in our more recent wars. However, Wilson's opponents rejected what he saw as his ultimate triumphs – the Versailles Treaty and the founding of the League of Nations – which were the direct fruit of his decision to go to war. America also paid a price when in the 1930s many had come to believe that America's entry into World War I was the result of collusion between the Wilson administration and big business, which made the American citizenry more reluctant to face the growing menace of the Axis powers.

WORLD WAR II

"Let no group assume the exclusive label of the 'peace bloc.' We all belong to it.

---

[330] The National Archives, "Teaching with Documents: the Zimmermann Telegram," http://www.archives.gov/education/lessons/zimmermann/.

-   FDR, 1940 Presidential Campaign[331]

"I have said this before, but I shall say it again and again and again: Your boys are not going to be sent into any foreign wars."

-   FDR, Boston, 30 October 1940, during the 1940 Presidential Campaign[332]

"I am fighting to keep our people out of foreign wars. And I will keep on fighting."

-   FDR, Brooklyn, 1 November 1940, during the 1940 Presidential Campaign[333]

*"To embargo oil to Japan would be as popular a move in all parts of the country as you could make. There might develop from the embargoing of oil to Japan such a situation **as would make it, not only possible but easy, to get into this war in an effective way**. And if we should thus be indirectly brought in, we would avoid the criticism that we had gone in as an ally of communistic Russia."* (Emphasis added)

-   Interior Secretary Harold Ickes, letter to FDR, 23 June 1941, the day after Germany attacked Russia[334]

---

[331] Message to Congress Urging Repeal of the Embargo Provisions of the Neutrality Law, September 21, 1939, *The American Presidency Project*, http://www.presidency.ucsb.edu/ws/index.php?pid=15813.

[332] William Henry Chamberlin, "How Franklin Roosevelt Lied America Into War," *Institute for Historical Review*, http://www.ihr.org/jhr/v14/v14n6p19_Chamberlin.html, from *The Journal of Historical Review*, Nov.-Dec. 1994 (Vol. 14, No. 6), pages 19-21. This piece was originally excerpted from the anthology, edited by Harry Elmer Barnes, *Perpetual War for Perpetual Peace* (1953), Chapter 8, pages 485-491.

[333] Chamberlin.

[334] Johnson 392.

*"The President predicted that we were likely to be attacked perhaps next Monday...**the question was how to maneuver them into the position of firing the first shot.**"*(emphasis added)

- Secretary of War Henry L. Stimson, wartime diary, entry for 25 November 1941[335]

"[Roosevelt,] the only American President who ever lied us into a war because he did not have the political courage to lead us into it."

- Congresswoman Clare Boothe Luce, October 1944, during the 1944 Presidential Campaign[336]

"But it was not a Republican President who dealt with the visibly rising menaces of Hitler and Mussolini and Hirohito. Ours was not the Administration that promised young [G.I.] Jim's mother and father and neighbors and friends' economic security and peace. Yes, peace. No Republican President gave these promises which were kept to their ears, but broken to their hearts. For this terrible truth cannot be denied: these promises, which were given by a Government that was elected again and again and again because it made them, lie quite as dead as young Jim lies now. Jim was the heroic heir of the unheroic Roosevelt decade: a decade of confusion and conflict that ended in war."

- Congresswoman Clare Boothe Luce, Keynote Address to the 1944 Republican National Convention[337]

---

[335] Timothy B. Benford, *The World War II Quiz and Fact Book* (New York: Berkley Books, 1982) 71.

[336] "Roosevelt 'Lied Us Into War,' Mrs. Luce Declares in Chicago," *The New York Times*, 14 October 1944, p 9, quoted in "Clare Boothe Luce: Representative, 1943-1947, Republican from Connecticut," http://womenincongress.house.gov/member-profiles/profile.html?intID=147.

[337] Quoted in Michael A. Davis, "Politics as Usual: Franklin Roosevelt, Thomas Dewey and the Wartime Presidential Campaign of 1944," (Ph.D. Dissertation: University of Arkansas, 2005) 110.

Our image of World War II is shaped by 70 years of Hollywood films, documentaries and frequently hagiographic histories of the main American leaders. Not surprisingly, domestic politics never really stopped. The charge of "presidential lying" about America's entry into wars, made before World War II and after, also occurred in this war, most dramatically in the 1944 presidential campaign.

Despite the generally positive journalistic and historical views of the FDR era, the 20-20 hindsight of history can birth enduring conspiracy theories. In the case of the Pearl Harbor attack, the conspiratorially-minded find it hard to believe that the Roosevelt administration did not know of Japanese plans, that our intelligence service lost the entire Japanese fleet as it sailed for Hawaii, and that Hawaii and other U.S. possessions in the Pacific were left unwarned of impending attack.[338] The historical record is clear that FDR wanted to get the U.S. into World War II before Pearl Harbor, but feared the potential electoral clout of the peace and isolation factions among the American electorate. For these reasons FDR waged an undeclared naval war against the Nazi submarine fleets in the North Atlantic, did the destroyer-for-bases deal with Great Britain, and plotted war strategy with Churchill well in advance of the Japanese attack. Yet, no concrete evidence of any conspiracy to let the attack on Pearl Harbor occur has ever surfaced. As with the attacks on 9-11, one might at most charge the sitting administrations with intelligence incompetence for not discovering the attacks in advance, given the accumulated raw evidence at hand.

FDR's critics were vociferous and direct in their accusations of his lying, particularly during election years. Although the more positive view of the Roosevelt administration now dominates, as late as 1953 one academic wrote,

---

[338] On the continuing conspiracy controversy, see for example, Sam Roberts, "Pearl Harbor Conspiracy Theory About 'Winds' Message Refuted," *The New York Times*, 7 November 2008, http://www.nytimes.com/2008/12/07/world/americas/07iht-pearl.4.18463914.html.

"One is left, therefore, with the inescapable conclusion that the promises to "keep America out of foreign wars" were a deliberate hoax on the American people, perpetrated for the purpose of insuring Roosevelt's re-election and thereby enabling him to proceed with his plan of gradually edging the United States into war."[339]

VIETNAM

"I don't think it had much to do with accelerating the war — we were already up to our eyebrows in war when the Gulf of Tonkin resolution came along. I had taken the Senate floor against our involvement there a full year before the Gulf of Tonkin incident. What happened there was a deception. We were told by the administration that two of our destroyers on the high seas, where we had always insisted on the freedom of the seas, were attacked — an unprovoked attack by elements of the North Vietnamese naval force. I didn't really want to vote for that resolution at the time, even though I believed what we were told about the Gulf of Tonkin. But I let the senators who were managing the bill on the floor convince me that it was more of a political move by President Johnson, who wanted to protect his political flanks, against the charge by his opponent, Senator Barry Goldwater, that he was not responding vigorously enough in the Vietnam War.

And I think a lot of us voted for it that way. We were assured by thoughtful men like Senator Fulbright that it didn't mean anything — that it was a gesture."

- Former Senator George McGovern, explaining his vote for the Gulf of Tonkin Resolution[340]

---

[339] Chamberlin.

[340] Joshua Tanzer, "George McGovern on Peace and Progress, Then and Now," 21 September 2005, http://www.offoffoff.com/opinion/2005/mcgovern.php.

"The greatest contribution Vietnam is making...is that it is developing an ability in the United States to fight a limited war, to go to war without necessity of arousing the public ire."
-   Secretary of Defense Robert McNamara[341]

The most contentious war in American history remains Vietnam, which was also our only strategic defeat, largely self-imposed. President Kennedy, a popular idealist at home and abroad, got America into Vietnam as a means of responding to Soviet Premier Khrushchev's "wars of national liberation." The involvement of several thousand American advisers and supporting troops was not very controversial initially, wrapped as it was in the soaring rhetoric of "pay any price, bear any burden, meet any hardship" of the Kennedy inaugural.

With Kennedy assassinated, and Lyndon Johnson assuming the presidency and wishing to continue the domestic transformation of America, Vietnam became a political burden and a distraction. Johnson did not even like calling it a war.[342] To deliver his domestic vision for America, LBJ needed to be re-elected, but was not nearly as charismatic nor as popular as the man he replaced. Worse, his Republican opponent in the 1964 elections, Senator Barry Goldwater, attacked LBJ and the Democrats for their weakness in the face of communist threats generally and in Southeast Asia in particular. Counterattacking Goldwater as a war-mongering extremist, while also demonstrating resolve and strength in Vietnam proved to be a successful electoral formula; Johnson won 61% of the popular vote in 1964.

Did LBJ lie about the Gulf of Tonkin and about what he eventually wanted to do in Vietnam? Senator McGovern certainly implies that he did, calling the Gulf of Tonkin incident a "deception." McGovern, though, was quite willing to go along with the deception, as were many others in the House and

---

[341] Schweikart 690.
[342] Schweikart 689.

Senate who shortly thereafter came to oppose the war. Voting for the Gulf of Tonkin Resolution provided the necessary election year political gesture to protect the president's flanks. In what surely must be one of the more cynical votes in U.S. history, these leaders of the President's own party voted "to take all necessary steps" – a de facto declaration of war– on 10 August 1964, for purely short-term political gains in an election only weeks away. Only two senators voted against the Gulf of Tonkin Resolution, as almost nobody wanted to be seen as weak. Two weeks later on 24 August, the Democrat Convention nominated LBJ for re-election. Once the election was safely won, many of those voting for the Gulf of Tonkin Resolution turned against their own votes.

THE CLINTON WARS

"The imagery was intentional: a President welcoming U.S. troops back from exemplary military intervention abroad. While the occasion was to honor their service in Somalia, its real object was to make Clinton look more like a Commander in Chief as he contemplates a much tougher operation in Bosnia."

- *Time*, 17 May 1993[343]

"As his aides have done previously, the president engaged in a bit of semantics to suggest that he actually is keeping to his original promise to withdraw [from Bosnia] next month because the follow-on force represents "a different mission," a distinction that seems to persuade few outside the White House...."

- *The Washington Post*, 16 November 1996[344]

---

[343] George J. Church, Ann Blackman, Andrew Purvis, "Mission Half Accomplished," *Time*, 17 May 1993, http://www.time.com/time/magazine/article/0,9171,978519,00.html.
[344] Peter Baker and Bradley Graham, "Clinton Decides to Keep U.S. Troops in Bosnia," *The Washington Post*, 16 November 1996, http://www.washingtonpost.com/wp-srv/national/longterm/inaug/issues/bostroop.htm.

In the 1980s, opponents often painted President Ronald Reagan as the cowboy adventurer in foreign policy – aggressive, belligerent, a war-monger. President Bill Clinton in the 1990s was painted by opponents as a Vietnam-era draft-dodger who had manipulated the selective service system to avoid military service. The draft-dodger would send many more troops into combat in more places than the cowboy ever did: in Somalia, President Clinton expanded a humanitarian mission into combat oriented nation-building; he removed the government of Haiti with the threat of armed assault and then occupied the island; he bombarded the Serbs and sent occupation troops to Bosnia and Kosovo; he attacked Saddam Hussein's regime repeatedly with missiles and airstrikes; and launched retaliatory missile strikes against suspected al-Qaeda positions in Sudan and Afghanistan. Opponents also accused President Clinton of being less than honest about his military actions, particularly in Somalia and Bosnia.

Somalia

In mid-May 1993, the White House hosted a welcome home ceremony. The President marched across the lawn alongside fatigue-clad soldiers and Marines to signal the end of a humanitarian operation in Somalia begun in the waning days of his predecessor's administration a few months previously. The successful famine relief mission was officially over, and the troops were coming home. The responsibility had been passed from a U.S.-led effort to a UN-led effort involving more than 20 nations. The scenes were reminiscent of the jubilant images at the end of the Gulf War.

The press coverage generally mentioned as an afterthought, if they mentioned it at all, that the US would leave 4000 troops behind to support the UN effort.[345] In the muted explanations of the Clinton administration, this stay-behind force was executing a different mission, not the same

---

[345] See for example, "Passing the Torch," *Time*, 10 May 1993, http://www.time.com/time/magazine/article/0,9171,978462,00.html.

mission that had terminated officially at the White House ceremony, thus setting a pattern that would be used again in Bosnia.

Three weeks later, on 5 June 1993, the Somali warlord Mohamed Farrah Aidid ambushed and killed 24 Pakistani troops serving under the UN flag. The residual US troops found themselves engaged for the first time since Vietnam in persistent combat stretching over weeks and months into the autumn of 1993. The Clinton administration reinforced the "new" mission with additional special troops to hunt down the renegade warlord, leading eventually to the humiliating episode now known via the popular book and film as "Blackhawk Down" where an American force was cut off and engaged over two days in early October 1993, resulting in 18 Americans killed, 73 wounded, 2 helicopters shot down, American corpses publicly mutilated, and one American taken prisoner. This came as a rude shock to a public that had witnessed the triumphant ceremony on the White House lawn, which would have led casual observers to believe that the U.S. was ending its Somali operation, not deepening its commitment.

Bosnia

Candidate Clinton had campaigned on adopting a more assertive U.S. policy in the Balkans than his predecessor had followed. As the *Time* citation above notes, as early as 1993, President Clinton was contemplating how to get into the Balkan conflicts, particularly in Bosnia.

His chance came in 1995, with the U.S.-led NATO bombing of Bosnian Serb forces after a series of Serbian outrages. The bombing led to the Dayton Accords, with its requirement for international forces to monitor the settlement. Before the Senate Armed Services Committee, two weeks after the signing of the Dayton Accords, Secretary of Defense William Perry and Chairman of the Joint Chiefs of Staff, GEN John Shalikashvili, stated the Clinton administration's intention that the deployment of U.S. troops would last only one year, with a very limited mandate for action. On 27 November

1995, President Clinton addressed the nation on Bosnia, also pledging publicly that the mission would "take about one year."[346] The troops began deploying in December 1995.

Yet, before that year was up, the Clinton administration was calling for the deployment of an additional 5000 troops, and extending the withdrawal from December 1996 until mid-March 1997. Reminiscent of Somalia, though, these additional troops were to be sent under a different mission – to cover the withdrawal of the original forces – and the name of the international effort was to be changed from the Implementation Force (IFOR) to the Stabilization Force (SFOR). On 3 October 1996, before the Senate Armed Services Committee, Senator McCain quoted to Secretary Perry and GEN Shalikashvili their withdrawal timetable and commitments from the previous year, and said, "I think you knew better at the time." Senator Thurmond questioned the motives and the timing of the change, given the 1996 elections a month hence, and asked the Defense Secretary for assurances on these points: "It appears that the deployment of the 5,000-man covering force may be a pretense to a further extension of the U.S. military presence in Bosnia which this administration is unwilling to admit because of the U.S. elections in November. *Can you assure us* that this is not so, and that there are no plans or commitments for U.S. forces in Bosnia beyond the March 1, 1997, withdrawal date for the covering force?"(emphasis added) Secretary Perry rejected the charge of election politics and responded that "I can assure you I have made no recommendation to the President on the follow-on force. He has made no decision ongoing to support a follow-on force at

---

[346] Transcript of President Clinton's Speech on Bosnia, CNN, 27 November 1995, http://edition.cnn.com/US/9511/bosnia_speech/speech.html.

this time." [347] Just six weeks later, safely re-elected, President Clinton announced an extension of U.S. troops in Bosnia well beyond the few extra months promised by Secretary Perry on 3 October.

President Clinton became famous for shading the truth. Did he lie about the missions in Somalia and Bosnia, relying on the possible semantic definitions of "mission?" In November 2004, headlines proclaimed that the U.S. mission in Bosnia had finally come to an end after nine years, and eight years after the Clinton administration promised it would end. In yet another Clinton-esque twist, 150 U.S. troops would continue to serve in Bosnia, albeit on a different mission. [348]

THE WAR ON TERROR: Bush Years

Democratic presidential candidate John Kerry said Wednesday that President Bush broke his promise to build an international coalition against Iraq's Saddam Hussein and then waged a war based on questionable intelligence.

"He misled every one of us," Kerry said. "That's one reason why I'm running to be president of the United States."

- Associated Press reporting , Lebanon, N.H., 18 June 2003 [349]

---

[347] Quotations from Elizabeth Farnsworth, "Early Withdrawal?" transcript of *PBS Online Newshour: Online Backgrounder*, 3 October 1996, http://www.pbs.org/newshour/bb/bosnia/october96/bosnia_troops_10-3.html. See also Steven Erlanger, "7,500 G.I.'s Staying in Bosnia to Next Spring, Perry Says," The *New York Times*, 4 October 1996, http://www.nytimes.com/1996/10/04/world/7500-gi-s-staying-in-bosnia-to-next-spring-perry-says.html.

[348] Associated Press, "U.S. Troops Mark End of Mission in Bosnia," The *Washington Post*, 25 November 2004, http://www.washingtonpost.com/wp-dyn/articles/A11164-2004Nov24.html.

[349] Ron Fournier, "Kerry Says Bush Misled Americans on War," Associated Press, 18 June 2003, found at http://www.commondreams.org/headlines03/0618-09.htm.

"There was no imminent threat. This was made up in Texas, announced in January to the Republican leadership that war was going to take place and was going to be good politically. This whole thing was a fraud."
- Senator Edward Kennedy, 19 September 2003[350]

The [Iraqi Air Force] document indicates that 13,000 chemical bombs were dropped by the Iraqi Air Force between 1983 and 1988, while Iraq has declared that 19,500 bombs were consumed during this period. Thus, there is a discrepancy of 6,500 bombs. The amount of chemical agent in these bombs would be in the order of about 1,000 tonnes. In the absence of evidence to the contrary, we must assume that these quantities are now unaccounted for."
- Dr. Hans Blix, Chief UN Weapons Inspector, Addressing the UN Security Council, January 27, 2003[351]

With the 9-11 attacks still fresh in the public memory, President George W. Bush asked Congress for an authorization to use force against Iraq, opening a new campaign in the multi-front war on terror. The House passed the measure by a vote of 296-133, and the Senate by 77-23; the Senate vote came thirteen months to the day after 9-11. Perhaps as significantly, the congressional votes came on the eve of the mid-term elections, when those adhering to President Bush and his firm post-attack leadership looked to do better than his critics.

U.S. and allied forces then waged a very quick ground campaign to remove Saddam Hussein and his Ba'athist Party from power. The aftermath of the ground campaign was not so quick, nor was the path to victory so clear. Moreover, the presidential election cycle for 2004 was due to begin. By mid-

---

[350] Joel Roberts, "Kennedy: Case for War a 'Fraud,'" CBS News, 19 September 2003, http://www.cbsnews.com/stories/2003/09/19/politics/main574154.shtml.
[351] Text published in *The Washington Post*, 27 January 2003, http://www.washingtonpost.com/wp-srv/world/transcripts/blix_012703.html.

2003, the Democrat opposition to Bush had settled on their principle theme that President Bush had misled Congress, the American public, and the world about Iraq. Since several of the leading Democrat contenders were senators that had voted for the authorization to use force in Iraq, they had to provide themselves with political cover. Arguing that Saddam was not a brutal, mass murdering dictator who aided and supported terrorists was not likely to be a winning strategy since the evidence was overwhelming. However, the search for Saddam's weapons of mass destruction (WMD) had failed to find the quantities and types of weapons expected. This quickly became the mantra, "No WMD in Iraq," which connected as quickly to the street and internet protest phrase, "Bush Lied, Kids Died."

The campaign theme took on a life of its own in 2003 and 2004. It did not matter that Bush's predecessor, President Clinton, had attacked Iraq militarily several times over the issue of WMD, citing the tens of thousands of supposed chemical munitions that Saddam possessed. Clinton would go so far as to say publicly, "There is no more clear example of this [WMD] threat than Saddam Hussein's Iraq. His regime threatens the safety of his people, the stability of his region and the security of all the rest of us.... And some day, some way, I guarantee you, he'll use the arsenal."[352] In his key State of the Union address a few weeks before the ground invasion began, President Bush had used similar language, also citing tens of thousands of chemical weapons, while also making the point that waiting until Saddam's threats became imminent before acting would be "[t]rusting in the sanity and restraint of Saddam Hussein," which was not an option for the post-9-11 world.[353]

---

[352] Address to the Joint Chiefs of Staff and Pentagon Staff, 17 February 1998, http://www.cnn.com/ALLPOLITICS/1998/02/17/transcripts/clinton.iraq/.

[353] Transcript, State of the Union address, 23 January 2003, http://articles.cnn.com/2003-01-28/politics/sotu.transcript_1_tax-relief-corporate-scandals-and-stock-union-speech/9?_s=PM:ALLPOLITICS.

Bush won re-election in 2004 despite the accusation of misleading America into war, but the accusation persisted and was damaging, no doubt contributing to the severe reversals that Bush's party experienced in the 2006 and 2008 elections. Would it have mattered to the critics if a single WMD had been found, so that the "No WMD" charge could be refuted? Or would it have taken a 100, or some other number? Almost lost in the electoral processes was a news article from June 2006 that a Defense Department intelligence unit reported more than 500 chemical munitions had been found in the period 2003-2006, and more discoveries were expected.[354]

THE WAR ON TERROR: Obama Years

"I suffer no illusions about Saddam Hussein. He is a brutal man. A ruthless man. A man who butchers his own people to secure his own power. He has repeatedly defied UN resolutions, thwarted UN inspection teams, developed chemical and biological weapons, and coveted nuclear capacity. He's a bad guy. The world, and the Iraqi people, would be better off without him. But I also know that Saddam poses no imminent and direct threat to the United States or to his neighbors…. I am not opposed to all wars. I'm opposed to dumb wars."

- Illinois State Senator Barack Obama, 2 October 2002[355]

I teach separation of powers and constitutional law. This is something I know. So I got together and brought a group of Constitutional scholars together and write a piece I'm going to deliver to the whole United States Senate in pointing out the president has no Constitutional authority to take this nation

---

[354] See "Report: Hundreds of WMDs Found in Iraq," *Fox News*, 22 June 2006, http://www.foxnews.com/story/0,2933,200499,00.html.
[355] Transcript: Obama's Speech Against the Iraq War," NPR, 20 January 2009, http://www.npr.org/templates/story/story.php?storyId=99591469, accessed 27 June 2011.

to war against a country of 70 million people unless we're attacked, or unless there is proof that we are about to be attacked. If he does, I would move to impeach him. The House obviously has to do that– but I would lead an effort to impeach him.

- Senator Joe Biden, presidential candidate, Hardball interview, responding to a question about bombing Iranian nuclear facilities, aired 4 December 2007[356]

"The President does not have power under the Constitution to unilaterally authorize a military attack in a situation that does not involve stopping an actual or imminent threat to the nation."

- Senator Barack Obama, presidential candidate, responding to a question about bombing Iranian nuclear facilities, 20 December 2007[357]

"[H]ad this been Bush exercising such brazen dishonesty, it would have been the lead story on every TV network news program – for days. But it was Obama and Biden who lied through their teeth..."

- Brent Bozell, conservative opinion columnist, referring to the Obama Administrations'' bombing campaign against Libya 29 March 2011[358]

"I will be very interested to see whether other senators support the candidate Barack Obama or now the hypocritical version that has become our

---

[356] "BIDEN FLASHB ACK: Launching an Attack without Congressional Approval Is an Impeachable Offense," Big Government, 23 March 2011, http://biggovernment.com/mrctv/2011/03/23/biden-flashback-launching-an-attack-without-congressional-approval-is-an-impeachable-offense/, accessed 27 June 2011.
[357] Charlie Savage, "Barack Obama's Q&A," *The Boston Globe*, 20 December 2007, http://www.boston.com/news/politics/2008/specials/CandidateQA/ObamaQA/, accessed 27 June 2011.
[358] Brent Bozell, "Obama's Libyan War," Newsbusters, http://newsbusters.org/blogs/brent-bozell/2011/03/29/bozell-column-obamas-libyan-war, accessed 30 March 2011.

president....He had utter disregard and contempt for the most important body in the United States that represents the people, the U.S. Congress....Utter contempt. He has gone to NATO, he has gone to the U.N., he has gone to our allies, he has gone to the Arab league, but he has not had one single minute to come to Congress....I do not use the word hypocritical lightly."

> - Senator Rand Paul (R-KY) upon introducing a motion to condemn the Obama administration's attack on Libya by quoting then-candidate Obama's 2007 views on attacking Iran[359]

As soon as he authorized air strikes against Libya, President Obama boarded a plane for Brazil, and remained strangely quiet for several days, leaving administration spokesman to carry the burden of explanation. Deputy National Security Advisor Ben Rhodes called the intervention a "kinetic military action;" a few days later the White House Press Secretary Jay Carney called it a "time-limited, scope-limited military action." Officials at the National Security Council were emphatic, "This is a limited humanitarian intervention, not war." Others added to the confusion by contending that the operations were conducted without regard to consistency or precedent, where U.S. participation had been volunteered by other nations, and that the removal of the Gaddafi regime was a desire, but that U.S. military involvement in "heavy kinetic military activity" would last "days not weeks." When the President finally did address the actions in a speech, on 28 March 2011, nine days after the operations began, his remarks on taking pre-emptive military operations to attack another sovereign country with the removal of that country's government as an aim were in startling contrast to positions he had taken as a candidate.

---

[359] Josiah Ryan, "Sen. Paul: Obama Is 'Hypocritical' for Engaging US in 'Third War,'" The Hill, 30 March 2011, http://thehill.com/blogs/floor-action/senate/152871-sen-paul-obama-is-hypocritical-for-engaging-us-in-third-war- accessed 1 July 2011.

Almost everything that State Senator Obama said about Saddam Hussein in 2002 could have been said about Moammar Gaddafi in 2011. By 2011, though, Gaddafi was no longer defying the international community on weapons of mass destruction. The Libyan dictator had very publicly revealed his programs and then terminated them as a consequence of the overthrow and capture of Saddam in the "dumb war" that Obama had opposed. Indeed, by 2011 many countries in the West were cultivating Gaddafi as he re-opened his oil fields for foreign investment and apparently sought to make amends for some of his past support for terrorists. Western performing artists and scholars flocked to Tripoli to take the dictator's money. As part of this outreach effort, in February 2011, just as the rebellion was beginning in Libya, the Obama administration supported a trip by one of Qaddafi's sons, Khamis, a brigade commander in the Libyan military, to various installations in the United States, including NASA and the U.S. Air Force Academy.[360] The intended visit of Khamis to West Point was cancelled when he was summoned home to take part in the defense of his father's regime.

Given the strident statements of candidates Obama and Biden, uttered with respect to a possible bombing of Iranian nuclear facilities should that country conclusively move toward the construction of nuclear weapons to mount on the missiles that Iran was simultaneously developing, the war commenced by the Obama and Biden administration against Libya without Congressional authorization was a particularly surprising event. Twelve weeks into the Libyan intervention, the Obama administration sent Congress a further explanation on 15 June 2011 stating that since "U.S. operations do not involve sustained fighting or active exchanges of fire with hostile forces, nor do they involve U.S. ground troops" the operation did not, in the view of the Obama administration, meet the definition of hostilities in the 1973 War

---

[360] John Warrick, "U.S. Officials Assisted Visit by Gaddafi Son Just Before Uprising," *The Washington Post*, 26 March 2011, http://www.washingtonpost.com/world/us-officials-assisted-visit-by-gaddafi-son/2011/03/25/AFT017YB_story.html, accessed 1 July 2011

Powers Resolution.[361] Two weeks later, U.S. military officials reported that 23% of the 3475 U.S. sorties flown since NATO had taken over control of the Libyan intervention were combat strike sorties, numbers at odds with the White House contention that the U.S. role was primarily in support, and did not involve much fighting. After fourteen weeks of combat, the notion that U.S. involvement was somehow limited in time was also hard to credit, since no schedule or desired end-state had so far been published.[362]

CONCLUSION

Accusations that Presidents have lied America into war are not uncommon in our history. Such accusations have a tendency to come with the electoral cycles. Congressmen and senators that vote for wars sometimes turn against the war in the next electoral cycle, a change that can come across as one of mere political convenience as it did in 1968 and in 2004. McGovern's admissions long after the fact seem to bear this out in the case of Vietnam – he was against the war before he was for it, and before he was against it again. As he put it, he thought the vote was a mere gesture, helping protect the political flanks of the president during an election year. It is difficult to accept that Senators and Congressmen, especially senior legislators with their vast access to information, could be simple, naive dupes.

Presidents share the blame, of course. Their policy choices must be wrapped in legislative compromises and the desire for re-election or an enduring legacy. In the view of the British historian, Paul Johnson:

---

[361] Charlie Savage and Mark Landler, "White House Defends Continuing U.S. Role in Libya Operation," The New York Times, 15 June 2011, http://www.nytimes.com/2011/06/16/us/politics/16powers.html, accessed 29 June 2011.
[362] David Majumdar, "AFRICOM: AF, Navy Still Flying Libya Missions," *Air Force Times*, 30 June 2011, http://www.airforcetimes.com/news/2011/06/defense-africom-air-force-navy-flying-libya-missions-063011/, accessed 1 July 2011.

"Peace has always been a vote-winning issue in the United States. Yet there is an instructive contrast in Democrat and Republican records. Wilson won in 1916 on a promise to keep America out of the war; next year America was a belligerent. Roosevelt won in 1940 on the same promise and with the same result. Lyndon Johnson won in 1964 on a peace platform (against Republican 'warmongering') and promptly turned Vietnam into a major war. Eisenhower in 1952 and Richard Nixon in 1972 are the only two Presidents in this century who have carried out their peace promises."[363]

Even Lincoln found himself adopting war measures he almost certainly would have opposed in other presidents. Wilson campaigned on peace, and shortly thereafter committed America to a "war of choice." FDR found it necessary to surreptitiously extend his war-making powers while saying one thing on the campaign trail and the opposite to his closest advisors. LBJ expanded the war in Vietnam to pose as the more responsible candidate. War truly is the continuation of politics by other means.

What of the current war? President Obama made many promises in the lengthy 2008 campaign. Candidate Obama promised to give the troops "a clear mission and a sacred commitment to give them the equipment they need in battle," and to take the war to the caves where al Qaeda was allegedly hiding in Pakistan, whether Pakistan cooperated or not.[364] His first year of policy making showed, though, a fractured approach, with at least four strategic reviews of the Afghanistan-Pakistan conflict, with a piecemealing of troops and equipment fed into the battle. The outcome of

---

[363] Johnson 460.

[364] Transcript, Barack Obama Acceptance Speech, Democrat Convention, *The New York Times*, 28 August 2008,
http://www.nytimes.com/2008/08/28/us/politics/28text-obama.html?pagewanted=5&_r=1; see also David E. Sanger, "New Debate Territory: Pakistan and Iran Policy," *The New York Times*, 26 September 2008,
http://www.nytimes.com/2008/09/27/us/politics/27policy.html.

the final strategic review determined that al Qaeda must remain the primary focus, and that the primary threat resided in Pakistan, *not* Afghanistan; therefore, more than 30,000 additional U.S. troops were dispatched to Afghanistan –not the main location of the threat - to deal with the Taliban, who were not the main threat. The decision logic and the consequent explanations were contorted at best. Still, it is too early to tell whether this strategy will result in overall strategic success.

DISSENT

America was born in dissent against the powers of taxation and other onerous acts from a distant government where Americans were not truly represented. The Founding Fathers of the American Revolution were traitors in the eyes of the British. Having won independence, those same Founders had to create a sense of national identity while maintaining the basic liberties for which they had fought. Almost immediately differences arose between those that sought a relatively stronger, centralized Federal government – the "Federalists" - and those that thought increases in Federal power would inevitably diminish the spheres of personal liberty and local democracy – the "Anti-Federalists" who later in the 1790s became known as "Republicans."

Having been born in dissent, the young Republic had difficulty defining the proper boundaries of future dissent. In the first 15 years after the Treaty of Paris secured American independence, the fledgling country experienced three revolts – Shay's Rebellion (1786-1787), the Whiskey Rebellion (1794), and Fries' Rebellion (1798) – over the issue of Federal powers of taxation that pitted veterans of the Revolution against each other. Thus, from the earliest years of the American Republic, its leaders and citizens have squabbled over where dissent crosses into sedition, rebellion, or treason, despite the constitution's definition of treason[365] and the protections afforded the right to free speech.[366] America has never had a war that did not feature some dispute over the proper venues and limits for popular dissent against the administration in power during the war.

---

[365] "Treason against the United States shall consist only in levying War against them, or in adhering to their Enemies, giving them Aid and Comfort." Article III, Section 3.
[366] "Congress shall make no law...abridging the freedom of speech, or of the press; or the right of the people peaceably to assemble...." 1st Amendment.

QUASI WAR

"We have given him the powers and prerogatives of a King....He holds levees like a King, receives congratulations on his birthday like a King, employs his old enemies like a King, takes advice of his counselors or follows his own opinions like a King."

> - Anti-Federalist editorial in New York, referring to President Washington[367]

"May he, like Samson, slay thousands of Frenchmen with the jawbone of a Jefferson."

> - A popular Federalist toast to President John Adams[368]

In 1789, America's main ally, France, collapsed into revolutionary fervor and chaos. The ideas and actions of Revolutionary France posed direct threats to the other monarchs of Europe and war soon followed, particularly with France's historic rival and Revolutionary America's enemy, Britain.

The new American Republic was also a geographical neighbor and trading partner with outposts of the British and French empires in the Americas. Indeed, despite the lingering enmity of the American Revolution, Britain was by far America's most important export market and source of imports. The French Revolution also arrived in the first few years of operation of the new U.S. Constitution. Perhaps because of the French assistance that was so crucial to American independence in the previous decade and perhaps because of the similar ideas that had animated both Revolutions, those that generally favored Revolutionary France were also those that generally favored the strictest interpretation of the U.S. Constitution - the Anti-

---

[367] Quoted in Joseph J. Ellis, *Founding Brothers: the Revolutionary Generation* (New York: Vintage, 2002) 126-127.
[368] Schweikart 151.

Federalists - clustered around Thomas Jefferson who served as the first Secretary of State. On the other side, clustered around the first Secretary of the Treasury, Alexander Hamilton, were those that favored improving relations with Great Britain - mainly the Federalists - including President Washington and Vice President Adams.

Given the geographical proximity and the trade relationships, America could not avoid involvement at some level in the Anglo-French wars. Given American military weakness, President Washington officially proclaimed neutrality in 1793. Critics of this policy pointed out that neutrality would redound to the favor of the stronger naval power, Britain, who took immediate advantage of that power to harass American shipping heading to French ports and to impress Americans sailors into the Royal Navy, thus causing the pro-French faction to agitate for an American military response. President Washington resisted such calls, and was vociferously condemned by the Anti-Federalist press.

In the late 1790s, when Adams was President and Jefferson was Vice President – both sides of the American domestic and foreign policy disputes serving side-by-side at the very pinnacle of government – the French Navy also began seizing American shipping, prompting the pro-British faction to pursue a military response. This period became known as the Quasi-War, and was in fact an undeclared naval war. Controlling the Presidency and Congress, the pro-British Federalists passed the Alien and Sedition Acts of 1798 as a war measure. Criticizing the President became a potential crime. Twenty-five people were convicted and sentenced under the Sedition Act, many of them Republican newspaper editors (by this time the Anti-Federalists had renamed themselves). One of those editors was also a congressman, Matthew Lyon of Vermont. In another case, a common citizen was fined $150 for criticizing the size of President Adams' posterior (among other demeaning nicknames, Adams was known as "His Rotundity")[369] Clamping down on dissent in such a manner hurt the Federalist cause, and in the elections of 1800, the Republicans gained decisive control of Congress and Jefferson won the Presidency.

WAR OF 1812

"Mr. Madison's War."
- The name given to the war by Federalist critics[370]

Twenty-three years after the French Revolution began, the Anglo-French wars continued, with the French under their new emperor, Napoleon. The vituperative politics of the founding era of the American Republic continued, with Federalists and Republicans still disputing the breadth and depth of federal powers, and still split politically and economically over relations with Britain. By 1812, New England had become even more entwined in the British trading system. Not a single Federalist in Congress had voted for the war. New England opposed the war by continuing to trade with Britain, selling supplies to British forces in Canada, denying financing to the U.S. government, and most importantly, refusing the use of state militia. In operational terms this last act severely hampered the planned invasion of British Canada by Federal forces.[371]

The New England dissent reached its climax almost at the same time as the war with the Hartford Convention of December 1814 with Delegates from Massachusetts, Connecticut, Vermont, and Rhode Island attending. The Convention discussed sending out separate peace feelers to Britain and proposed constitutional amendments that would limit the power of southern and western states; implied in all of this was a threat of secession (New

---

[369] Schweikart 152. See also David McCullough, *John Adams* (New York: Simon and Schuster, 2001, Kindle version) locations 9264-9269.
[370] Millett 108.
[371] Millett 108.

England had also implied such a threat in 1804 if Jefferson was re-elected)[372] Meanwhile, peace had been concluded with the signature of the Treaty of Ghent, signed 24 December 1814. American forces then won the lopsided victory at the Battle of New Orleans on 8 January 1815.

News traveled very slowly in those days, and word of the Hartford Convention, the Treaty of Ghent, and the victory in New Orleans arrived in the capital at about the same time. The victory at New Orleans smoothed passage of the Treaty in the Senate, while the dissent of New England spelled the end of the Federalist Party, verging as it did on secession after their actions had already impeded the war effort.[373]

CIVIL WAR

"I had reason to believe that the administration was a little afraid to have a decisive battle at that time, for fear it might go against us and have a bad effect on the November elections. The convention which had met and made its nomination of the Democratic candidate for the presidency had declared the war a failure. Treason was talked as boldly in Chicago at that convention as ever been in Charleston. It was a question whether the government would then have had the power to make arrests and punish those who talked treason."

-   Ulysses S. Grant[374]

*"Grant is a butcher and not fit to be at the head of an army. He loses two men to the enemy's one. He has no **management**, no regard for life...."* (emphasis in original)

-   Mary Todd Lincoln[375]

---

[372] Schweikart 175.
[373] Millett 118-119; Schweikart 175.
[374] Grant, locations 16928-16937.
[375] Sam Grant, "1864: Most Hallowed Ground," Geoffrey C. War, ed., *The Civil War* (New York: Vintage, 1990) 255.

"I will violate the Constitution if necessary to save the Union."

- President Lincoln's statement to the Treasury
Secretary, Salmon Chase, on the issue of printing
paper money.[376]

To stifle extreme dissent, officials in the Lincoln Administration took extreme
measures. Lincoln suspended habeas corpus, and when the courts ruled
against him, he ignored the ruling and imprisoned thousands of dissidents,
including editors of opposition newspapers that he closed. This is the same
Abraham Lincoln who as a Congressman had chided President Polk over the
Mexican War, "[Y]our view places our president where kings have always
stood."[377]

Lincoln, though, did not suspend elections, and the unpopularity of his
actions cost the Republicans several seats in the 1862 elections, as well as
control of his home state legislature in Illinois.[378] After more than three years
of fighting, the war was inevitably going to impact the presidential elections
in 1864. In the first nine months of 1864, more than 100,000 Union soldiers
became casualties, and 65,000 of them came between May and July.[379] Many
citizens in the North still seethed over the Draft and the resulting bloody
riots of 1863. Lincoln's detractors dubbed him "King Lincoln" for his vigorous
suppression of dissent. Dissent went very high indeed in 1864 as the toll of
battle came in, even into the White House itself, as Mary Todd Lincoln's
quote above shows.

---

[376] Len Fullenkamp, Review of Geoffrey Perret, *Lincoln's War: The Untold Story of
America's Greatest President as Commander in Chief* (New York: Random House,
2004), *Parameters*, Vol. 35, Summer 2005, p. 157,
http://www.carlisle.army.mil/usawc/Parameters/Articles/05summer/sum-rev.pdf,
accessed 1 May 2011.

[377] Fullenkam 156.

[378] Schweikart 341-342.

[379] James M. McPherson, "War and Politics," Geoffrey C. War, ed., *The Civil War*
(New York: Vintage, 1990) 285.

Influential newspaperman Horace Greeley, editor of the New York *Tribune*, a Radical Republican, in his disgruntlement with Lincoln's policies would say, "Our bleeding, bankrupt, almost dying country...longs for peace, shudders at the prospect of...further wholesale devastation, of new rivers of human blood."[380] The Radical Republicans went so far as to seek an alternative Republican candidate, the adventurer and former Union general, John C. Fremont. The Democrats termed the entire war effort a failure, and proposed a peace platform to end the war: "After four years of failure to restore the Union by the experiment of war...[we] demand that immediate efforts be made for a cessation of hostilities...."[381] The Democrats chose a disgruntled, dissident general of their own as candidate, George McClellan.

In the end, though, Fremont withdrew before the elections and Lincoln won 54% of the popular vote. He may have taken as much as 74% of the absentee voting that nineteen Union states allowed for their citizen soldiers. Why did the victims of "Grant the Butcher" vote the way they did, rejecting the Democrats' peace platform? As a New York private explained, "I cannot afford to give three years of my life to maintaining this nation and then give the Rebels all they want."[382]

What of the Constitutional issues raised by Lincoln's policies against dissent? The end of the war and Lincoln's death essentially relegated the issues to history and academic discussion. The other great hero-leader of the Civil War, LTG Grant, who would himself rise to the Presidency in 1868, provided this summation of the issues: "The Constitution was therefore in abeyance for the time being, so far as it in any way affected the progress and termination of the war."[383]

---

[380] McPherson 286.
[381] McPherson 287.
[382] McPherson 289.
[383] Grant, location 20267.

WORLD WAR I

"The foreign minister of Germany once said to me, 'Your country does not dare to make a move against Germany, because we have in your country 500,000 German reservists who will rise in arms against your government if you dare to make a move against Germany.' Well, I told him that that might be so, but that we had 500,001 lamp posts in this country, and that that was where the reservists would be hanging the day after they tried to rise."

- AMB James W. Gerard, former U.S. Ambassador to Germany, April 1918[384]

"The War of 1812 was opposed and condemned, the Mexican War was bitterly condemned by Abraham Lincoln, Charles Sumner, Daniel Webster, and Henry Clay. They were not indicted. They were not tried for crime. They are honored today by all of their countrymen. The war of Rebellion was opposed and condemned. In the year 1864 the Democrat Party met in convention at Chicago and passed a resolution condemning the war as a failure. What would you say if the Socialist Party were to meet in convention today and condemn the present war as a failure? Were the Democrats of 1864 disloyalists and traitors because they condemned the war as a failure?"

- Eugene V. Debs, American Socialist, addressing the jury before his sentencing to 10 years in prison under the Espionage and Sedition Acts, 1 September 1918.[385]

The America of 1917 had large communities of Irish-Americans and German-Americans that still felt some connection to their original homeland. These

---

[384] "Ambassador James W. Gerard Encourages German Americans to be Loyal to the United States – Or Else," Senator Robert Torricelli and Andrew Carroll, eds., *In Our Own Words: Extraordinary Speeches of the American Century* (New York: Washington Square, 1999) 46.

[385] "Socialist Leader Eugene V. Debs Defends Himself in Court Against Charges of 'Disloyalty' and 'Sedition,'" Torricelli and Carroll, 49.

groups were not generally supportive of the British- and French-led alliance against Germany. Socialists, Communists, and anarchists likewise did not want the U.S. to enter a war they deemed capitalistic or imperialistic. In the 1916 presidential campaign, Woodrow Wilson's policies of strict neutrality and his slogan, "He kept us out of war," attracted support from those agitating for peace, or at least for non-intervention, in a race decided by only 500,000 popular votes. Wilson won the Electoral College by the slim margin of 23 votes, 277 to 254.

Weeks after his victory on a peace platform, when Wilson decided to take America into World War I on the side of the Alliance – a "war of choice" in today's parlance - his Democrat administration had to pivot politically 180 degrees, from strict neutrality to demonization of Germany and her allies. Society, industry, and manpower required mobilization, and the potentially restive immigrant populations had to be kept under control. The Democrats created the Committee on Public Information under the leadership of a journalist, George Creel, to manage the propaganda effort, waged in the days before radio by posters and newspaper articles.

Part of the Committee's effort was to encourage citizens to report to the Justice Department any anti-war activities. Like the Federalists of the Quasi War, President Wilson and his fellow Democrats passed the Espionage Act of 1917 within two months of the declaration of war, and then reinforced this with the Sedition Act of 1918. These acts criminalized the "uttering [of] words intended to cause insubordination and disloyalty within the American forces, to incite resistance to the war, and to promote the cause of Germany."[386] The Committee also monitored journalists' coverage of the war in a form of bland censorship.

Under these laws and consistent with the propaganda effort, the Post Office refused to mail Socialist Party materials. One German-American in St Louis

---

[386] Torricelli 47.

was lynched, perhaps to encourage other German-Americans to behave as AMB Gerard famously suggested. However, of the millions drafted to serve in the American forces in World War I, some twenty percent were foreign-born, including large numbers from the German-American community.[387] On the other hand, two thousand dissidents were prosecuted under the Espionage Acts, including Eugene V. Debs, the prominent Socialist leader.[388] As in previous American wars, dissent came at a high price to the dissenters.

Anarchist Emma Goldman and her aid, Alexander Berkman, convicted of conspiracy against the draft law and sentenced to two years in penitentiary and fined $10,000 each, July 9, 1917[389]

---

[387] Schweikart 514-515.

[388] "Sedition and Domestic Terrorism – The Espionage Acts of 1917 and 1918," http://law.jrank.org/pages/2025/Sedition-Domestic-Terrorism-Espionage-Acts-1917-1918.html#ixzz0sKwQaglm, accessed 2 May 2011. Although sentenced to 10 years in prison, Debs served only two years and was later pardoned by Republican President Harding in 1921.

[389] National Archives, **Woman anarchist leader and aid in draft war. Emma Goldman and Alexander Berkman convicted of conspiracy against draft law and sentenced to two years in penitentiary and fined $10,000 each, July 9, 1917. International Film Service.: 1917 - 1919**, ARC Identifier 533643 / Local Identifier 165-WW-164B(6), Still Picture Records Section, Special Media Archives Services Division, College Park, MD, Item from Record Group 165: Records of the War Department General and Special Staffs, 1860 – 1952.

WORLD WAR II

"There are also American citizens, many of them in high places, who, unwittingly in most cases, are aiding and abetting the work of these agents. I do not charge these American citizens with being foreign agents. **But I do charge them with doing exactly the kind of work that the dictators want done in the United States.** *These people not only believe that we can save our own skins by shutting our eyes to the fate of other nations. Some of them go much further than that. They say that we can and should become the friends and even the partners of the Axis powers."* (emphasis added)

- President Franklin Delano Roosevelt, Fireside chat, 29 December 1940[390]

"I have said before, and I will say again, that I believe it will be a tragedy to the entire world if the British Empire collapses. That is one of the main reasons why I opposed this war before it was declared, and why I have constantly advocated a negotiated peace. I did not feel that England and France had a reasonable chance of winning. France has now been defeated, and...it is now obvious that England is losing the war...But they have one last desperate plan remaining: They hope that they may be able to persuade us to send another American Expeditionary Force to Europe and to share with England militarily, as well as financially, the fiasco of this war...and I have been forced to the conclusion that we cannot win this war for England, regardless of how much assistance we extend."

- Charles A. Lindbergh, one of America's most admired public figures, 23 April 1941[391]

---

[390] Fireside chat on national security and the common cause, Washington, D. C., December 29,1940, "Arsenal of Democracy" Speech, World War II Resources, Paper XXI, p 72, Pearl Harbor History Associates, Inc., http://www.ibiblio.org/pha/7-2-188/188-21.html, accessed 27 April 2011.

[391] "Famed Pilot Charles Lindbergh Argues That the United States Would Meet with 'Defeat and Failure' Against the German Army," Torricelli 126-127.

It would be difficult to find a better example of an American president questioning the patriotism of his domestic critics than the quote above from Democrat Franklin Delano Roosevelt. The largest pre-war organized block of dissent came from the Committee to Defend America First, which had several hundred thousand members. We know them today as "isolationists." In the run-up to Pearl Harbor, the isolationist and neutrality sentiments were so strong, however, that Congress passed the series of Neutrality Acts and other measures designed to hem in a Chief Executive thought to be too inclined toward intervention. This also forced Roosevelt to run on a peace platform in 1940 not unlike his Democrat predecessor, Wilson, in 1916. The American Firsters counted among their supporters public figures like Henry Ford (who had also prominently opposed intervention in World War I), AMB Joseph Kennedy, and Charles Lindbergh. America First also attracted the youth, who would be called upon to fight in the advent of war, including future presidents John F. Kennedy and Gerald Ford. Polls showed that most Americans agreed with Lindbergh's position, which led to FDR seeking to undermine the aviation hero by having him called a Nazi by others.[392]

According to the American First Committee, the members wanted the focus of foreign and defense policies to be on defending America, rather than on intervention in foreign wars. When Pearl Harbor happened, the America First movement dried up, its younger members gone off to war, except for Lindbergh, against whom the Roosevelt Administration maintained animosity for his leading role in hindering their pre-war policies. Although Lindbergh, who had held the rank of Colonel in the Army Air Corps Reserve and had been awarded the Medal of Honor for his solo transatlantic flight in 1927, volunteered to serve in any capacity, the influential Secretary of the Interior, Harold Ickes, wrote to advise the President, "I ardently hope that this confirmed fascist will not be given the opportunity to wear the uniform of the United States."[393] Refused re-entry into the Air Corps, Lindbergh served

---

[392] Schweikart 585.
[393] Torricelli 129.

as a civilian adviser to his fellow isolationist, Henry Ford, in Ford's aircraft production effort, eventually making several combat flights in the Pacific as an observer.

Roosevelt's salvo against his dissenters "doing the work that the dictators want done" was accurate at least with respect to the German-American Bund and the American Peace Mobilization Committee, both of whom very much functioned as front organizations for the dictators Hitler and Stalin respectively.

The Bund was able to assemble a crowd of 20,000 in Madison Square Garden in February 1939 to hear denunciations of FDR and his alleged linkages to the British, Jews, and Bolsheviks. The Bund's membership was part of an estimated 400,000 German-Americans suspected of having ties to Germany or otherwise supporting Hitler.

Not to be outdone, the Communists called out 22,000 anti-war, anti-Roosevelt supporters for its national convention in June 1940. The American Peace Mobilization Committee (or APM), operating as a communist front organization, pulled in support from members of the left-wing veterans that had fought in the Abraham Lincoln Brigade in the Spanish Civil War. One of APM's vice-chairs was a sitting Congressman, Vito Marcantonio, and its National Council included the poets Carl Sandburg and Langston Hughes. The APM published pamphlets and maintained vigils outside the White House in support of the Soviet Union which was then cooperating with the Nazis under the Molotov-Ribbentrop Pact. APM agitated against any support to Britain as it fought alone after the fall of France. The APM continued these activities until the very day that Hitler invaded the Soviet Union on 22 June 1941, then immediately adopted the opposite stance, always taking their cues from Moscow. This brazen reversal in protest policy was too much to sustain, and the APM all but disappeared as a mass movement in October 1940.[394]

5 Planks to Defend America
Program of APM

1. Get out and stay out of the European War.
2. Defeat Militarism and Regimentation. Repeal Conscription. No M Day for the American people.
3. Restore the Bill of Rights. Restore free speech, freedom of assembly, freedom of thought. Take special privilege away from the top and give it back to the whole American people.
4. Stop War Profiteering. Put lives ahead of profits. Put profits last on democracy's list. What helps democracy helps you.
5. Guarantee a decent standard of living for all. Work for more social and labor legislation. End discrimination.

THIS PROGRAM IS SIMPLE JUSTICE, MAKE IT REAL AND AMERICA IS DEFENDED.

The American Peace Mobilization's anti-Roosevelt and anti-war agenda on behalf of the Soviet Union.[395]

TIME magazine lumped these dissenters together amorphously as "communazis" during the period when the Nazis and Communists had cooperated in starting World War II in Europe, and also called them a "Fifth Column" that numbered more than a million. *TIME* recommended that citizens report suspicious behavior of these groups to the government.[396] The Federal government and local governments did indeed investigate the activities of these organizations, and proposed legislation that would be considered an affront to civil liberties today, aside from eventually interning

---

[394] "American People's Mobilization Collected Records, 1940-1941," Collection CDG-A, http://www.swarthmore.edu/library/peace/CDGA.A-L/ampeoplesmob.htm, accessed 1 May 2011.

[395] *Volunteer for Liberty*, Vol III, No. 2, February 1941, p. 1, Abraham Lincoln Brigade Archives, http://www.alba-valb.org/search?SearchableText=volunteer+newsletter+1941, accessed 1 May 2011.

[396] See "RADICALS: Fifth Column," *TIME*, 10 June 1940, http://www.time.com/time/magazine/article/0,9171,763992-2,00.html, and WAR & PEACE: Science of Treason, *TIME*, 26 August 1940, http://www.time.com/time/magazine/article/0,9171,764451,00.html, both accessed 2 May 2011.

more than a 120,000 residents of Japanese, German, and Italian origins – a sort of prospective repression of potential dissent. Both before and during the war, the House Committee on Un-American Activities, led by Texas Congressman Martin Dies, was active in investigating both leftist and rightist organizations, a decade before the Committee became synonymous with the McCarthy era in the 1950s. After the war began in 1941, with press censorship and full societal mobilization, dissent became muted. Some Americans nonetheless continued to agitate for those who were now declared enemies of the United States, and chose to do so in very public ways via radio broadcasts.

Tokyo Rose

A name given by American GIs to female broadcasters on Japanese radio that included an Australian, Filipinos, and Japanese-Americans. One of the Japanese-Americans, Iva Toguri Ikoku (also known as Rosa D'Aquino) broadcasted from Tokyo under the name "Orphan Ann." After the war, Ikoku was sentenced to 10 years in jail and a $10,000 fine, but was released after serving 6 years. In January 1977, President Ford pardoned her as one of his last official acts.[397]

Axis Sally

This nickname applied to two American women that made Axis radio broadcasts in Europe. The first, Mildred Elizabeth Gillars, a failed actress and artist, broadcasted German radio propaganda from Berlin. After the war, she was convicted of treason, and given a 12-year sentence but was paroled in 1961.[398] The second Axis Sally was Rita Zucca, of Italian descent, who made

---

[397] Dear 1119.
[398] Dear 97. See also, "Treason: I wish…,"*Time*, http://www.time.com/time/magazine/article/0,9171,933785,00.html, and "People," *Time*, 25 June 1973, http://www.time.com/time/magazine/article/0,9171,907459,00.html.

radio broadcasts on behalf of the Mussolini government from Rome and Milan. Since Zucca had renounced her American citizenship upon her return to Italy, the American government did not prosecute her, although the post-Fascist Italian government did, and she spent several months in an Italian prison.

Ezra Pound

Artists and intellectuals have a strange fascination for totalitarianism. Before becoming a political pariah, Mussolini attracted many to view his works. Others went on to see the Potemkin villages of Stalin. Hitler, too, had his admirers. Of this parade of intellectuals, one of the most noted poets of his day, Ezra Pound, founder of the *Imagist* school of poetry, took up residence in Italy. During the war, he made pro-Axis, anti-Semitic broadcasts from Rome and Milan. Having many friends in the literary community, after the war he was conveniently found mentally unfit to stand trial, and was placed into an asylum until 1958, all the while continuing to work on his epic, *Cantos*. In 1958, he was released as incurably insane, and returned to live out his last 14 years of life in Italy. All seemed forgiven in the name of art, as Pound continued to receive prizes and accolades until his death.[399]

---

[399] For the views of Pound's protectors and benefactors, see the historical description at "Letter, Ernest Hemingway to Archibald MacLeish discussing Ezra Pound's mental health and other literary matters", 10 August [1943],(Archibald MacLeish Papers), *Words and Deeds in American History: Selected Documents Celebrating the Manuscript Division's First 100 Years*, The Library of Congress, http://memory.loc.gov/cgi-bin/query/r?ammem/mcc:@field(DOCID+@lit(mcc/035)).

Iva Toguri Ikoko in September 1945[400]

VIETNAM

"These were not men who had been tortured. These were not men who had been starved. These were not men who had been brainwashed."

- "Hanoi Jane" Fonda, referring to the American POWs tortured into holding a fake Press Conference with her in Hanoi before members of the international media.[401]

---

[400] "Correspondents interview `Tokyo Rose.' Iva Toguri, American-born Japanese." September 1945. 80-G-490488. (ww2_174.jpg), http://www.archives.gov/research/military/ww2/photos/#prisoners

[401] "Hanoi'd with Jane," http://www.snopes.com/military/fonda.asp, accessed 29 April 2011.

The once oft-quoted saying about American foreign policy was, "All politics stops at the water's edge." This may have expressed more myth than reality (see the Hartford Convention mentioned above), but during the Vietnam era, the saying simply was not applicable. Domestic dissent came into public awareness as never before through the new medium of television, although radio continued to play a significant role. During the Vietnam years, domestic dissent was allowed a degree of latitude never before seen during American conflicts. The history of the Vietnam War is replete with images of American protestors carrying the flags of the enemy, rooting for enemy victory, and encouraging American troops to shirk their duties and desert their posts. Some Americans went so far as to engage in bombing campaigns against government facilities in a form of domestic guerrilla warfare.

Wealth and ease of jet travel made it possible for some dissenters to visit the capital of the enemy in Hanoi, much like their intellectual predecessors once flocked to Rome, Berlin, and Moscow before World War II. The major difference during the Vietnam War, though, was that the dissenters that went to the enemy capitol either in support of the enemy's policy or in protest against U.S. policy were not thereafter tried and imprisoned like Iva Toguri Ikoku and Mildred Elizabeth Gillars, nor declared insane like Ezra Pound.

Hanoi Jane

The most notorious visitor to Hanoi was the wealthy, successful actress, Jane Fonda, daughter of the American Hollywood icon, Henry Fonda. During her 1972 trip, even as American involvement in the war effort was winding down, Fonda made ten radio broadcasts on behalf of the enemy. She declared American soldiers to be "war criminals," praised the North Vietnamese and thanked the Soviet Union for their support to the enemy efforts. She also appeared at a "press conference" with international journalists jointly with eight American POWs. After their release, these POWs reported that they had been tortured into appearing; Fonda called them liars.[402]

American film star, Jane Fonda, mugging for the cameras in Hanoi[403]

Fonda was a not a solitary totalitarian pilgrim. Others trooped to Hanoi, including Fonda's future husband, the leftwing activist Tom Hayden, who had made his first trip as early as 1965.[404] Another was David Ifshin, the President of the National Student Association, who travelled to Hanoi in 1970 to make radio broadcasts encouraging dissent among American troops on the front lines. His broadcasts were piped into the cells of American POWs to demoralize them.[405]

---

[402] See "Hanoi'd with Jane."

[403] Pictures from Kurt Schlichter, "Forever 'Hanoi Jane,'" Big Hollywood, 7 April 2010, http://bighollywood.breitbart.com/kschlichter/2010/04/07/forever-hanoi-jane/, accessed 29 April 2011.

[404] See http://tomhayden.com/biography

[405] Wolfgang Saxon, "David M. Ifshin, Capital Lawyer and Lobbyist," New York Times, 2 May 1996, http://www.nytimes.com/1996/05/02/us/david-m-ifshin-47-capital-lawyer-and-lobbyist.html, and Margaret Carlson, "Friends, 12-Steppers, Freshmen," "Time This Week"..., "All Politics," CNN TIME, 13 May 1996,

Serving enemy propaganda purposes in the style of Tokyo Rose, Axis Sally, or Ezra Pound proved to be no impediment to high political office in the case of Hayden, who served several terms in the California Legislature and twice on the Democrat Party's National Platform Committee, or for Ifshin, who served as a general counsel for the Mondale campaign in 1984 and the Clinton campaign in 1992 or to the lucrative film career and other business interests of "Hanoi Jane." These and other activist dissenters became celebrated icons of America's political Left. Much as the well-known domestic terrorist from the same period, William Ayers, famously described his own situation, these Americans that had traveled to Hanoi to give aid and comfort to America's enemy in a very public manner were "Guilty as hell, free as a bird...."[406]

Resentment lingers: Blackhawk crewman's helmet patch, November 2005, near Saddam's hometown of Tikrit, Iraq, 33 years after Hanoi Jane's radio broadcasts. The crewman wearing this patch would have been born more than a decade after the broadcasts.[407]

---

http://www.cnn.com/ALLPOLITICS/1996/analysis/time/9605/13/carlson.shtml, both accessed 29 April 2011.

[406]See the flattering portrait of the unrepentant bomber, William Ayers, standing on an American flag in Marcia Froelke Coburn, "No Regrets," ChicagoMag.com, August 2001, http://www.chicagomag.com/Chicago-Magazine/August-2001/No-Regrets/index.php?cparticle=2&siarticle=1#artanc.

[407] Author's personal photo.

WAR ON TERROR

In rhetoric reminiscent of his Democrat Party ancestors of the Civil War, the former Klansman, Senator Robert Byrd (Democrat -West Virginia), said that President George W. Bush sought a "boundless authority" to wage war with the sort of "powers reserved only for kings and potentates."[408] President Bush was in good company, because as noted above, domestic critics in the midst of conflict also accused Washington, Polk, and Lincoln of seeking the power of kings. Caricatures of Bush as "King George" became common on the internet.

For the 2004 and 2006 election campaign, the Democrats fashioned some themes that came to resonate with their own voters and with independents: Bush lied about WMD in Iraq; Bush was tied to the Saudi royal family and the Bin Laden family; maybe the 9-11 attacks were somehow an inside job done with knowledge and complicity of the administration (known as the Truther conspiracy); Bush had committed the crime of being Absent Without Leave (AWOL) as a Texas Air National Guard pilot, who was accepted into the National Guard only because of family connections, the records of which were missing or incomplete; Bush was exceeding his constitutional authorities as Commander-in-Chief; Bush authorized torture; Bush wanted to create a police state through the Patriot Act. Critical to these lines of argument was the idea that the Bush administration was trying to quash domestic dissent, either through the legal means of the Patriot Act, the use of warrantless wiretaps, or by questioning the patriotism of dissenters in war time (see the Ashcroft quote below).

When Bush left office after eight years of constant criticism of this sort, and the Democrats controlled the House, Senate, and White House, the new

---

[408] "No President Is above the Law," Remarks by U.S. Senator Robert C. Byrd, 19 December 2005, West Virginia Patriots for Peace, http://www.wvpatriotsforpeace.org/speeches/byrd_2005_12_19.html, accessed 27 April 2011.

Obama administration counted among its members many of those that had been harshly critical of the previous administration. The Obama administration nevertheless retained almost all of the national defense leadership and maintained almost all of the most controversial policies that they had just campaigned against. Obama himself would face vituperative and demeaning criticism that depicted him in the garb of an aloof, dandified French monarch, but as a reaction to domestic issues rather than war policy.

The Bush Years

*"To those who pit Americans against immigrants, citizens against non-citizens, to those who scare peace-loving people with phantoms of lost liberty, my message is this: **Your tactics only aid terrorists for they erode our national unity and diminish our resolve**. They give ammunition to America's enemies and pause to America's friends. They encourage people of good will to remain silent in the face of evil."* (emphasis added)

- Attorney General John Ashcroft, 6 December 2001, testimony to Senate Judiciary Committee[409]

"I am sick and tired of people who say that if you debate and you disagree with this administration somehow you're not patriotic. We should stand up and say we are Americans and we have a right to debate and disagree with any administration."

- Sen. Hillary Rodham Clinton, at the annual Democrat Party Jefferson-Jackson-Bailey Day fund raising dinner in Connecticut, 28 April 2003[410]

---

[409] "Ashcroft: Critics of new terror measures undermine effort," CNN.com, 7 December 2001 http://archives.cnn.com/2001/US/12/06/inv.ashcroft.hearing/, accessed 29 April 2011.
[410] Elizabeth Hamilton, "Hillary Clinton Rallies Democratic Troops," *Hartford Courant*, p. B1, 29 April 2003.

A major theme for the opposition in the first years of the War on Terror was that the Bush administration was in fact trying to silence them, a claim that sounds bizarre in hindsight given the very large number of protests held during the period and the constant criticism of the Bush administration in print and on radio, television, and internet. This theme of governmental repression of dissent, though, harkens back to the heyday of anti-war protests during Vietnam, when the phrase, "Dissent is the highest form of patriotism" became commonly used by those protesting the war, and became identified almost exclusively with leftwing dissent.[411] During an interview conducted in July 2002, well before the controversial decision to open a campaign front in Iraq, Howard Zinn, the historian beloved by the modern American Left, responded to an interviewer's statement that, "Dissent these days seems to be a dirty word. The Bush administration has, at least since September 11th, usually termed any criticism of its policies 'unpatriotic,'" by saying, "While some people think that dissent is unpatriotic, I would argue that dissent is the highest form of patriotism."[412] Less than a year after the 9-11 attacks, when the American military commitment to the War on Terror still numbered in the low thousands, the dissenters had re-birthed a theme that had worked so well for them in an earlier generation.

Far from being hindered in the Bush years, dissent and protests against the War on Terror or its various campaigns were ubiquitous.

---

[411] The phrase is often attributed to Thomas Jefferson, but see http://www.monticello.org/site/jefferson/dissent-highest-form-patriotism-quotation, accessed 27 April 2011, which suggests that the first use was in 1961.

[412] Sharon Basco, "An Interview with Historian Howard Zinn: Dissent in the Pursuit of Equality, Life, Liberty, and Happiness," TomPaine.com, 3 July 2002, http://www.tompaine.com/Archive/scontent/5908.html, accessed 4 May 2011.

Baghdad Sean and the Human Shields

Reminiscent of the intellectuals and artists that trooped to Europe in the 1930s to admire the totalitarians, the actor Sean Penn traveled to Baghdad on the eve of Operation Iraqi Freedom in December 2002 "to pursue a deeper understanding of the conflict."[413] Also traveling to Baghdad before hostilities began were 30 other Americans whose stated purpose was to act as human shields for Saddam's key infrastructure.[414] Lacking the courage of their stated convictions, all of the visitors survived the experience, apparently leaving before the bombing began. Penn would return to Baghdad after liberation, traveling with Medea Benjamin (see below) whose "Occupation Watch" website regularly accused Allied soldiers of human rights abuses.[415] Penn later also visited Caracas to sit at the feet of Hugo Chavez as the Venezuelan caudillo insulted America.

CodePink and the Crawford Ditch-dwellers

In November 2002, female activists, among them well-known Communist sympathizer, Medea Benjamin, and Democrat Party activist, Jodie Evans, created CodePink to oppose the war policies of the Bush administration.[416] CodePink came into public prominence by outrageous acts that disrupted a congressional hearing, the Democrat and Republican Conventions in 2004, the 2005 Inauguration, and by insulting wounded troops and their families at

---

[413] Alistair Lyon, "Sean Penn Says War in Iraqi Is Avoidable," 15 December 2002, Reuters, http://www.commondreams.org/headlines02/1215-10.htm, accessed 4 May 2011.

[414] Human Shields Face 12 Years' Jail for Visiting Iraq," *The Guardian*, 13 August 2003, http://www.guardian.co.uk/world/2003/aug/13/usa.politics, accessed 27 April 2011.

[415] See Ben Johnson, "Sean Penn's Baghdad Homecoming," FrontPageMagazine.com, 21 January 2004, http://archive.frontpagemag.com/readArticle.aspx?ARTID=1450, accessed 4 May 2011.

[416] See the CodePink website, http://www.codepink4peace.org/article.php?list=type&type=3.

the entrance to Walter Reed Medical Center. In 2005, CodePink members also established a camp in the ditch across from the entrance to President Bush's ranch in Crawford, TX. It later became known that Democrat members of Congress arranged tickets for CodePink to attend the 2005 Inaugural, as they did for the 2006 State of the Union Address, and the address to Congress by Iraqi Prime Minster Maliki in 2006, all of which were disrupted by CodePink members.[417] Worst of all, Democrat congressmen and one Democrat Senator aided CodePink's late 2004 mission to Fallujah, Iraq, to present $600,000 of aid to "the other side."[418] Far from coming from the fringe element of Leftwing politics, one CodePink founder, Jodie Evans, had been a campaign manager for perennial Democrat candidate, Jerry Brown, and a speaker at the 1992 Democrat National Convention, and was invited to the Obama White House in 2009 as a result of her fundraising activities for Democrats in the 2008 campaign.[419]

The relentless political and media attacks on President Bush personally and on his administration generally had an impact, dropping his popularity to abysmal levels. Not surprisingly, by mid-2007, 61% of Democrats polled thought the Bush administration knew in advance of the 9-11 attacks (35%)

---

[417] Michelle Malkin, "Dems Gave Code Pink Disrupters Tickets," 21 January 2005, http://michellemalkin.com/2005/01/21/dems-gave-code-pink-disrupters-tickets/;Michelle Malkin, "Democrat Rep. Lynn Woolsey: Capitol Hill's Lindsay Lohan," 18 March 2011, http://michellemalkin.com/2011/03/18/democrat-rep-lynn-woolsey-capitol-hills-lindsay-lohan/;

[418] Jim Hoft, "Barbara Boxer Approved Code Pink Trip to Fallujah to Donate $600,000 to Extremists to Murder US Soldiers," Big Peace, 13 October 2010, http://bigpeace.com/jhoft/2010/10/13/barbara-boxer-approved-code-pink-trip-to-fallujah-to-donate-600000-to-extremists-to-murder-us-soldiers/email/, accessed 4 May 2011.

[419] See for example, Kristinn Taylor and Andrea Shea King, "Obama Funder Jodie Evans: Democrat Rep. Alan Grayson Supports Code Pink Kidnapping Karl Rove," Big Government, 12 April 2010, http://biggovernment.com/taylorking/2010/04/12/obama-funder-jodie-evans-democrat-rep-alan-grayson-supports-code-pink-kidnapping-karl-rove/, accessed 27 April 2011.

or were not sure (26%) thus entertaining the notion that the administration might have known.[420] The latter percentage was surely helped in its opinion by the hints and insinuations in the movie, *Fahrenheit 9-11,* that filmmaker Michael Moore turned into millions in profit for himself and Miramax, and the similar positions of leading Democrats in the 2004 and 2006 campaigns that sought to cast doubt on President Bush's veracity, intellect, and loyalty. The negative climate did have its limits: as in 1864 when the "failed war" of "King Lincoln" and "Grant the Butcher" attracted 74% of the votes in the Union Army, some 73% of the American military indicated in October 2004 that they intended to vote to re-elect "King George," the president that had sent them to war allegedly under false pretexts and with inadequate equipment.[421]

Dissent in the Bush Years[422]

---

[420] "22% Believe Bush Knew About 9/11 Attacks in Advance," http://www.rasmussenreports.com/public_content/politics/current_events/bush_a dministration/22_believe_bush_knew_about_9_11_attacks_in_advance.

[421] Dave Moniz, "Troops in survey back Bush 4-to-1 over Kerry," *USA Today*, 3 October 2004, http://www.usatoday.com/news/politicselections/nation/president/2004-10-03-bush-troops_x.htm, accessed 4 May 2011.

[422] From http://farm1.static.flickr.com/6/6789848_7e8675334b.jpg as linked to by James Taranto, "How Code Pink Supports the Troops: A 'Peace' Group Appeals to the

The Obama Years

"Politically motivated criticism and unfounded fear-mongering only serve the goals of al-Qaeda....too many in Washington are now misrepresenting the facts to score political points, instead of coming together to keep us safe." (emphasis added)

- Deputy National Security Adviser John Brennan, Op-ed, *US News and World Report*, 9 February 2010[423]

"When a radical fringe element of demonstrators and others begin to attack the president of the United States as an animal or as a reincarnation of Adolf Hitler or when they wave signs in the air that said we should have buried Obama with Kennedy, those kinds of things are beyond the bounds."

- Former President Jimmy Carter, speaking to Students at Emory University, September 2009. Carter attributed much of the criticism of Obama to racism.[424]

"But the bottom line is, whose side are you on? Are you on Qadhafi's side or are you on the side of the aspirations of the Libyan people and the international coalition that has been created to support them?"

- Secretary of State Hilary Clinton, 22 June 2011, questioning the motives of Congressional critics of

---

Authority of a Mass Murderer," *The Wall Street Journal*, 16 November 2009, http://online.wsj.com/article/SB10001424052748704431804574539601006447292.html?mod=wsj_share_twitter#articleTabs%3Darticle, accessed 30 April 2011.

[423] Jake Tapper, "WH: Some Critics 'Serving the Goals of al Qaeda,'" Political Punch Blog, ABC News, 9 February 2010, http://blogs.abcnews.com/politicalpunch/2010/02/wh-some-critics-serving-the-goals-of-al-qaeda.html, accessed 27 April 2011.

[424] Transcript of Former President Jimmy Carter's Remarks on Racism at an Emory University Townhall Meeting on Wednesday, Sept. 16, 2009, Op-Eds/Speeches, The Carter Center, Emory University, http://www.cartercenter.org/news/editorials_speeches/emory-racism-091609.html, accessed 1 May 2011.

the Libyan intervention, thus providing an ironic contrast to her statement as a Senator in 2003, quoted above.[425]

American politics frequently has a high content of irony. John Brennan's quote in 2009 sounds very much like John Ashcroft's quote in 2001 that did so much to create the idea that the Bush Administration was seeking to silence critics of its war policies. Similarly, former President Carter made no such criticisms during the Bush presidency of those portraying Bush as an animal or a Hitler, but rather invited Michael Moore to sit in the Presidents' Box at the 2004 Democrat Convention in full knowledge of the dark, vitriolic implications against President Bush in Moore's award-winning firm.[426] Perhaps equally ironic, Emory University hosts both the Carter Center and the Jane Fonda Center.[427]

The general thrust of the "dissent is patriotic" theme, 2002-2008, was that the Bush administration was trying to foreclose debate on war policies by appeals to patriotism. After the 2008 election, most of the anti-war fervor of the previous 6 years suddenly evaporated.[428] Critics of the new president's policies were described as unpatriotic or racist if they did not want to pay higher taxes or opposed the new President's anti-terror policies. Such tactics by the Democrats certainly seemed to be just as intent on foreclosing debate as anything the Republicans had done since the war began.

---

[425] "Remarks With Jamaican Foreign Minister Kenneth Baugh and St. Kitts and Nevis Deputy Prime Minister Sam Condor," U.S. State Department, 22 June 2011, http://www.state.gov/secretary/rm/2011/06/166752.htm, accessed 23 June 2011.

[426] See http://zombietime.com/ for photos of anti-Bush signs used at various protests.

[427] See http://janefondacenter.emory.edu/.

[428] John Stossel, "Where Did All the Anti-War Protestors Go?" Fox Business, 25 April 2011, http://www.foxbusiness.com/on-air/stossel/blog/2011/04/25/where-did-all-anti-war-protestors-go, accessed 4 May 2011.

Turnabout in American politics is also fair play. After the Democrats in 2004 had demanded the release of all possible records of Bush's National Guard service in the hopes of finding some incriminating hidden secret, Senator, then President Obama, was placed into an ironic position when members of his own party in the hotly contested primary races in 2008 began questioning the location of his birth certificate and other personal records, thereby launching the Birther conspiracy.[429] This was doubly ironic because earlier in 2008, Democrat activists and their media allies had questioned the eligibility of Republican candidate, John McCain, since he had been born in the Panama Canal Zone. Tripling the irony, the first leading Birther, lawyer Philip J. Berg, a supporter of Senator Hillary Clinton in the Democrat primaries, was also a Truther. Obama's willingness to spend allegedly millions defending against suits seeking his original birth certificate, and the dearth of other documents from his 1981 trip to Pakistan, or his records at Occidental, Columbia, and Harvard became grist for the conspiracy mills. By April 2011, as the presidential primary races were about to start again, one early Republican aspirant, businessman Donald Trump, began hitting the President hard on his unwillingness to release his original long-form birth certificate, and suggesting that his academic grades were not good enough for the young Obama to have been admitted and maintained at Ivy League schools like Columbia and Harvard.[430] One poll reported that only 38% of Americans believed that President Obama was definitely born in the United States.[431] After three years of resisting, President Obama finally released his long-form

---

[429] Ben Smith and Byron Tau, "Birtherism: Where It All Began," Politico, 22 April 2011, http://www.politico.com/news/stories/0411/53563.html, accessed 4 May 2011.

[430] "Donald Trump: Obama Was a 'Terrible Student,'" Real Clear Politics Video, 25 April 2011, http://www.realclearpolitics.com/video/2011/04/26/donald_trump_obama_was_a_terrible_student.html, accessed 27 April 2011.

[431] Susan Page, "Poll: What Kind of President Would Donald Trump Make?" USA Today, 25 April 2011, http://www.usatoday.com/news/politics/2011-04-25-trump-president-poll.htm, accessed 26 April 2011.

birth certificate on 27 April 2011, but critics then demanded that he release the rest of his records.[432]

CONCLUSION

From the Founding until the present day, American wars and conflicts have always had American dissenters. Many times the Federal government took direct action against the dissenters for the simple act of publishing or speaking. More recently, dissenters have enabled enemy propaganda or provided other support to the enemy and emerged unscathed. Of note, one Truther, Van Jones, would rise to hold the position of "Green Jobs Czar" in the Obama White House until his previously stated beliefs became a political liability; he then left the White House to assume a prominent position at Princeton University. Meanwhile, the most prominent Birther, Donald Trump, briefly became a leading contender in the early polls for the 2012 Republican presidential nomination until the President finally released his birth certificate. Thus continues the modern trend, first established during the Vietnam era, where even the most absurd and disgusting political dissent in war time poses no impediment to continued popularity and high public position.

---

[432] See for example, "Trump to Obama: Now Release Your College Records," Real Clear Politics, 27 April 2011, http://www.realclearpolitics.com/video/2011/04/27/trump_to_obama_now_releas e_your_college_records.html, accessed 27 April 2011.

THE MEDIA

Closely connected to dissent is the manner in which dissent is transmitted. We use the word Media in a generic sense to communicate what our Founders would have called the Press. The Founders thought that a Free Press was fundamental to the proper functioning of a democratic republic. So much so that the sceptics at the Constitutional Convention - those who did not have absolute trust in a government limited by Enumerated Powers - sought a special protection by the passage of a Bill of Rights that specifically protected freedom of speech and the freedom of the press among other key rights reserved to "the people." The Press then or the Media today carry messages in the public debate. Since we now have printed material, photography, radio, television, movies and the internet, the "Media" available to carry messages has never been so omnipresent, so robust, and so democratically available to individual citizens.

However, a Free Press need not be a subsidized press or an irresponsible press. The "Press" or the "Media," like the "Market," is neither moral nor immoral; only the individuals involved are moral or immoral. The current war is certainly not the first war where the Media have been hostile to the war effort or to the sitting president, going beyond the simple conveying of messages to inject its own viewpoints into the debate. This chapter provides examples of the sometimes conflicting relationship between the government and military on one side, and the various media and participants in the media on the other.

CURRENT SITUATION

"I guess I would say if you're under the impression that the press is neutral in this war on terror, or that we're agnostic--and you could get that impression from some of the criticism--that couldn't be more wrong. We have people traveling in the front lines with soldiers in Iraq and Afghanistan. We've had people who've been murdered in trying to figure out the terrorist threat. You

*know, we live in cities that are targets, proven targets, for the terrorists. So we--**we're not neutral in this**."* (emphasis added)

- Bill Keller, Executive Editor, New York Times, "CBS News' Face the Nation," 2 July 2006, commenting on the New York Times recent publication of the details of a secret government program used to track terrorist financing[433]

QUASI-WAR

"For God's sake, my dear sir, take up your pen, select his most striking heresies, and cut him to pieces in the face of the public."

- Secretary of State Thomas Jefferson writing to James Madison, referring to Secretary of the Treasury Alexander Hamilton[434]

"[Let] nothing pass unanswered; reasoning must be answered by reasoning; wit by wit; humor by humor; satire by satire; burlesque by burlesque and even buffoonery by buffoonery."

- Vice President John Adams' advice on responding to Anti-Federalist attacks in the Press[435]

As described in the chapter on Dissent, the first decade after the ratification of the Constitution was one filled with political vitriol among the Founding Fathers. The sides divided over support to the French Revolution, and over Jay's Treay with the hated Britain, negotiated from a position of weakness. The factions coalesced around Jefferson and Hamilton. To Jefferson, Hamilton was a monarchist "bottomed on corruption."[436] To Hamilton, the

---

[433]Transcript at http://www.cbsnews.com/htdocs/pdf/face_070206.pdf, accessed 5 May 2011.
[434] Schweikart 150.
[435] Schweikart 150.
[436] McCullough, location 7473.

Jefferson faction was too much taken with French revolutionary fervour, and too willing to ignore the economic realities of the relationship with Britain.

The Founders quickly found printers and journalists willing to take part in the political squabbles. The Media of the day included newspapers, pamphlets, books, and caricatures. Jefferson found willing publishers and writers like Philip Freneau, editor of the *National Gazette*, and Benjamin Franklin Bache, the editor of the *Aurora*. Bache was the grandson of Benjamin Franklin and a childhood friend of John Quincy Adams. This did not stop him from heavy criticism of George Washington, John Adams, and Alexander Hamilton, going so far as to allege that Washington had been a traitor, like Benedict Arnold, conspiring with the British.[437] Jefferson, as Vice President, paid the journalist James Callender, a writer for the *Aurora*, to allege that President John Adams had royalist tendencies, and to make public the notorious case of Hamilton's adultery.[438] The Federalists, as John Adams recommended, replied in kind through their favourite papers like the *Gazette of the United States*, to which Hamilton was a frequent contributor, and the *Porcupine Gazette*.

Those in the Media became partisans themselves, and not just neutral vehicles to deliver messages or report the news. The editor of the *Gazette of the United States*, John Fenno, said of his rivals at the *Aurora*, "In the name of justice, how long are we to tolerate this scum of party filth and beggerly [sic] corruption....?"[439] The Federalist Fenno thus claimed the mantle of non-partisanship and moral probity for the undefined "we." Some of the Anti-Federalist editors and writers, or Republicans as they were later known, or "scum" as Fenno called them, spent time in jail for their partisan activities under the Alien and Sedition Acts. Jefferson's hired journalist, Callender, was one of them. When Jefferson's payments were late, Callender used the power of the pen to publish the Vice President's letters to him on the subject

---

[437] McCullough, location 7847; See also Ellis 126, 146, 160, 190.
[438] See Ellis 198, 201, 208-209.
[439] Quoted in McCullough, location 8586-8588.

of the President's royalist leanings as well as the payment terms, and then also alleged that Jefferson was having an affair with the slave, Sally Hemings. Even with a free press, journalists once bought do not stay bought, unless the payments are on time.

CIVIL WAR

"On one of these six Cold Harbor days, when my battery was in action, I saw a party of horsemen riding towards us from the left. I smiled as the absurdity of men riding along a battle-line for pleasure filled my sense of the ridiculous; but as I looked I saw that the party consisted of a civilian under escort. The party passed close behind our guns, and in passing the civilian exposed a large placard, which was fastened to his back, and which bore the words, "Libeller of the Press". We all agreed that he had been guilty of some dreadful deed, and were pleased to see him ride the battle-line. He was howled at, and the wish to tear him limb from limb and strew him over the ground was fiercely expressed."

- Union soldier Frank Wilkeson recording the punishment of correspondent Edward Crapsey by MG Meade, who explained, "The race of newspaper correspondents is universally despised by the soldiers."[440]

"Correspondents of the press were ever on hand to hear every word dropped, and were not always disposed to report correctly what did not confirm their preconceived notions, either about the conduct of the war or the individuals concerned in it."

- LTG Ulysses S. Grant[441]

---

[440] Hastings, *Anecdotes,* 276-277.
[441] Grantlocations 6819-6823.

In the Civil War, the dominant medium continued to be print. Dissent was partisan and vicious, verging on treasonous in the eyes of a government that closed opposition newspapers and imprisoned opponents. The new technology of photography added a medium for reporting and recording the sickening horrors of war, though its impact was more historical than political, as photographs were engraved before publishing.

The relationship between journalists, often called "correspondents," and troops in the field was at least as rancorous as the relationship between journalists and politicians. In 1863, Sherman said of newspapermen that, "the day must come when the army will make short work of this class of enemies."[442]

In the event recorded by Wilkeson (see above), the correspondent, Edward Crapsey, had angered MG Meade by publishing that Meade had recommended retreat to LTG Grant after the Battle of the Wilderness, 5-6 May 1864. The potentially deadly treatment of Crapsey no doubt reflected an accumulation of military rancor against a Press of suspect loyalty in the midst of an incredibly bloody series of battles that were having negative repercussions in the vital presidential campaign year of 1864. In that campaign the prominent newspaper publisher, Horace Greeley, a dissident Republican, recruited a Union general to run against the sitting Commander-in-Chief and the Democrats' candidate was another serving general. The Civil War generation would have scorned the notion of the Press as a neutral conveyor of facts and events.

---

[442] Mark Moyar, *Triumph Forsaken: the Vietnam War, 1954-1965* (New York: Cambridge, 2006) 176.

The new medium of photography brought home the horrors of the Civil War as never before.[443]

---

[443] The National Archives; On left: **Pennsylvania, Gettysburg. A Harvest of Death: 07/1863, ARC Identifier 533310 / Local Identifier 165-SB-36,** Still Picture Records Section, Special Media Archives Services Division, College Park, MD, Item from Record Group 165: Records of the War Department General and Special Staffs, 1860 – 1952; On right: **Virginia, Cold Harbor. A burial party on the Battlefield: 04/1865, ARC Identifier 533367 / Local Identifier 165-SB-94,** Still Picture Records Section, Special Media Archives Services Division, College Park, MD, Item from Record Group 165: Records of the War Department General and Special Staffs, 1860 – 1952.

SPANISH-AMERICAN WAR

"You furnish the pictures, and I'll furnish the war."

> - Widely attributed to William Randolph Hearst in a telegram response to artist Frederic Remington and correspondent Richard Harding Davis, January 1897[444]

The 1890s was the age of Yellow Journalism – sensational headlines, graphic illustrations, and comic strips used to excite the readership. The publishers, editors, and journalists adopted the mantle of fighting for the common man against the powerful in the Gilded Age. Mass media itself became big, profitable, powerful business. Two of the largest contending media empires belonged to Joseph Pulitzer with its flagship, the *New York World*, and Randolph Hearst with its flagship, the *New York Journal*.

Both Pulitzer and Hearst had ties to the national Democrat Party, although the local New York Democrats were still under the influence of the corrupt Tammany Hall machine, the very antithesis of the two contending media empires' professed concern for the poor and downtrodden. The sensationalism of foreign policy issues was just another tactic in the circulation wars with both empires exaggerating the conditions in Cuba, then in rebellion against the Spanish empire, and with both calling for the U.S. government to take action.

The new medium of photography was once again a minor player as photojournalism was in its infancy. Lacking cheap, fast technology for printing photographs, pictures were still engraved after development before printing, and drawings were still frequently used for illustration. Another

---

[444] Some question whether Hearst actually sent this message. See W. Joseph Campbell, "You Furnish the Legend, I'll Furnish the Quote," *American Journalism Review*, Dec. 2001, http://www.ajr.org/Article.asp?id=2429, accessed 22 Apr. 2011.

new invention, motion pictures, made its debut with two film companies sending teams to cover the war. The teams took footage of war preparations in Florida, some limited footage of troops landing in Cuba, troops coming home, and naval vessels underway. This silent footage was shown in theatres and other stage venues, but had little impact on the course of the war.

The Spanish-American War was short, glorious, and victorious, lasting less than four months (25 April-12 August 1898), and the cheerleading Press did not have time to become jaded and discontented with the main military operations. The subsequent counter-insurgency campaign in the Philippine Insurrection, lasting another four years until 1902, did cause some political and social opposition as America transitioned to managing an overseas empire. Using politics and social anxiety to sell papers and earn profits continued, but yellow journalism suffered a blow when Hearst's New York paper ran a couple of items that seemed to encourage the assassination of President McKinley, a Republican, despite McKinley having delivered the war that Hearst and the other yellow journalists had demanded. When McKinley was indeed shot in September 1901, outrage was expressed against the paper and circulation fell. The new president, Teddy Roosevelt, called such reporting "reckless utterances," implying that yellow journalism had inflamed the situation thus contributing to the violence.[445]

---

[445] See Frank Luther Mott, *American Journalism: A History of Newspapers in the United States Through 250 Years, 1690-1940* (London: Routledge, 2000) 541.

Teddy Roosevelt and Volunteers near San Juan Hill[446]

WORLD WAR I

"These requests go to the press without larger authority than the necessities of the war-making branches. Their enforcement is a matter for the press itself."

> - The explanation on the "Request for Censorship" cards sent to every newspaper in the country by the Committee on Public Information (The Creel Committee) in 1917[447]

In World War I, newspapers generally complied with the Creel Committee. The printed media of newspapers and magazines still dominated. The Press, like the infant film industry, was supportive of the mobilization and the war effort. The Creel Committee used newspapers, magazines, and posters to drum up support for the war effort, and to sell war bonds. Photo journalism now became available, but photos had to be transported back to the States

---

[446] Official Army photo, "Spanish American War," http://usmilitary.about.com/library/milinfo/arhistory/nlspanish-8.htm, accessed 16 May 2011.
[447] George Creel, "The Plight of the Last Censor," *Collier's*, 24 May 1941, 13.

for publication. Artists still contributed to the war effort, mainly through posters. The innovation of newsreels represented the early combination of news and entertainment, playing as they did just before feature films in most theatres. The Committee also used these reels and short propaganda films to get out the Government's message, providing competition to print media over content and audiences for the first time.

The film industry had a new nationwide audience for its products, and movies got into the act of supporting the war effort. Charlie Chaplin, for example, financed his own film, "The Bond," to aid in the sale of Liberty Bonds.[448] Other film stars also pitched in to help the government sell bonds. As with the Spanish American War, victory came too soon for war fatigue to manifest itself, especially given government repression of dissent under the Espionage Acts.

WORLD WAR II

Media covering this war had expanded to include print, photography, radio, and film. Each would impact society and politics. Newspapers continued to be important, but had forever lost their dominance. During the war, 700 journalists followed US forces into theater; 450 were present at D-Day alone.[449] While most of these were still print journalists, among them were also radio announcers, photographers, and filmographers. The government once again imposed censorship and set forth rules of what could and could not be published. Like in World War I, this was mostly self-censorship enforced by a Press that saw itself as part of the larger effort. Nonetheless military censors did review material before it was sent back for use, which was why the public did not find out about the dimensions of disasters and blunders like Kasserine Pass, Tarawa, Peleliu, or Slapton Sands until well afterwards.

---

[448] See http://www.archive.org/details/CC_1918_09_29_TheBond.
[449] Benford xii.

Newspapers

While the Press was generally supportive of the war effort, newspapers did not entirely stop their criticism of the FDR administration. The *Chicago Tribune* had been highly critical of FDR before the war, and pro-isolationist. Before the attack on Pearl Harbor, the paper had published allegedly secret documents that exposed the Roosevelt administrations plans for war, and Hitler made indirect references to these published plans in his declaration of war against the United States. In perhaps the most egregious example of violating the censorship rules with potentially disastrous results for the lives of servicemen, the *Chicago Tribune* published the secret, obtained from anonymous sources, that the U.S. had cracked the Japanese naval codes, which had been crucial to the U.S. victory at Midway. The administration seriously considered prosecuting the paper under the 1917 Espionage Acts, but decided otherwise for fear that the prosecution would only confirm the story to the Japanese.[450]

Balancing such behaviour, some journalists went beyond just coverage of the war and became combat soldiers. One of the most notable of these was Ralph M. Ingersoll who had been managing editor of *Fortune* and *The New Yorker*, and general manager of Time, Inc. Bald and middle-aged, Ingersoll was commissioned as a Lieutenant in the Army Engineers and fought in the European Theater of Operations.[451] This was different time and a different type of journalist.

---

[450] For a fuller discussion of the Chicago Tribune case, see Gabriel Schoenfeld, "Has the 'New York Times' Violated the Espionage Act?" Commentary Magazine, March 2006, http://www.commentarymagazine.com/cm/main/viewArticle.aip?id=10036, accessed 20 May 2011.
[451] Atkinson, location 8808.

Photography

Although the technology for wire photos and radiophotos emerged in the 1920s much news travelled physically until the written copy or the photograph could reach a location to be sent by wire or radio. Days would go by before news got home. The battles at Tarawa and Saipan, for example, were over before the first news accounts and photos reached the U.S. By the time of Iwo Jima, though, news took only 24 hours to reach home as American logistical capabilities improved across the entire Pacific, but for text only; wire photos still took two more days to get back to the U.S. from Iwo. For the famous 23 February 1945 photo of the flag-raising on Mt Suribachi, the rolls of film went on a mail plane to Guam, were developed there, and then the product was sent by "radiophoto" back to the States. The famous photo first appeared in papers on 25 February. The battle on Iwo was also the first in the Pacific where radio news broadcasts were made while the battle was still going on.[452]

Foreshadowing debates in the current war about photos of the dead in order, according to journalists, to bring home the true cost of war, publishing photos of the dead in WWII also caused controversy. The decision to publish photos and newsreels of dead Marines at Tarawa horrified the public and led to widespread indignation over the operation: "This Must Not Happen Again" was a newspaper editorial theme.[453] After seeing the published photos, one distraught mother wrote to Admiral Nimitz, "You killed my son."[454] To soldiers and their relatives, such photos always smacked of macabre voyeurism, if not vulturism. To critics of the self-proclaimed purity of the Press, the publication of such photos raises questions about journalistic motives – the desire of many journalists to win prizes and earn money at the expense of the agony of others.

---

[452] Bradley, *Flags,* especially 218-219.
[453] Bradley, *Flags*, 97.
[454] Manchester 242.

Photography could still move the nation. The government used this picture to sell more than $26 billion in War Bonds to finance the last efforts in World War II.[455]

---

[455] National Archives; **Photograph of Flag Raising on Iwo Jima: 02/23/1945 - 02/23/1945** , **ARC Identifier 520748 / Local Identifier 1221,** Still Picture Records Section, Special Media Archives Services Division, College Park, MD, Item from Record Group 80: General Records of the Department of the Navy, 1804 – 1983.

Photo of American dead in the battle for Buna and Gona, New Guinea, January 1943. Photos like these from Tarawa later in 1943 caused widespread consternation.[456]

---

[456] Photo 24, "Captured: The Pacific and Adjacent theaters in WWII," *pLog: Photo Blogs from the Denver Post*, 18 March 2010, http://blogs.denverpost.com/captured/2010/03/18/captured-blog-the-pacific-and-adjacent-theaters/1547/?source=ARK_plog, accessed 16 May 2011.

Radio

After World War I, radio emerged as a vital new medium and tool to reach wide audiences. Radio news and entertainment became big business. Demagogues like Huey Long and Father Coughlin became the forerunners of today's TV and radio talk shows, providing a continuing fusion of information, news, and entertainment – or "infotainment." Even radio entertainers like Will Rogers were not above using political wit. Governments also made immediate use of the tool. In the United States, audiences were treated to FDR's fireside chats. In Europe, Germans and Italians sat through the harangues of their leaders. When war broke out in Europe, Americans were transfixed by the reporting of Edward R. Murrow on-scene during the Blitz of London. Later, as noted in the previous chapter on Dissent, the Axis powers would use American and British traitors to make radio broadcasts in an attempt to undermine Allied troop morale.

Hollywood

Motion pictures became the other medium that had mass appeal and mass impact. "Hollywood" became synonymous with the worldwide motion picture industry, whether situated in Hollywood or not. Hollywood came into its golden age in the three decades after World War I, and joined the war effort even before the Japanese attacked Pearl Harbor. Perhaps because of the artists', actors', directors', and producers' identification with the oppressed in Asia and Europe, or because they simply sought to fill a voracious public appetite, Hollywood churned out dozens of war movies and hundreds of training films, documentaries, and newsreels while the war was being waged. As many as 80 million Americans attended movies every week, and watched in particular the newsreels that played before the feature films. Audiences saw an easily stereotyped enemy, whose caricatures have stayed with us to this day, coloring our perceptions of World War II. These films were not critical of the war effort, or America's participation in the war. Indeed, it was the isolationists who were viewed critically. American soldiers were held up as heroes of the everyman variety, reflective of the ethnic and occupational make-up of the country (but with much less coverage for non-white minorities), and easily outwitting members of the allegedly superior races of the Axis powers.

Hollywood went to war literally as well as figuratively. Many of the biggest stars served in some capacity making training films or propaganda films for the Office of War Information. Big studio names got commissions into the Signal Corps to make propaganda films - COL Frank Capra, LTC Darryl F. Zanuck, MAJ John Huston - and some stars even went into combat units, risking death despite their celebrity status – those like Jimmy Stewart, Tyrone Power, Clark Gable, Douglas Fairbanks, Jr., and Robert Montgomery. In all, 132 members of the Screen Directors Guild and more than 40,000 others from the film industry served in uniform. [457]

As long-time Hollywood writer, Bill Katz, noted in 2007, "During World War II the war movies were very popular. And that was even true early in the war, when we were struggling, and when there were questions about FDR's leadership. (People forget that the GOP made important gains in the 1942 elections, only 11 months after Pearl Harbor.) When 'Wake Island' appeared, also in 1942, the Marine Corps set up recruiting booths in movie theatres....There was never any question about which side the film industry was on." [458]

KOREA

In the Korean War, all the same media were present as in World War II which had ended less than five years before, but the war was waged without societal mobilization. The cohesiveness and solidarity of World War II still

---

[457] Benford 86.
[458] "The Eternal Return of Hollywood Politics," 11 November 2007, http://www.powerlineblog.com/archives/2007/11/018997.php, accessed 19 May 2011.

largely prevailed despite political scandals at home with the House Un-American Activities Committee and in the military with the dismissal of GEN MacArthur, although journalists did indulge in some questioning and coverage that was critical of early American tactics and the quality of South Korean forces.

The military command authorized only 270 journalists to cover the war on the Korean Peninsula itself.[459] Early on MacArthur relied on official dispatches from his Tokyo headquarters to get out the government's views. Any reporter that did not follow the rules was denied access. These daily dispatches, dutifully reported by compliant reporters, actually published news of the landing of troops, including an announcement of the landings at Inchon some 10 hours before the actual landings occurred. Decades later, an aide to Chinese General Peng explained, "It was very easy to get intelligence in the beginning. There was no censorship in the West at the time about troop movements. We gained much vital information from Western press and radio."[460] With the Chinese intervention and the UN retreat, controls on information and censorship rules tightened. The UN Command specifically asked reporters not to cover the UN evacuation of Seoul, but one journalist evaded the censors to report the story within hours of the event.[461] By March 1951, all battlefield reporting had to flow back through a censorship office in Japan.

In World War II, TV was in its infancy, with only a few thousand sets in existence in the U.S., and had no effect on the war or its coverage.[462] By 1950, though, America had 9.7 million sets which exploded to over 28 million

---

[459] Andrew F. Smith, "Activity 6E: The Press and the Military: The Korean Conflict," The American Forum For Global Education, http://www.globaled.org/curriculum/cm6e.html, accessed 21 May 2011.
[460] Hastings 172.
[461] Hastings 172.
[462] "Annual Television Set Sales in USA" http://www.tvhistory.tv/Annual_TV_Sales_39-59.JPG, accessed 19 May 2011.

sets in 44.7% of American homes by the war's end in 1953.[463] Thus, war news began to filter directly into American homes daily, without the public having to wait to attend movies, generally on the weekends, to see news reels. The news product had not changed much, but its frequency and availability was beginning to change how the broadcast networks reported the news, and how the public consumed information.

Unlike in World War II, Hollywood did not get into the act so early, although the Army Signal Corps did produce some Korean-specific documentaries, like *The Crime of Korea* (1950) and *The Big Lie* (1951).[464] The most notable Korean War commercial films of the sort seen in the previous war were not produced until after the war with the Oscar-winning *The Bridges at Toko-Ri* appearing in 1954, based on the novel of the same name written by James Michener, who had been a war correspondent with the Navy in Korean waters. Perhaps this is not surprising since many of the World War II films were still being circulated in theaters and appearing on TV, and the studios were still making new World War II movies. Not for nothing did Korea become known as the "forgotten war," sandwiched as it was between a very popular war with almost total societal participation and America's most unpopular war in Vietnam – the two conflicts that defined the polar opposites of Press and entertainment viewpoints and products that still reverberate today.

VIETNAM

President Merkin Muffley: *But this is absolute madness, Ambassador! Why should you **build** such a thing? [A Doomsday Machine; emphasis in the*

---

[463] For percentages see "Number of TV Households in America," http://www.tvhistory.tv/Annual_TV_Households_50-78.JPG.
[464] *The Crime of Korea* (U.S. Signal Corps, 1950), http://www.archive.org/details/CrimeofK1950, accessed 3 May 2011; The Big *Lie* (U.S. Army Signal Corps, 1951), http://www.youtube.com/watch?v=Cl1By29Ee_Y, accessed 3 May 2011.

original]

Ambassador de Sadesky: *There were those of us who fought against it, but in the end we could not keep up with the expense involved in the arms race, the space race, and the peace race. At the same time our people grumbled for more nylons and washing machines. Our doomsday scheme cost us just a small fraction of what we had been spending on defense in a single year. The deciding factor was when we learned that your country was working along similar lines, and we were afraid of a doomsday gap.*

President Merkin Muffley: *This is preposterous. I've never approved of anything like that.*

Ambassador de Sadesky: *Our source was the New York Times.*

- Dr. Strangelove, 1964[465]

"He was a friend to virtually every journalist who covered the war, and was the source for some of the most crucial press reporting of the war."

- Referring to Pham Xuan An, a Colonel in the North Vietnamese intelligence service, and a reporter for *Time.*[466]

The Vietnam era brought major turning points in American history – the daily presence of news and entertainment in American life through the medium of television, and a major cultural shift in the attitude of American journalists and entertainers generally against the military and generally against those societal and governmental themes that had resounded for the previous decades; it was a major shift leftward in a political sense when, as the

---

[465] Memorable Quotes for "Dr Strangelove or: How I Learned to Stop Worrying and Love the Bomb," 1964, The Internet Movie Database, http://www.imdb.com/title/tt0057012/quotes, accessed 6 May 2011.

[466] James H. Willbanks, Book Review of *Perfect Spy: The Incredible Double Life of Pham Xuan An, Time Magazine Reporter and Vietnamese Communist Agent*, Larry Berman, HarperCollins, 2007, in *Military Review*, May-June 2008, p. 120, http://usacac.army.mil/CAC2/MilitaryReview/Archives/English/MilitaryReview_2008_0630_art018.pdf, accessed 22 May 2011.

historian Paul Johnson put it, the Press "moved into permanent opposition."[467] If the adage, "all politics stops at the water's edge," ever had any meaning, it certainly ceased in this era.

The military command in Vietnam had rules governing, or censoring, what journalists could report based on whether the command considered such information useful to the enemy. The rules prohibited publishing American casualty figures or pictures of American dead, and required the use of prescribed language to describe certain weapons, such as napalm (called "selective ordnance"), or certain types of operations (the prescribed name for "search and destroy" was "search and clear").[468] The military command also gave regular, sometimes daily, briefings to the assembled Press corps in Saigon. Members of the Press would later maintain that these controls and briefings misled them, and consequently the public. Members of the military came to consider the Press as a whole to be biased. This mutual distrust continues to linger.

Newspapers and Magazines

Print media continued in importance if not dominance. Like other media, the print journalists in the early 1960s were generally supportive of the activist foreign policy of the Democrats under President Kennedy, including his desire to combat the "wars of national liberation" sponsored by the Soviets. This included support for deepening U.S. involvement in South Vietnam. Despite this support, South Vietnam in the early- to mid-1960s was not seen as a major location for the Press, and often junior reporters were sent.[469]

---

[467] Johnson 647.

[468] Mark Hillel Samisch, "Comparison of the Media Coverage of the Vietnam War to the Media Coverage of the Invasions of Grenada and Panama," Master Thesis, University of Maryland, 1991, p. 37, http://www.dtic.mil/cgi-bin/GetTRDoc?AD=ADA245458&Location=U2&doc=GetTRDoc.pdf, accessed 22 May 2011.

[469] For these early years see Moyar 170-172.

These reporters, while initially supportive, were critical of American tactics, the South Vietnamese allies, and especially the South Vietnamese leadership. As the war continued, and the Democrats under President Johnson deployed 550,000 American soldiers to the fight, the Press began shifting its attitudes against the style of military involvement, then against American involvement in general.

As the *Dr. Strangelove* quote above indicates, even before the major cultural and political shift that came in the later years of Vietnam, the "Press" in general and certain newspapers in particular were already suspect for their penchant for publishing what the government wished to keep secret. By the last years of the war, much of the pretense of objectivity disappeared along with accuracy. When Nixon ordered the bombing of North Vietnamese targets in December 1972, journalist Stanley Karnow, writing a decade later, noted that "the Christmas bombings of Hanoi have been depicted as another Hiroshima," which they clearly were not. *The New York Times* called the decision "Stone Age barbarism," while *The Washington Post* called it "savage and senseless." Yet, the bombing was effective and the number of fatalities officially reported by the North Vietnamese government – slightly more than 1600 – was surprisingly low given the hyperbolic characterizations by journalists and editors.[470]

After the war, the victorious North Vietnamese communists revealed that one of their spies, Pham Xuan An, a Colonel in their intelligence service, had infiltrated American news agencies, becoming a reporter for *Time and* using his privileged access to collect intelligence on U.S. military activities. Colonel An became the only Vietnamese full staff correspondent in any American news agency. For an age when American journalists were extremely protective of the concept of press neutrality, many were strangely tolerant of the revelation of an enemy spy that had penetrated their organizations. Colonel An was treated as a hero by the North Vietnamese, which can only

---

[470] For quotes and casualties, see Karnow, 653.

lead to the reasonable assumption that his penetration led to successful attacks on American installations and forces. Even so, his former colleagues contend that the news he reported through mainstream American channels was accurate, as if that is somehow exculpatory.[471]

Radio

In Vietnam, this medium lost much of the importance that it had in World War II and Korea, where it served a public thirst for on-the-spot reporting while action, like the London Blitz, was on-going. Nonetheless, enemy radio broadcasts retained importance as a tool. As the previous chapter on Dissent noted, the North Vietnamese used radio broadcasts by notable Americans to undermine the morale of American soldiers and American POWs.

Television

By 1965, more than 92% of American households had at least one TV set.[472] The Vietnam era represented the real coming of age for television. What radio lost as a medium that gave the audience the feel of being at the front, television gained. The vast majority of Americans tuned into the nightly news on one of their favorite broadcast network channels. While not truly an instantaneous experience, the daily news reports replaced the old weekly

---

[471] See for example the warm recollections in Stanley Karnow, "The Man Who Loved 2 Countries," *The Los Angeles Times*, 13 May 1990, http://articles.latimes.com/1990-05-13/opinion/op-52_1_american-press, accessed 22 May 2011, and Patricia Sullivan, "Pham Xuan An, 79, Reporter for Time, Spy for Viet Cong," *The Washington Post*, 21 September 2006, http://www.washingtonpost.com/wp-dyn/content/article/2006/09/20/AR2006092001904.html, accessed 22 May 2011, and Dennis Hevesi, "Pham Xuan An Dies at 79; Reporter Spied for Hanoi", The New York Times, 22 September 2006, http://www.nytimes.com/2006/09/22/world/asia/22an.html, accessed 22 May 2011.
[472] "Number of TV Households in America," http://www.tvhistory.tv/Annual_TV_Households_50-78.JPG.

news reels. By the mid-1960s, an opinion poll named the newscaster Walter Cronkite of CBS news the "most trusted man in America." On 27 February 1968, while the fighting in the Tet Offensive was still underway, Cronkite broadcasted a negative report on his recent trip to South Vietnam, calling the struggle a stalemate from which the U.S. would have to negotiate an exit, but not as victors. This report, coming from such an influential personage with a huge audience, helped convince President Johnson not to run for re-election in 1968 thus denoting the new, incredible power of a now almost ubiquitous medium. Ironically, the visual images of and accompanying commentary on the Tet Offensive created the impression that American and South Vietnamese forces were suffering major defeats – the very opposite of the true situation.

Hollywood and the Film Industry

The military services continued to produce training films and Public Affairs documentaries, as they had since the 1940s. Despite the length of the war, Hollywood continued the trend begun in the Korean War, and only dealt commercially with the theme of Vietnam after the war was over, with the notable exception of *The Green Berets* in 1968 (the same year as Cronkite's famous broadcast), an unabashedly pro-American film starring John Wayne, which was a box-office success and included a hit song. The film industry, though, continued to make blockbuster films about the safer subjects of World War II all during the Vietnam era.

Hollywood stars continued to make USO visits to forward deployed trips, often led by the incomparable Bob Hope. Others, led by Jane Fonda and Donald Sutherland, "went to war" by launching the "Free The Army" tour as an alternative to the USO with the object of causing dissension in the ranks;

a film of this tour was released in 1972 as *F.T.A.*[473] Fonda and Donald Sutherland also supported the Vietnam Veterans Against the War (VVAW). In the Winter Soldier protest held by the VVAW, veterans professed to have participated in a range of war crimes. When Federal officials tried to investigate the claims, the veterans refused to cooperate, and some of those on stage admitting to crimes were shown to be frauds.[474] One of the principal leaders of VVAW was Al Hubbard, who claimed to be a former Air Force Captain wounded in Vietnam. His records showed that he had never served a tour in Vietnam, had only risen to the rank of Sergeant (E5) and was injured playing sports.[475] To those actors supporting the VVAW, and eventually to Hollywood as an industry, the themes became more important than mere facts, a precursor to the "fake but accurate" standard in the current war.

GULF WAR

Reporter #2: Sir, knowing what you know, where would you say our forces are most vulnerable to attack, and how could the Iraqis best exploit those weaknesses?

Reporter #5: I understand that there are passwords that our troops use on the front lines. Could you give us some examples of those?

Reporter #7: Sir, what would be the one piece of information that would be most dangerous for the Iraqis to know?

Reporter #9: Is there anything that you can tell us that would lower the morale of our fighting men?

---

[473] See http://www.imdb.com/reviews/302/30294.html, accessed 22 May 2011. See also "Show Business: Typhoon Jane," *Time*, 3 January 1972, http://www.time.com/time/magazine/article/0,9171,879060-2,00.html.

[474] Guenter Lewy, *American in Vietnam* (New York: Oxford University Press, 1978) 316-317.

[475] These events were widely covered at the time, and replayed during the 2004 Presidential Campaign. See the accounts in B.G. Burkett, *Stolen Valor: How the Vietnam Generation Was Robbed of its Heroes and its History* (New York: Summit Publishing, 1998).

- *Saturday Night Live* spoof of reporters' questions at Pentagon press conferences during the Gulf War, 9 February 1991[476]

In the 1980s, research reports began circulating demonstrating what many Americans could already sense – that the Press was largely liberal, or left-wing. By 1981, more than 80% of elite journalists admitted to having voted Democrat in the elections 1964-1976.[477] In the 1980 election, a study showed that 75% of the journalists at the 50 major newspapers in the U.S. voted against Reagan.[478] In the 1984 elections, a study of the news and editorial staff at 621 newspapers showed that 67% had voted for Mondale, while more than three quarters supported the most left-wing elements of the Democrat Party's foreign policy agenda in the 1980s – a unilateral nuclear freeze, cuts to the defense budget, and stopping aid to the Contras.[479] As described in the chapter on Preparedness, the 1980s was also the decade when journalists and policy-makers maintained the common belief that the U.S. military was a decrepit force equipped with machinery that would not work, and low-quality troops that could not fight, all of which cost far too much. This was the stage set for the coverage of the Gulf War.

As in all previous wars in the Twentieth Century, the military imposed controls on what the Press could report in order to keep certain information from being widely available to the enemy. Whereas in Vietnam journalists could move about the battlefield whenever they could find space on military aircraft or vehicle convoys, the military in the Gulf War reduced the ability of journalists to travel freely through the battle zone on military assets by

---

[476] "Desert Storm Press Briefing," *Saturday Night Live*, Season 16: Episode 12: Kevin Bacon / INXS (9 Feb. 1991; NBC, Broadway Video), http://snltranscripts.jt.org/90/90lgulfwarbriefing.phtml (accessed 4 May 2011).

[477] L. Brent Bozell III and Brent H. Baker, *And That's the Way It Isn't* (Alexandria, VA: Media Research Center, 1990) 19.

[478] Bozell 32.

[479] Bozell 33.

requiring them always to be accompanied by an assigned military escort. The difficulty of gaining access to Saudi Arabia, a tightly controlled Islamic country, further constricted the number of journalists gaining entry to military staging areas. To be accredited and gain access to the military, journalists had to sign a pledge to follow the established rules; breaking the rules resulted in denial of access.[480] An additional complication was the need to ship visual products from the front back to an airport in the rear. This meant that camera footage might take a day to reach headquarters back in the U.S. Journalists eventually demanded that the military put precious helicopters to work ferrying their products.[481]

In the brief military interventions in the 1980s, the Press and the Defense Department had developed the concept of a "Press Pool" where certain reporters were always on stand-by to accompany American forces into battle, filing reports that the Press in aggregate could use. The pool was initially used for the deployments to Saudi Arabia during the Gulf War, but the major news organizations fully expected that once the military was deployed and established in base camps, the Press would be allowed independent or "unilateral" reporting, as in Vietnam, with credentialed reporters free to roam. Saudi Arabia eventually allowed some 1600 reporters to enter the country to cover the war. Faced with these huge numbers, the Pentagon decided to maintain the pool concept and allowed only 400 reporters to accompany the frontline troops.[482] Pool reports then had to flow through the Joint Information Bureau at Dhahran for review before

---

[480] Jason DeParle, "AFTER THE WAR; Long Series of Military Decisions Led to Gulf War News Censorship," *New York Times,* 5 May 1991, http://www.nytimes.com/1991/05/05/world/after-the-war-long-series-of-military-decisions-led-to-gulf-war-news-censorship.html?pagewanted=all&src=pm, accessed 5 May 2011.

[481] John J. Fialka, *Hotel Warriors: Covering the Gulf War,* (Washington, DC: Woodrow Wilson Center Press, 1992) 17.

[482] Gary C. Woodward, "The Rules of the Game: The Military and the Press in the Persian Gulf War," chap. in *The Media and the Persian Gulf War,* ed. Robert E. Denton, Jr. (Westport, Connecticut: Praeger, 1993) 11-12.

release.[483] Given military control over access and transport of product, and the final security review, some news agencies took to using the old phrase from World War II and Korea, "Reports reviewed by military censors."[484]

Even though the Press continued in "permanent opposition" mode, and despite the irritants of enhanced military control, journalists were not as openly hostile to the war effort or to the military as they had been in the latter years of Vietnam or in the skirmishes that occurred in the final two decades of the Cold War. For the first time in decades, some journalists openly used "we" in their accounts of military efforts, much to the chagrin of generally left-wing critics that wanted at least neutrality in coverage, if not the outright hostility to the military or to Republican administrations that they had grown accustomed to having.[485] More importantly, the public supported the military measures and polls indicated the public would have supported even more stringent censorship.[486] So many negative reports had been made early in the deployment about poor U.S. military capabilities that would inevitably lead to extremely high casualties, reaching potentially tens of thousands of dead, that the public may have taken the war as a very serious endeavor requiring some measure of societal solidarity.

Any criticism of military control via reduced access and use of pools applied only to the U.S., of course, and not to Iraq. Only one prominent western journalist remained in Baghdad, reporting frequently – the Vietnam veteran reporter, Peter Arnett of CNN. This was significant because in the 1980s

---

[483] Pete Williams, "Statement before the U.S. Senate Committee on Governmental Affairs," chap. in *The Media and the Gulf War*, ed. Hedrick Smith, (Washington, DC: Seven Locks Press, 1992) 40.

[484] DeParle, "AFTER THE WAR."

[485] For example see Jim Naureckas, "Gulf War Coverage: The Worst Censorship Was at Home," *FAIR: Special Gulf War Issue*, 1991, http://www.fair.org/index.php?page=1518, accessed 3 May 2011.

[486] Gary C. Woodward, "The Rules of the Game: The Military and the Press in the Persian Gulf War," chap. in *The Media and the Persian Gulf War*, ed. Robert E. Denton, Jr. (Westport, Connecticut: Praeger, 1993) 22.

television news went from a daily presence with the nightly news to a ubiquitous 24-hour-per-day presence via the cable news channel, CNN. Moreover, satellite technology now allowed Arnett to broadcast live from Baghdad. Americans could literally watch war news all day long. Later it became known that Arnett's reports were subject to, and made at the sufferance of, the Iraqi regime that selected his reporting locations and reviewed his material before broadcasting.[487]

As in the Spanish-American War, the Gulf War was too short and victorious for a deep animosity to develop among the media or for massive protests to develop on campuses or in the streets. It was also too short for Hollywood to get decisively engaged, although television entertainers were quicker to sense the shift in public sentiment than news executives. The seminal moment was the *Saturday Night Live* skit a few days before the ground phase of the war. The skit illustrated the changing attitudes of Hollywood (with respect to the waging of this brief war) and the public at large. The skit famously lampooned journalists for asking military spokesman to provide specific information that might help the enemy's effort, and provided an amazing contrast for a comedy crew that normally portrayed President Bush as an inarticulate fool. In short order after the war, though, Hollywood returned to the major media themes of the post-Vietnam era with the Gulf War films, *Courage Under Fire* (1996) and *Three Kings* (1999), and later, *Jarhead* (2005), showing American soldiers as dimwitted, burned out, misogynist victims from the downtrodden class of American citizens, prone to lying and cover-ups.

---

[487] See "Press Freedom Versus Military Censorship," Constitutional Rights Foundation, http://crf-usa.org/america-responds-to-terrorism/press-freedom-versus-military-censorship.html, accessed 16 May 2011. Arnett would eventually fall from grace when a joint CNN-*Time* hit piece, "The Valley of Death," alleged that the U.S. government used chemical weapons on deserting American soldiers in Laos in 1970. CNN later retracted the report, firing several and reprimanding Arnett.

WAR ON TERROR

(BEGIN VIDEO CLIP) OSAMA BIN LADEN (through translator): Your security is not in the hands of Kerry or Bush or al Qaeda. Your security is in your own hands. Any nation that does not attack us will not be attacked. (END VIDEO CLIP)

LARRY KING: OK, Walter. What do you make of this?

WALTER CRONKITE: Well, I make it out to be initially the reaction that it's a threat to us, that unless we make peace with him, in a sense, we can expect further attacks. He did not say that precisely, but it sounds like that when he says...

KING: The warning.

CRONKITE: What we just heard. So now the question is basically right now, how will this affect the election? And I have a feeling that it could tilt the election a bit. **In fact, I'm a little inclined to think that Karl Rove, the political manager at the White House, who is a very clever man, he probably set up bin Laden to this thing.** (Emphasis added)

> - *Larry King Live*, 29 October 2004, a few days before the presidential election; Cronkite, a journalist once considered "the most trusted man in America," indulged in petty politics of the vilest, Truther variety[488]

"We are at war, and if the government doesn't move decisively to find and stop the leaks, they will only continue. [The New York]Times columnist Frank Rich once whined: 'Since 9-11, our government has asked no sacrifice of civilians other than longer waits at airline security.' Well, Messrs. Rich and Keller, your government asked you to forego your next Pulitzer to protect you, your subscribers and the rest of us. You refused. Walk a few blocks,

---

[488] "Bin Laden Releases New Videotape," CNN Larry King Live, 29 October 2004, http://transcripts.cnn.com/TRANSCRIPTS/0410/29/lkl.01.html, accessed 6 May 2011.

gentlemen, and see where the World Trade Center used to be. It could have been the Times."

- *Investor Business Daily* editorial, June 2006[489]

"I understand that people have a hard time with the concept that we get to decide what is news and what isn't, and what is fair and what isn't."

- David McCumber, Managing Editor of *The Seattle Post-Intelligencer*, explaining why the newspaper would not help the FBI track suspicious characters travelling on Seattle ferries in a time of war and frequent terrorist threats, 22 August 2007[490]

Hoping to relive the hey-day of the anti-war movements of the 1960s, various organizations around the world held protests, marches, and vigils in the weeks leading up to Operation Iraqi Freedom. Cumulatively, the numbers involved were in the millions spread across 300 cities worldwide.[491] As one observer, Patrick Tyler, in *The New York Times* put it, "...the huge anti-war demonstrations around the world this weekend are reminders that there may still be two superpowers on the planet: the United States and world public opinion."[492] According to another observer, Micah L. Sifry, the coordination of these mobilizations was "undoubtedly aided by the

---

[489] "All the U.S. Secrets Fit to Print," *Investor Business Daily,* quoted in Michelle Malkin, "How About a Nice Big Glass of...," 24 June 2006 http://michellemalkin.com/2006/06/24/how-about-a-nice-big-glass-of/ , accessed 6 May 2011.

[490] David McCumber, "A ferry captain, the FBI and Benjamin Franklin," Seattle's Big Blog, *Seattle Post-Intelligencer*, 22 August 2007, http://blog.seattlepi.com/thebigblog/2007/08/22/a-ferry-captain-the-fbi-and-benjamin-franklin/, accessed 22 May 2011.

[491] Micah L. Sifry, "The Second Superpower," in Micah L. Sifry and Christopher Cerf, *The Iraq War Reader: History, Documents, Opinion* (New York: Touchstone, 2003) 486-489.

[492] Patrick E. Tyler, "A New Power in the Streets," *The New York Times*, 17 February 2003, http://www.nytimes.com/2003/02/17/world/threats-and-responses-news-analysis-a-new-power-in-the-streets.html, accessed 22 May 2011.

networking power of the internet," a new medium hitherto unavailable to anti-war movements.[493]

Tyler's coining of the phrase almost created a new media theme – a "meme" – that suggested that the U.S. and "world public opinion" were inherently at odds with each other, with a unilateralist nation facing a truly global popular movement. Yet the "Second Superpower" epically failed as 40 nations sent troops to liberate and rebuild Iraq, and a half dozen others provided vital basing, and the participants maintained the coalition effort for almost 6 years until the new Iraqi Security Forces assumed responsibility in January 2009. The new medium of the internet, so crucial to the notion of the Second Superpower, was the tool used to defend the Bush administration against the attempt to swing the 2004 elections through the use of faked documents, and in countless other fact-checking of the big media conglomerates and news agencies. Tyler and many others made the basic error common to modern journalism since Vietnam of mistaking pictures of chanting, marching crowds capable of filling the TV screen (or the front page above the fold) as representing a sustainable popular movement. The cumulative millions protesting across dozens of countries simply did not equal enough democratic power as percentages of their home electorates to modify significantly their governments' policies toward Iraq.

As noted above, a new medium has been added to print, radio, photography, and television – the internet – and like new media before it, the internet has fundamentally changed the flow of information whether for entertainment or for news or for "infotainment." As the first decade of the current war closes, it seems likely that the internet has weakened in particular printed media, since the same information can now flow to most households without the use of presses and paper. Combined with the advent of cheap digital cameras, the internet also brings a unique spread of democratization of media, wherein those controlling printing presses, photographic

---

[493] Sifry 488.

reproduction, or motion picture production have lost a substantial measure of their ability to decide what gets printed or shown.

Even with so many media available, and with soldiers accessing the internet even from remote outposts, control of militarily sensitive information proceeded much as it had in the Gulf War. The Pentagon established ground rules and established a process for credentialing reporters. Given the terrorist nature of the enemies, few reporters ventured out to become "independents" or "unilaterals" roaming the battlefields, although some did hole up in hotels in Baghdad and Kabul, relying on local stringers to mingle with the populace. The military also followed a policy of embedding reporters with combat units, not unlike the 400 pool reporters allowed in forward units in the Gulf War, or the correspondents that accompanied combat units in World War II.

Newspapers and Magazines

In the current war, after a very brief period of national grief and solidarity, print journalism came to reflect the partisanship and the "permanent opposition" of earlier times. One newspaper decide to publish the details of top secret programs, and two magazines of wide circulation published stories of dubious accuracy that fit the memes they favoured.

Like the *Chicago Tribune* in World War II, the *New York Times* in the current war published secrets that could only help the enemy, prompting Keller's statement that paper was not, in fact, neutral in the war. On 16 December 2005, the *Times* published an article that detailed how the Bush administration was tapping into terrorist communications, setting off a political firestorm about "illegal wiretapping" or "warrantless wiretapping," issues never adjudicated against the administration, but which fed into a general opposition to the war methods of the Bush administration.[494] On 23 June 2006, the *Times* published an article blowing another top secret program, this one designed to track electronic transfers of funds to terrorist organizations.[495] According to the *Times*, in the first article, the Bush administration asked them not to publish the details given the potential damage to the anti-terror campaigns, and the paper held off for a year. Their article appeared just days before a book on the same topic appeared. [496]

What about the leakers? The Bush administration launched probes to find the source of the leaks, since clearly some government officials had violated their most fundamental oaths to reveal the information to the journalists. These investigations became just another example to administration critics of police state tendencies. However, the Obama administration continued to investigate leakers, just as the Bush administration had done. In April 2011, though, the Obama administration made known its decision not to prosecute former Justice Department lawyer Thomas Tamm. In December 2008, at the very end of the administration he had served and opposed, Tamm admitted his illegal leaking of the terrorist wiretapping program to *The New York Times*.[497] This action by the Obama administration stands in strange contrast to its vigorous program of combating leaks in other circumstances – the

---

[494] James Risen and Eric Lichtblau, "Bush Lets U.S. Spy on Callers Without Courts," *The New York Times*, 16 December 2005, http://www.nytimes.com/2005/12/16/politics/16program.html?ei=5090&en=e3207 2d786623ac1&ex=1292389200&partner=rssuserland&emc=rss&pagewanted=all, accessed 23 May 2011.

[495] Eric Lichtblau and James Risen, "Bank Data Is Sifted by U.S. in Secret to Block Terror, *The New York Times*, 23 June 2006, http://www.nytimes.com/2006/06/23/washington/23intel.html, accessed 23 May 2011.

[496] For an excellent discussion of the ramifications of the *Times* actions in the wiretapping case, see Schoenfeld, *Commentary Magazine*.

[497] Josh Gerstein, "Wiretapping Leak Probe Dropped," Politico, 26 April 2011, http://www.politico.com/news/stories/0411/53718.html, accessed 1 May 2011.

toughest of any first-term U.S. president so far.[498] Those sworn to uphold the laws of the U.S., which include the laws and regulations covering protection of classified information, hold a very dim view of other government employees that willfully leak such information for fun, politics, or profit, whether or not enticed to do so or suborned to so by journalists. The average American might fairly ask what sort of idiot would publish governmental secrets in time of war that could even marginally help the enemy. In the case of the wiretapping and the terrorist finance exposés the sad conclusion is that this sort are the types looking to sell books and win Pulitzers.

While not engaging in the egregious acts of publishing top secret programs in the midst of war, certain magazines did earn notoriety for simply getting war stories spectacularly wrong, phenomena stemming from a readiness to believe almost anything bad about American soldiers and American actions in the current war. In the case of the *"Newsweek* riots," a once respectable weekly news magazine fell for governmental sources that were at best incomplete, and at worst fraudulent. On 9 May 2005, *Newsweek* published an article alleging that U.S. soldiers had flushed a Koran down a toilet at Guantanamo. The story caused riots in Islamic countries, including Afghanistan, where several people were killed. Yet one week later, *Newsweek* recanted the story when its main government source recanted. The magazine's editor, Mark Whitaker, said, "Based on what we know now, we are retracting our original story that an internal military investigation had uncovered Quran [sic] abuse at Guantanamo Bay."[499] The retraction came too late to save lives or to prevent damage to America's image abroad.

---

[498] Scott Shane, "Obama Is Already Toughest President on leaks," The New York Times, 12 June 2010, http://www.msnbc.msn.com/id/37653773/ns/politics-the_new_york_times, accessed 23 May 2011.

[499] "Newsweek Retracts Quran Story," CNNWorld, 16 May 2005, http://articles.cnn.com/2005-05-16/world/newsweek.quran_1_retraction-newsweek-editor-mark-whitaker-quran?_s=PM:WORLD, accessed 23 May 2011.

In mid-2007, *The New Republic* published a series of three stories called "Baghdad Diaries," written by a pseudonymous "Scott Thomas," a common soldier. The tales contained laughably false portrayals of American soldiers and equipment in Kuwait and Iraq, which were immediately attacked by conservative media and veterans. *The New Republic* defended "Scott Thomas" for months in what it called "re-reporting" but which critics could safely say was "report then verify," in the process revealing that the author's real name was Scott Thomas Beauchamp, and that Beauchamp was married to one of the magazine's employees – ironically a fact-checker. Finally, in December 2007, the editor, Franklin Foer admitted, "[W]e cannot stand by these stories."[500] Like the Koran story in *Newsweek*, the story may have been wrong, but it fit easily into the general view *The New Republic* had of the war and of American soldiers.

While fake stories were popular, fake soldiers also made a comeback to be used as props in biased journalism or in political campaigns, much like the role played by the fabulists in the Winter Soldier protests that proved useful in the early 1970s. Gullible journalists and certain Democrat political campaigns embraced several fake veterans that fit the memes of the anti-war, anti-Iraq campaign, and anti-Bush movements that arose after the 9-11 attacks. On at least two occasions in campaign ads, Democrats used men making fraudulent claims about their service in Iraq, one in Missouri (appearing jointly with retired General Wesley Clark) and the other in Colorado.[501] In another story, a female sailor claimed injury and mental trauma caused by service in Iraq, dutifully reported in *The New York Times*

---

[500] Franklin Foer, "Fog of War: The Story of our Baghdad Diarist," *The New Republic*, 10 December 2010, http://www.tnr.com/article/fog-war, accessed 23 May 2011.
[501] For Missouri, see Michelle Malkin, "The Dems Embrace an Anti-war Hoaxer," Michelle Malkin, 4 November 2006, http://michellemalkin.com/2006/11/04/the-dems-embrace-an-anti-war-hoaxer/, accessed 23 May 2011; for the Colorado example, see Michael Riley, "Dems Red-faced over Veteran Impostor," Denverpost.com, 21 May 2009, http://www.denverpost.com/ci_12373595#ixzz1LlITgVgi, accessed 8 May 2011.

Magazine, but the Navy had no record of her service there, nor any record of injuries.[502] Fake soldiers and fake tales that fit a given meme got attention, especially during political seasons.

Hey, Bill Keller! How about a nice big glass of shut the hell up?

STOP COMPROMISING NATIONAL SECURITY FOR PROFIT!

A spoof on an old Operations Security poster from World War II; posted on some bulletin boards in Multinational Force-Iraq headquarters, 2007.[503]

Radio

As a medium, radio experienced resurgence with the emergence of talk shows dominated by conservative hosts. Like the radio personalities of the 1930s, the modern versions were often populist and demagogic. The shows

---

[502] Robert Hodierne, "War Story Told by Former Sailor Disputed," *Navy Times*, 25 March 2007, http://www.navytimes.com/news/2007/03/navy_timesmagazine_veteranrape_070 322w/, accessed 23 May 2011.

[503] Originally from Michelle Malkin, "How About a Nice Big Glass of...," 24 June 2006 http://michellemalkin.com/2006/06/24/how-about-a-nice-big-glass-of/ , accessed 6 May 2011.

took their daily themes from the headlines or news appearing in other media. The conservative slant balanced not only the government-subsidized liberal viewpoints of National Public Radio, but also the leftward tilt of most broadcast TV news. Any perceived bias in the newspapers, the nightly news or cable news was immediately answered within hours by the talk show hosts with counterpoints or simply ridicule.

Television

By 2001, broadcast and cable news had become so ubiquitous and powerful that television news readers became major public personalities earning millions of dollars. Whereas CNN dominated cable news in the Gulf War, multiple 24-hour news channels competed to cover the Global War on Terror. One of them, Fox News, was as overtly conservative as the others were overtly liberal.

After Saddam Hussein fled Baghdad in April 2003, CNN's news chief, Eason Jordan, admitted that the cable news network had cut a deal with the Iraqi dictator after the Gulf War to tone down their reporting from Iraq in return for maintaining access. Jordan admitted that CNN had covered up news of tortures, murders, and assassination plots. In other words, CNN officials willingly submitted to a censorship in Iraq that they would have hotly contested in the U.S. Jordan had made 13 trips to Baghdad to cultivate the relationship and maintain the deal.[504] Slanting the news in Saddam's favor was not a firing offense in the years before 2003, and neither was accusing U.S. soldiers of the arrest and torture of journalists in Iraq, which Jordan did in November 2004.[505] Just a few months later, though, at the World

---

[504] Franklin Foer, "CNN's Access of Evil," Opinion Journal, *Wall Street Journal*, 14 April 2003, http://www.rcgroups.com/forums/showthread.php?t=110206, accessed 23 May 2011. Foer was the managing editor of *The New Republic* that would publish the false tales from Scott Thomas Beauchamp four years later.
[505] Claire Cozens, "US Military 'Still Failing to Protect Journalists in Iraq,'" *The Guardian*, 19 November 2004,

Economic Forum in Davos, Switzerland, in February 2005, Jordan implied that U.S. troops may have been fatally targeting journalists in Iraq. When critics roundly slammed Jordan and CNN for these remarks, Jordan stepped down after a 23-year career at the channel, and so exited a news executive more willing to give slack to a mass murdering dictator than to the troops of his own country.[506] Like journalists' curious acceptance of Colonel Pham Xuan An's treachery, a case like Eason Jordan's and CNN'S deal with Saddam Hussein calls into question Press objectivity.

In the 2004 presidential campaign, intended fraud met willing gullibility on the major CBS news show, *60 Minutes II*, hosted by veteran anchor, Dan Rather. Democrats and other critics of President Bush had made his service in the Texas Air National Guard a major issue in the campaign, with Terry McAuliffe, the head of the Democrat National Committee, going so far as to accuse Bush of committing the crime of AWOL, while many others alleged that he got preferential treatment to avoid service in Vietnam. When retired Lieutenant Colonel Bill Burkett of the Texas Army National Guard contacted CBS with purported documents from Bush's military personnel files, the network rushed the story forward as the presidential campaign heated up, claiming that an expert had authenticated the documents. In the days following the September 2004 broadcast, the Kerry campaign would launch the "Fortunate Son" ad campaign making similar insinuations. That the documents provided by Burkett were fakes was painfully obvious, as many on the internet quickly pointed out. CBS initially vigorously defended the documents, but then caved and appointed an Independent Review Panel headed by former U.S. Attorney General Dick Thornburgh. The investigation reported that the documents had not been properly authenticated, and that the segment's producer, Mary Mapes, had called officials in the Kerry

---

http://www.guardian.co.uk/Iraq/Story/0,2763,1355027,00.html, accessed 23 May 2011.
[506] Howard Kurtz, "CNN's Jordan Resigns Over Iraq Remarks," *The Washington Post*, 12 February 2005, http://www.washingtonpost.com/wp-dyn/articles/A17462-2005Feb11.html, accessed 23 May 2011.

campaign to alert them to the show and to offer to put their campaign in contact with Burkett.[507] Eventually Mapes and three others were fired or resigned from CBS as a result of the investigation, but the man who placed his 40-plus-year reputation on the line to read the report, Dan Rather, continued with CBS until June 2006.

As other major media outlets investigated CBS' handling of the faked memos, the famous headline by *The New York Times* summarizing the recollections of a retired Texas National Guard secretary was "Fake, but Accurate."[508] These were not the actual words of the secretary, but the spin put on it by the *Times* reporters. Yet, it summed up both the factual situation and the hope of the journalists – the story may have been falsified but it fit the meme that journalists wanted to sell in the 2004 campaign. Given that the print media also fell for its share of "fake but accurate" military stories, it is fitting that *The New York Times* accurately named the phenomena. LTG Grant's summary on journalism in wartime is as apt now as it was when he put it in his memoirs: "[Journalists] were not always disposed to report correctly what did not confirm their preconceived notions, either about the conduct of the war or the individuals concerned in it."

Internet

In the decade between the end of the Gulf War in 1991 and the 9-11 attacks in 2001, the internet had become almost ubiquitous in the United States. Coupled with this was the availability of cheap digital cameras that could

---

[507] For a good summary of the Thornburgh report, see "The Thornburgh Report: What It Says, and What It Doesn't Say," 10 January 2005, http://www.powerlineblog.com/archives/2005/01/009066.php, accessed 23 May 2011.

[508] Maureen Balleza and Kate Zernike, "Memos on Bush Are Fake but Accurate, Typist Says," *The New York Times*, 15 September 2004, http://www.nytimes.com/2004/09/15/politics/campaign/15guard.html, accessed 11 May 2011.

take high quality still photographs or film clips. Software for personal computers permitted the modification of these products, and the rapid dissemination via video or social media websites, or just via email.

The combination of digital cameras, photo modification software, and the internet led to "fauxtography" where digital photographs were enhanced or otherwise changed to reflect certain viewpoints. Quite a few news agencies and newspapers were duped into using "fauxtographs." In one of the most absurd cases, in 2005, some press outlets published Iraqi insurgents' claim to have captured a U.S. soldier, complete with picture. The figure in the picture was actually a toy.[509]

One fake soldier, Jesse MacBeth, gained worldwide fame via a video alleging that he and other Americans committed war crimes. The video went viral on the internet attracting attention from anti-war and mass media groups. For anyone with even limited military experience, MacBeth's claims were absurd – that he had entered the Army at 16 but left at age 20, that he had been a Ranger and a Special Forces soldier, that he held several awards that were impossible for him to hold. His on-line picture in uniform was filled with simple errors.[510] That the video went viral speaks volumes about the preconceived notions that many in the media and on the Left have of American soldiers and American tactics.

The internet during the current war also represents the breakdown of major news and media outlets' control of information. So-called media moguls can no longer control the spread of information when anyone with a digital camera, a laptop, and an internet connection can become a "citizen

---

[509] For a list of "fauxtography" duping media outlets, see "Fauxtography," MediaMythbusters, http://mediamythbusters.com/index.php?title=Fauxtography, accessed 23 May 2011.
[510] See Michelle Malkin, "The Fables of Jesse/Jessie MacBeth," Michelle Malkin, 23 May 2006, http://michellemalkin.com/2006/05/23/the-fables-of-jessejessie-macbeth/, accessed 23 May 2011.

journalist." A spectacular example of the power of the internet to damage governments has been the publication of U.S. State Department emails by the website, Wikileaks. Many of the emails were stolen by Army Private First Class Bradley Manning by simply downloading them from the government's Secret computer system onto CDs. The internet is also providing a check on the older journalistic media. Bloggers broke the news on the fraudulent documents in the *60 Minutes II* scandal that eventually brought down Dan Rather. Others on the internet attacked the credibility of the fauxtography and fake soldier incidents sometimes within minutes of their appearance in the mass media.

Secrets are harder to keep, and control has ebbed from the dominant media to the citizen. Surprisingly, no Ernie Pyles have appeared among the major press outlets in the War on Terror. The American troops surrounding Pyle could sense that he was on their side, and understood their sacrifice. Pyle could use the word "we" when writing about combat in WWII, and the troops and their families back home understood. In the past decade of war, some independent writers, appearing mainly on the internet, like Bill Roggio and Michael Yon, have established a similar long association and close relationship with American soldiers, which the large scale media largely ignore. But the democratizing power of the internet also allowed hundreds of individual soldiers and military family members to launch blogs, collectively known as "milbloggers."[511] Had it not been for the internet, these important voices probably would not have been heard at all.

Hollywood

After 9-11, presidential adviser Karl Rove went to Hollywood to get help, meeting with film industry executives including Paramount Pictures

---

[511] See James Dao, "Military Blogging Goes Mainstream," *The New York Times*, 1 May 2011, http://www.nytimes.com/2011/05/02/us/02bloggers.html, accessed 23 May 2011.

Chairman Sherry Lansing, a prominent Democrat, and Jack Valenti, the head of the Motion Picture Association of America. The Bush administration wanted the industry's help to get out the message on America's war aims, and, as Valenti put it, to "make it clear to the millions of Muslims in the world that this is not an attack on Muslims. This is an attack on people who murder innocent people."[512]

And Hollywood went to war, but not entirely in the way the administration had hoped. The film industry found it difficult to shake the stereotypes so carefully crafted in the decades since Vietnam. From the hagiographic portrayals in World War II films of the American soldier as an "everyman" serving in a squad that inevitably had some cross-section of American society, often including stereotypical quasi-illiterate ploughboy and a wise-cracking Jewish kid usually from New York, the stereotypes shifted to a new post-Vietnam theme of the American soldier as a degraded human being made worse by military service. In this reigning theme the soldier or veteran (or intelligence agent) becomes a crazed victim of racism, sexism, and an incompetent, murderous government held in thrall by conspiratorial corporate interests. In movies since the Vietnam era, this disdainful view is cast backwards to earlier wars. Consider *Kelley's Heroes* (1970) where the troops are thieves, *Saving Private Ryan* (1998) with its wanton murdering of surrendering enemy troops, or *The Patriot* (2000) where the hero is actually a war criminal.

The Hollywood stereotypes occasionally find a reflection in other media. Even in the week that Osama bin Laden was finally brought to justice by elite American forces, *The New York Times Magazine* published an article on the

---

[512] Dana Calvo, "Hollywood Signs on to Assist the War Effort," *The Los Angeles Times*, 12 November 2001, http://articles.latimes.com/2001/nov/12/news/mn-3236, accessed 18 May 2011.

Crazy Vet theme.[513] Statistically, though, these stereotypes are simply not true as veterans have higher employment rates and commit crimes at lower rates than non-veteran civilians in the same age category.[514] These negative stereotypes feed from, and support a negative view of soldiers and veterans, birthed in the Vietnam War, that the self-appointed intellectual elites dominating large press organizations, academia, and the film industry find convenient and self-justifying. Such stereotyping would be considered anti-social bigotry if applied to other social, ethnic, or religious groups. Like other bigotries, this stereotype is deeply entrenched.

In many of the films appearing about the War on Terror, particularly about Operation Iraqi Freedom, the anti-military and anti-government bias of the film industry was readily evident. The multimillionaire Michael Moore's award-winning anti-Bush, anti-war film, *Fahrenheit 9-11*(2004), grossed $119 million in U.S. sales alone.[515] The film, financed in part by Democrat campaign contributors, did much to implant the idea that President Bush might have conspired to bring about, or allow, the 9-11 attacks to further some darker agenda. The negative stereotypes of American soldiers, the American government, or America in general were fundamental to anti-war films such as *Syriana* (2005), *Home of the Brave* (2006), *In the Valley of Elah* (2007), *Rendition* (2007), *Redacted* (2007), *Lions for Lambs* (2007), *Stop-Loss* (2008), and *Green Zone* (2010). Most of these films flopped in American box

---

[513]Luke Mogelson, "A Beast in the Heart of Every Fighting Man," *The New York Times Magazine*, 27 April 2011, http://www.nytimes.com/2011/05/01/magazine/mag-01KillTeam-t.html?_r=1&pagewanted=all, accessed 8 May 2011.

[514] See "Employment Situation of Veterans Summary," Bureau of Labor Statistics, 11 March 2011, http://www.bls.gov/news.release/vet.nr0.htm, accessed 8 May 2011. See also John Whiteclay Chambers II. "Veterans." The Oxford Companion to American Military History. 2000. *Encyclopedia.com*, http://www.encyclopedia.com, accessed 8 May 2011.

[515] Steven Zeitchik, "Michael Moore Sues Weinstein Brothers Over 'Fahrenheit 9/11' Profits," *The Los Angeles Times*, 7 February 2011, http://latimesblogs.latimes.com/entertainmentnewsbuzz/2011/02/michael-moore-harvey-weinstein-fahrenheit-911.html. Accessed 23 May 2011.

offices as the public rejected the negativism, even though each of these films had A-list stars or directors or otherwise received critical praise. TV entertainers and TV talk show hosts joked about the deaths of President Bush or Vice President Cheney, and the *Lil' Bush* cartoon (2007-2008) demeaned the president even further. Finally, worthy of mention is Gary Busey's role in the anti-American, anti-Semitic Turkish film, *Valley of the Wolves: Iraq* (2006).

According to former Hollywood writer, Bill Katz, the film industry makes anti-military and anti-U.S. films because of social reasons as much as for political reasons. Producers, directors, and stars see it as their social responsibility, plus it's hard to get invited to the right cocktail parties otherwise. Although their anti-war, anti-military, and sometimes anti-American themes do not generally sell well in the U.S., Hollywood trades on its brand appeal to sell these films to foreign audiences, where anti-Americanism earns larger returns. Without foreign sales which can average more than 65% of the total box office take, most of the negative films listed above would not have earned back their production costs.[516] And one wonders why some foreign publics have such a negative view of U.S. society, culture and politics – because we ourselves feed that image to them with our news broadcasts and our entertainment products.

The film industry was not, however, uniformly negative. *We Were Soldiers* (2002), based on a true story, was a brief return to the hagiographic past, especially surprising given that it's a Vietnam movie. *United 93* (2006), *World Trade Center* (2006), *Path to 9-11* (2006), *Hurt Locker* (2008), and *Taking Chance* (2009), all broke the usual negative stereotypes, and earned well both at home and abroad. Despite being grossly inaccurate about actual tactics in Iraq, *Hurt Locker* won a number of Oscars for its portrayal of

---

[516] "Anti-US Fervor in Hollywood," 25 February 2011, http://politicalcalculations.blogspot.com/2011/02/anti-us-fervor-in-hollywood.html, accessed 23 May 2011.

American soldiers in something other than a demeaning light. The TV series *24* (2001-2010) and the movies *The Kingdom* (2007) and *Body of Lies* (2008) show American intelligence agents and agencies in a more positive light than normal, but using practices that the average Hollywood denizen would find objectionable, if actually used in reality. Finally, the popular *Army Wives* (2007-2011) also does not follow the negative stereotyping, but is only tangentially connected to the on-going war. *United 93* and *Taking Chance* were closely based on true stories, which had more heroism and honor in them than most of Hollywood's fictional artistic creations. The same is true of *Restrepo* (2010), a documentary about the 173d Airborne Brigade in Afghanistan.

The role of the entertainment industry in the current war would not be complete without mentioning that the USO shows continue. The singer Wayne Newton and the actor Gary Sinise have generously supported the USO and a variety of other military-related charities and events. Many of the visiting USO artists seem to come from country music or professional sports cheerleading squads, but Arnold Schwarzenegger, Bruce Willis, and James Gandolfini among other actors have visited forward-deployed troops in Iraq and Afghanistan, as have comedians like Al Franken (before his election to the Senate), Robin Williams, Drew Carey, and Kathy Griffin. Still, in World War II, as many as 7000 entertainers made the rounds for the USO.[517]

Another important aspect of Hollywood has changed over the years – while the stars still makes fortunes acting in war movies, they avoid military service. To paraphrase a recent commercial, "The actors may not be real men like their Hollywood predecessors, but they play them in war movies."

---

[517] Martin Kasindorf and Steven Komarow, "USO Cheers Troops, but Iraq Gigs Tough to Book," *USA Today*, 22 December 2005, http://www.usatoday.com/news/world/iraq/2005-12-22-uso-cover_x.htm, accessed 23 May 2011.

CONCLUSION

Closely related to dissent is the form of dissent. We are fortunate to live in an age of many forms of media which provide endless, instant access to streams of data in the form of news, entertainment, and infotainment. The quality can be, and often is suspect, but that is no less true in the 21st Century than it was in the 18th. Such information streams have political impacts, by design and by happenstance.

As he accurately described so many aspects of war, Ernie Pyle also understood the peculiarity of those covering conflict: "War makes strange giant creatures out of us little routine men who inhabit the earth."[518] The media that carry information flows are also industries within which are numerous large businesses and wealthy individuals. Since the dawn of the age of industrialized warfare, identifying and decrying "war profiteers" – those who make money from war, usually individuals or firms supplying armaments – has been a favorite theme of those working as journalists and entertainers. But are the journalists, writers, and film makers that make millions off of the blood and suffering of others just another subspecies of war profiteer? Michael Moore made over $220 million from his war film, but is suing his financial backers, the Weinstein brothers, for a few dollars more of the profits. Is their conduct any better than the corporate war profiteers so many writers and filmmakers regularly denounce?

Our Founding Fathers experienced first-hand that the participants in the media are not themselves neutral. One can imagine if America had today's press corps in World War II, and if that press corps had not been muzzled by the Democrat administration of the day. While the public would certainly have had more and better information that they did, would the war effort

---

[518] "Ernie Pyle Quotes/Quotations," http://www.icelebz.com/quotes/ernie_pyle/, accessed 24 May 2011.

have been strengthened? Would any of the many troops who suffered and died from the World War II blunders and disasters have been saved? Or, would the war effort have been weakened? Would FDR's leadership have been called into question, especially in the 1944 elections? Would leaders crucial to our victory, like Marshall, Eisenhower, Bradley, and MacArthur have been pressured from command for purely domestic political reasons in response to press accounts? Equally unimaginable would have been film products that demeaned and belittled FDR. As America has changed, so have its journalists and entertainers. The Press and Hollywood of World War II bought into the war, and became de facto participants when not literal participants, especially in the "information operations" that the Roosevelt administration and the military commands found necessary.

Sometime in the middle of the Vietnam years that all changed, and most of the collective Media became institutionally hostile to the sitting government, though slightly less so when a liberal Democrat is in office, and institutionally hostile to the military. This has gone to the degree that the Press in particular now likes to see itself as purely objective and preferably a neutral on the battlefield, and is willing to give the enemy's side of the story equal billing or better than it does the official American or Allied line. And Hollywood (or the broader entertainment industry) now produces anti-American-themed products to tap into foreign audiences. These themes pass back and forth between the various media, such that reputable news agencies are open to being duped in furtherance of a good story – see the Texas National Guard letter, fauxtography, fake soldiers and fantastic tales that have appeared in major news outlets in the past decade.

With the inauguration of the Obama administration, the anti-war movement and the daily bombing and casualty counts have all but disappeared from news coverage. One comes to the necessary conclusion that the vitriol of the period 2002-2008 was much more anti-Republican and anti-Bush than it was anti-war. In early 2004, a British journalist described his encounter with a respected American colleague beside a hotel pool in recently liberated

Baghdad. The former was struck by the "moral degeneracy" of the latter who was positively rooting for America to fail in Iraq because it was essential that Bush failed. The American described "giggling editors" on the East Coast talking about "how awful it would be if this worked out" in Iraq, even if that meant that thousands more Iraqis had to die.[519] The media participants are not neutral. We can take Bill Keller at his word on that. Keller could have said, "I want the U.S. and its allies to *win* in Iraq, Afghanistan, or anywhere else we need to fight in this war." But he didn't; rather he made a bland statement about not being neutral, leaving the audience to guess at his and his paper's motivations.

Bush is gone, and American journalists thankfully are not now likely to root for an American defeat. We are also not likely to see entertainers joking about the assassination of the current president, nor are we likely to see *Lil' Obama* appear on cable comedy channels. Although America faces great challenges abroad, so many in the various media are really focused on local politics, and the issues of war and peace and grand strategy just provide useful ammunition to fight the local political battle in the next electoral cycle. This is something that the Federalists and Anti-Federalists would have understood.

---

[519] See Glenn Reynolds, Instapundit, 13 May 2004, http://pajamasmedia.com/instapundit/45849/, accessed 24 May 2011.

HEROES

No account of domestic issues during war time would be complete without mentioning how we treat our heroes. The wars since 9-11 have had their heroes, like all American wars. What has changed perhaps is that we have heard or seen little of these heroes compared to earlier wars, even when the war was unpopular, like Vietnam. Below are vignettes of some of America's heroes from earlier wars, a heroine from Iraq, and a hero from Afghanistan. The former are fitting company to the latter two.

CURRENT SITUATION

"First time I saw 10th Mountain Division, you guys were in southern Iraq. When I went back to visit Afghanistan, you guys were the first ones there. I had the great honor of seeing some of you because a comrade of yours, Jared Monti, was the first person who I was able to award the Medal of Honor to who actually came back and wasn't receiving it posthumously."

- President Obama, confusing posthumous Medal of Honor winner Jared Monti of the 10th Mountain Division with living Medal of Honor winner Salvatore Giunta of the 173d Airborne Brigade, 23 June 2011.[520]

REVOLUTIONARY WAR: Alexander Hamilton

Born in the West Indies, Hamilton arrived in New York City only in 1772. By 1776, he had become enamored with the cause of American independence, and formed his own volunteer artillery company before becoming General Washington's aide-de-camp. After the Revolution, Hamilton served as a Member of Congress, and then played a critical role in the Constitutional

---

[520] Jake Tapper, "Obama Flubs Medal of Honor Winner, ABC News, 24 June 2011, http://blogs.abcnews.com/politicalpunch/2011/06/obama-flubs-medal-of-honor-winner.html, accessed 29 July 2011.

Convention. He wrote most of the crucial *Federalist Papers* that sold the ideas behind the new Constitution to the broader public. Washington then appointed him the nation's first Secretary of the Treasury. These personal successes and the successful birth of Hamilton's adopted nation, though, were grounded on the personal bravery of Hamilton leading a nighttime frontal assault in the most important battle of the war.

In the Yorktown campaign in 1781, as the Franco-American siege lines closed in on the British positions, the capture of two British strong points, known as Redoubts 9 and 10, became crucial. The task was given to the division commanded by the Marquis de Lafayette, who assigned Redoubt 9 to a 400-man French force, and Redoubt 10 to an equal-sized American force. Washington had recently put Lieutenant Colonel Alexander Hamilton in command of a battalion, and Hamilton demanded to lead the Americans as the senior Battalion commander in the division. Lafayette granted his wish.

On the night of 14 October 1781, the two forces set out with unloaded muskets to prevent any accidental misfires that would alert the British defenders. The Redoubts were raised earthworks surrounded by pointed stakes driven into the low ground. With unloaded weapons, the forces would conduct frontal assaults with just bayonets and sabers. Redoubt 10 was closest to the river and thus covered any British approach to or from the river bank and also threatened the flank of the French assault on Redoubt 9. Hamilton led the charge in the darkness. The fighting was over in only 30 minutes, with the two Redoubts captured. The loss of the Redoubts unhinged the British lines, prompting them to ask for surrender terms on 17 October.[521] Yorktown proved to be the pivotal battle in the American victory in the Revolution, and the engagement at Redoubt 10 was the pivotal action bringing about that victory.

---

[521] For an account of the Yorktown campaign and Hamilton's role in it, see "Yorktown Battlefield: Lieutenant Colonel Alexander Hamilton," National Park Service, http://www.nps.gov/york/historyculture/hamiltonbio.htm, accessed 22 July 2011.

CIVIL WAR: Joshua Chamberlain

Joshua Chamberlain was a professor at Bowdoin College in Maine when the Civil War began. He had absolutely no military training before the war, but accepted a commission from the Governor of Maine as a Lieutenant Colonel of Volunteers. In July 1863, Chamberlain was commanding the 20th Maine Regiment when it was assigned to anchor the far left of the Union battle line on Little Round Top hill at Gettysburg on the battle's second day, 2 July. The Union forces had been forced back on the first day to occupy defensive positions on the high ground. Confederate leaders sought to turn the Union's left flank, seen as key to winning the battle, and thus launched multiple uphill assaults on the 20th Maine. Under Chamberlain's vigorous leadership, the 20th Maine stood firm until late in the day when the regiment was exhausted and low on ammunition. At this point, Chamberlain ordered and personally led a bayonet charge down the hill that caught the Confederates by surprise, ending the threat to the Union line.

Had the Confederates turned the Union flank on 2 July, the Union would probably have lost the battle and might very well have lost the Civil War. Chamberlain's role in the victory was recognized with the Medal of Honor, with the simple citation: "Daring heroism and great tenacity in holding his position on the Little Round Top against repeated assaults, and carrying the advance position on the Great Round Top."[522] At Appomattox on 12 April 1865, Chamberlain and the 20th Maine were accorded the prestige of being the official honor guard for the surrender ceremony that ended the major fighting between North and South.

WORLD WAR I: Douglas Macarthur

General MacArthur is remembered mostly for his exploits in the Pacific during World War II, and for his famous relief from command in Korea. As a younger Engineer officer, though, MacArthur routinely displayed personal

---

[522] "Chamberlain, Joshua L.," Congressional Medal of Honor Society, http://www.cmohs.org/recipient-detail/238/chamberlain-joshua-l.php

courage in the face of the enemy. During the U.S. occupation of Vera Cruz, Mexico, in 1914, MacArthur led a reconnaissance behind enemy lines that led to the recommendation that he be awarded the Medal of Honor, which was not granted. Four years later on the Western Front, MacArthur would again be recommended for the Medal of Honor, and again denied. In total, for his courage in battle on the Western Front, MacArthur won seven Silver Stars and two Distinguished Service Crosses (DSCs). His first DSC was awarded for actions in March 1918, when MacArthur was serving as the Chief of Staff of the 42d Division. Despite his high-ranking staff position, MacArthur joined an infantry company in defense of its position, providing the leadership necessary to keep them from breaking. His second DSC came in October 1918, again as Chief of Staff of the 42nd and as commander of the 84th Brigade, his units captured key terrain on the Meuse River. The citation for this action said, "On a field where courage was the rule, his courage was the dominant feature." [523]

MacArthur would finally win the Medal of Honor for his unsuccessful defense of the Philippines in the Japanese onslaught launched in December 1941, and won a third DSC in January 1945 upon his return to the Philippines when he advanced to within 75 yards of the Japanese positions when visiting front line troops. While vain and frequently controversial politically, MacArthur's personal courage and willingness to lead from the front was never in doubt and still stands as an incredible example to American officers and soldiers.

WORLD WAR II: Theodore Roosevelt, Jr.

The eldest son of the famous Rough Rider and President and already a wealthy man through his own efforts, Teddy, Jr. served in World War I with distinction earning a Distinguished Service Cross and two Silver Stars for actions in the trenches. In the interwar years, he became a founder of the

---

[523] Douglas MacArthur, Military Times Hall of Valor, http://militarytimes.com/citations-medals-awards/recipient.php?recipientid=676, accessed 20 July 2011.

American Legion, an early supporter of the NAACP, and Chairman of American Express. He also served as Assistant Secretary of the Navy and as the Governor of Puerto Rico and the Philippines. Throughout, he had maintained a commission in the Army Reserve. When mobilization began in 1940, Teddy, Jr. was recalled despite his physical infirmities (he frequently walked with a cane), and was promoted to Brigadier General. In the chaotic North African landings, he was one of the senior officers noted for leading straggling soldiers and fragmented units inland to seize and hold the beachhead. In one famous engagement, General Roosevelt mounted a frontal attack on a French colonial cavalry unit, firing over the windshield of his Jeep.[524] On D-Day, 6 June 1944, General Roosevelt requested to land with the first wave of troops on Utah Beach, and was the most senior officer to land on the beaches that day. Just as he had done in Africa, Roosevelt walked the beaches with his cane, policing up stragglers and forming them into assault forces, and then directing them against German positions. His Medal of Honor citation noted his "seasoned, precise, calm, and unfaltering leadership" that was crucial to the success of the landings.[525] A month later, General Roosevelt died of a heart attack, still on the battlefield.

VIETNAM: Captain Humbert R. "Rocky" Versace

In the early years of Vietnam, only a few thousand Americans served there as advisors. In late October 1963, less than a month before the JFK assassination, CPT Versace and two other American advisers were taken prisoner in South Vietnam. As the senior man, Versace assumed leadership in the jungle prison, and set about antagonizing the communist guards with his command of French and Vietnamese. This particularly upset those communist agents sent to indoctrinate the POWs and get them to confess to war crimes. He also tried to escape three times. As a result, Versace was

---

[524] Atkinson, locations 1894-1900.

[525] Theodore Roosevelt, Jr., Military Times Hall of Valor, http://militarytimes.com/citations-medals-awards/recipient.php?recipientid=2922, accessed 21 July 2011.

beaten, shackled, and starved. His irritating actions kept attention away from the other prisoners. Finally, the communists isolated Versace from his fellow POWs, preparatory to executing him in September 1965, an event announced on Radio Hanoi. The last the other POWs heard of Versace was his singing "God Bless America" at the top of his lungs. As his fellow prisoner, Dan Pitzer, remembered, "[Versace] got a lot of pressure and torture, but he held his path. As a West Point grad, it was duty, honor, country. There was no other way. He was brutally murdered because of it."

Despite this incredible tale of valor, President Nixon's original request in 1969 to award a Medal of Honor to Versace was downgraded by the Army to a mere Silver Star, but his friends and fellow prisoners kept agitating for an upgrade, which finally came through 33 years later in 2002.[526] After World War II, America and her allies tried hundreds of Axis soldiers for similar offenses against POWs, and spent decades looking for escaped Nazi concentration camp guards. However, having chosen strategic abandonment of our Southeast Asian allies as an exit strategy in 1975, America has not searched for those who murdered Rocky Versace or those who mistreated our other prisoners. Rocky Versace still awaits justice.

IRAQ: Sergeant Leigh Ann Hester, Kentucky Army National Guard

SGT Hester, a store manager in civilian life, was a member of a squad of gun trucks guarding a convoy of 30 civilian supply vehicles. South of Baghdad on 20 March 2005, Iraqi insurgents attacked the convoy. SGT Hester led three armored HUMVEES into a counterattack. In the ensuing 90-minute battle, at one point SGT Hester dismounted and led a few soldiers in an attack on an insurgent trench-line. Hester and her unit killed 27 insurgents and captured another 7.

SGT Hester's actions certainly rank with those of the other heroes mentioned here; her squad leader, SSG Timothy F. Nein, won the second-highest award

---

[526] See Steve Vogel, "Honoring the Defiant One," <u>Washington Post Online</u>, 27 May 2001, at http://www.mishalov.com/Versace.html, accessed 29 July 2011.

for valor – the Distinguished Service Cross – for the same action, and five other members of the squad were also decorated. In a different, less politicized war, perhaps SGT Hester's degree of leadership and personal bravery under fire would have brought a higher award.

AFGHANISTAN: Specialist Salvatore A. Giunta

On a night patrol returning to their base on 25 October 2007, 22-year-old Specialist Giunta's squad walked into a classic L-shaped ambush by Taliban fighters, high on a ridge in the Korengal Valley of eastern Afghanistan. The enemy opened up from ranges as close as 15-20 feet, too close for aircraft or adjacent units to provide supporting fires. Every man in Giunta's squad was immediately hit; Giunta took bullets in his front ceramic breast plates and in his assault pack. In a close ambush, the only viable tactical move is too attack into the ambush, which the squad then proceeded to do despite their wounds. Advancing into the fire throwing grenades, Giunta and two others made it to one of their wounded comrades, who was clearing his weapon. Leaving the other three behind to lay down a base of fire, Giunta then advanced alone to find the one man still missing in the dark – Sergeant Josh Brennan. As he came over the ridge, Giunta saw two Taliban dragging Brennan away into the brush, and charged them, killing one and causing the other to flee. Giunta then began treating Brennan's wounds.[527]

Later investigations concluded that the ambush may have been set up to capture one or more of the Americans probably for the propaganda value, a goal foiled by Giunta's bravery in saving Brennan. In response to those trying to understand why men under fire take such actions, Giunta replied, "I didn't run through fire to do anything heroic or brave. I did what I believe **anyone**

---

[527]For an account of the ambush, see Sebastian Junger, *War* (New York: Hachette, 2010, Kindle version), locations 1430-1456, and 1516-1522. See also "Giunta, Salvatore A.," Congressional Medal of Honor Society, http://www.cmohs.org/recipient-detail/3471/giunta-salvatore-a.php, accessed 29 July 2011.

would have done."[528] (emphasis original) Yet, the President could not remember his name or his unit just six months after presenting him the Medal of Honor.

CONCLUSION

Celebrated publicly nowadays are those that expose government secrets in war time, or those that courageously interrupt diplomatic visits, camp in a ditch outside a President's ranch, or fly off to consort with enemy leaders. Rarely do the purveyors of public information allocate much space to the heroes in today's war. Few Americans even know their names, let alone what they did. Now that an American student can go through twelve years of school without learning very much about American history, the names appearing above from earlier wars may also be unfamiliar to many readers. By the time of his June 2011 mistake, President Obama had presented six Medals of Honor, of which only three went to heroes from the current campaigns in Iraq and Afghanistan. Of these six, only one went to a surviving hero, Salvatore Giunta. In a country where the public can spend weeks transfixed by murder trials or maintain consistently high ratings for ever more bizarre reality shows, not even the President could remember the details of the few heroes he had honored.

Every time America has been tested, heroes emerge. Where do we get such men and women? There is steel in the soul of a free people, as we have re-learned again since 9-11. The average American may not hear of them and the President may not be able to remember their names, but still the heroes come when needed, and the Republic endures.

---

[528] Junger, locations 1482-1483.

CONCLUSION

*"We want peace too...**honorable** peace, won in the full light of day at the bayonet's point, with our grand old flag flying over us as we negotiate it, instead of a cowardly peace purchased at the price of national dishonor."*
(emphasis in the original)

- A Colonel from Ohio, a Democrat turned Republican, during the presidential campaign of 1864[529]

"After leaving Afghanistan, the Muslim fighters headed for Somalia and prepared for a long battle, thinking that the Americans were like the Russians," bin Laden said. *"The youth were surprised at the low morale of the American soldiers and realized more than before that the American soldier was a paper tiger and after a few blows ran in defeat. And America forgot all the hoopla and media propaganda ... about being the world leader and the leader of the New World Order and after a few blows they forgot about this title and left, dragging their corpses...."*

- Osama bin Laden, May 1998[530]

In the water at Pearl Harbor lie the remains of the *USS Arizona*, still leaking oil that slicks the surface. Concrete sign posts mark where the other warships were anchored along Battleship Row on the morning of 7 December 1941. This is the Alpha. Behind *Arizona's* grave the *USS Missouri* floats at anchor. You can stand on the spot where the Japanese surrender documents were signed on 2 September 1945, look out over the bow, and see the Arizona Memorial. It doesn't take much to think that the Mighty Mo', mothballed

---

[529] James M. McPherson, "War and Politics," in Geoffrey C. War, ed., *The Civil War* (New York: Vintage, 1990) 289.

[530] John Miller, "Greetings America. My Name is Osama bin Laden...," in "Hunting Bin Laden," *Frontline*, PBS, April 1999, updated September 2001, http://www.pbs.org/wgbh/pages/frontline/shows/binladen/who/miller.html, accessed 30 May 2011.

after its service off of Kuwait in 1991, is standing eternal watch, guarding the memory of its sunken sister. This is the Omega.

The USS *Missouri* stands its eternal watch over the remains of the USS *Arizona*[531]

The attack at Pearl Harbor temporarily crippled an American fleet. The 9-11 attacks in New York, Washington, and Pennsylvania temporarily crippled the American economy. Our country responded in a radically different manner to the two attacks. In the first, we mobilized the entire society, took 16 million men under arms, ramped up our industry, and made sure that every citizen knew that the price of victory was going to be high. We then set out to change the map of the world. In the second, we have chosen to wage a "just-in-time, just enough" war. In the decade since 9-11 the two presidents involved have not called for volunteers, have not asked industry to mobilize, and have not fully and consistently explained to the citizens the cost of victory...or the cost of defeat.

In World Wars I and II, one way the average citizen could participate was through the purchase of special bonds used to finance the war effort. The bond drives brought home some sense of the cost, and allowed those "back home" to participate in a least a small way. In the War on Terror, few citizens

---

[531] Author's photograph.

know the costs, although war funding has become a perennial political football, blamed conveniently for government deficits, wasteful spending, and being a major contributor to the onset of the Great Recession of 2008-2010. The actual costs do not bear this out (see chart below).

Fiscal Year	Federal Deficits	Iraq-Afghanistan War Costs	War Costs as % of Deficits
2002	157.8	20.8	13%
2003	377.6	67.7	18%
2004	412.7	90.4	22%
2005	318.3	105.5	33%
2006	248.2	120.6	49%
2007	160.7	170.4	106%
2008	458.6	185.6	40%
2009	1412.7	155	11%
2010E	1342.0	165.1	12%

All costs in billions of current year dollars[532]

The total cost of defense in the midst of war in 2011 will be 4.5% of GDP, versus the average 6.2% of GDP spent in the Reagan years, and the 7.5% of

---

[532] Composite numbers from: Amy Belasco, "The Cost of Iraq, Afghanistan, and Other Global War on Terror Operations Since 9/11," Congressional Research Service, 29 March 2011, "Summary" and p. 3, http://www.fas.org/sgp/crs/natsec/RL33110.pdf, accessed 28 May 2011; "Statistical Abstract 2011: Federal Gov't Finances & Employment: Federal Budget--Receipts, Outlays, and Debt," The 2011 Statistical Abstract, U.S. Census Bureau, http://www.census.gov/compendia/statab/cats/federal_govt_finances_employmen t/federal_budget--receipts_outlays_and_debt.html, accessed 28 May 2011; CBO, "The Budget and Economic Outlook: an Update," August 2010, p. 2.http://cbo.gov/ftpdocs/117xx/doc11705/08-18-Update.pdf, accessed 30 May 2011

GDP spent on average for defense during the Cold War.[533] Of the total defense spending since 2002, the cost of the campaigns in Iraq and Afghanistan has been about 20%, and the annual Defense budget itself has averaged less than 20% of the Federal government's budget. If America had not responded militarily after 9-11, saving all the money spent in Afghanistan and Iraq, only in Fiscal Year 2007 would our government have run close to break-even. If America had not spent a dime on Iraq, Afghanistan or any other item in the defense budget since Fiscal Year 2002 began on 1 October 2001 – an unrealistic choice even in the most extreme case - the nation's budget would still have been trending into deficit by 2008 due to domestic spending. The campaigns in Iraq and Afghanistan have cost a total of about $1.3 trillion in the ten years since the 9-11 attacks. In the same period, the U.S. government debt has risen from $5.8 trillion in 2001 to over $14 trillion in mid-2011, an increase of well over $8 trillion of which the war costs are less than 16%. The war did not break the budget, and only costs about 1% annually of our $14 trillion GDP, roughly equivalent to the 1% of the population serving in any capacity in the military. This is the "just enough" approach.

A critic might argue that the comparative vignettes herein are ridiculous because Saddam was no Hitler; he wasn't even a Mussolini. Or, that the effort expended in Afghanistan was not worth the cost in blood and national treasure simply because the Taliban and al Qaeda might be able to pull off a 9-11-style attack every now and then, but they could never really threaten our national existence. Such arguments are really no different than those who might once have said that the US overreacted to the Pearl Harbor attack, since the Japanese might have conquered a few islands, but could never have realistically threatened the US homeland. Japan would have needed years to absorb and consolidate its conquests in Asia, especially the

---

[533] "The Gates Farewell Warning," Wall Street Journal, 28 May 2011, http://online.wsj.com/article/SB10001424052748703779704576074273918974778.html, accessed 28 May 2011.

enormity of coastal China, before building air, naval, and land forces strong enough to threaten mainland America. We might have requested a negotiated peace and some sort of indemnity for the damage of 7 December, and just accepted the loss of some inconsequential islands.

At least the Japanese had a blue-water navy, which could transport large numbers of troops thousands of miles. Neither Hitler nor Mussolini had this capability, nor were they close to its development though the Nazis did have superior research programs for future "super weapons." America could have ignored Hitler's and Mussolini's declarations of war just as we did al Qaeda's declaration of war in 1996. As the "arsenal of democracy," we could then have continued funding and equipping Great Britain and the Soviet Union, hoping that at a minimum these two countries would be able to tie down Germany and Italy for years.

After buying ourselves this time behind the sacrifices of others, hopefully building up our industry and armed forces, we could then have either negotiated with the victors, or built a strategy around western hemispheric defense. These strategic options were available to America's leaders in the 1940s, but would this have been the right thing to do? The world can be grateful that we had the leaders we did, and that they chose the harder right over the easier wrong.

The current war is far more contentious, perhaps because of the manner in which we have chosen to wage it. Osama Bin Laden and al Qaeda declared war on the U.S. in 1996, and we sadly focused on this mostly as a law enforcement problem until the ultimate bloody failure of that policy on 9-11. In the 1990s, a favorite saying among those studying issues of national or international security was that "terrorism has no return address." We discovered on 9-11, or perhaps re-discovered, that international events always have a return address. Terrorism cannot exist absent terrain. The 9-11 attacks were hatched with the support or active acquiescence of the Taliban government of Afghanistan, which then opted to stand with al Qaeda in the ensuing war. Al Qaeda and its allies prefer the gray zones created by anarchical chaos, or the zones where governments hold little sway. Hence, their cells were found in the jungles of the Philippines, the chaos of Somalia and earlier, Sudan, and in the interstices between territory controlled by Saddam and the Kurdish zone in Iraq before Operation Iraqi Freedom, and amongst the rebel Sunnis and Baathists after Saddam fell. Their cells have also found safe havens within civilized countries, including our own, playing on the sentiments and legal protections of liberal democracies. Lax enforcement of existing immigration and anti-terror laws, and fears of being accused of being politically incorrect for racial profiling, helped make 9-11 and the subsequent terror attacks or attempted attacks possible. There is always a return address.

We hunted Osama bin Laden since the Embassy bombings of 1998. The U.S. took 13 years to track him down through three presidential administrations, causing great domestic and international political stress. Our old alliances held for some campaigns, while new alliances were required for others. In the process we liberated 30 million in Afghanistan and 27 million in Iraq. The U.S. and its allies created a new Iraqi Security Force, composed of Muslims, of 700,000 that fought alongside the allies, and took over control of their own security on 1 January 2009. By the time of Bin Laden's death, we had created a new Afghan Security Force, also composed of Muslims, of over 300,000, who fought daily side-by-side with the forces of 49 other nations to defeat the Taliban. With these successes, and the death of the spiritual and intellectual leader of the most radical and most successful group of Islamic fanatics, the free peoples of the world can hope that we are now looking at the beginning of the end of this war.

Why does the end matter? We now know that the U.S. policy incoherence in Somalia, followed by the failure to resource appropriately the uncertain mission, and the subsequent ignominious withdrawal emboldened Osama Bin laden and Al-Qaeda to assume that the U.S. was so weak internally that killing a few Americans, especially in a very public manner, would weaken

American resolve and force a political defeat all out of proportion to the actual military damage done. This is the essence of what was called "asymmetric warfare" in the 1990s.

And we know that other potential adversaries have learned this lesson in their study of the U.S. In 2000, one of the consensus views in a formal Defense Department study of the future security environment out to 2025 was that "U.S. public opinion will be seen as a center of gravity."[534] Writing a few months before 9-11, another observer wrote of China that "Among the most dangerous elements in U.S.-China relations is the fairly widespread belief in America's limited national willpower."[535] The reactions of the political and media elites to casualties in Iraq and Afghanistan – light by historical terms – lend substantial credence to this point of view among our current enemies and potential future adversaries. To combat this perception, America need not absorb casualties the way we did at Cold Harbor or Iwo Jima, but rather we must demonstrate a willingness to see policies through to conclusions consistent with our long-standing, oft-stated interests without indulging in the strategy of wishful thinking and the politics of misplaced hope.

The current war is not unlike the frontier wars of Britain's Victorian empire; however, rather than defending along a geographical line of mountains or rivers, our forces are arrayed along a bloody, jagged edge of civilized thought – individual freedom and the political liberty that sustains it are after all concepts that become embodied in other ideas known as laws and the rule

---

[534] Sam J. Tangredi, "Toward a Consensus Scenario," *All Possible Wars? Toward a Consensus View of the Future Security Environment, 2001-2025* (Washington, D.C.: National Defense University, 2000) in *Warfighting*, Book 1, 14th edition, (Maxwell AFB: Air University, December 2003) p. 66.

[535] Thomas J. Christensen, "Posing Problems Without Catching Up: China's Rise and Challenges for U.S. Security Policy," *International Security*, Vol. 25, No. 4, Spring 2001, pp. 5- 40, reprinted in *International Security Studies*, book 2, 13th edition (Maxwell AFB: Air University, November 2002) p. 166.

of law. As that great British-American, Winston Churchill, so presciently put it in 1943 at Harvard University, "The empires of the future are the empires of the mind." Our force of American volunteers serves on that frontier of thought just as their forebears, also mostly volunteers, defended the geographical frontiers of the earlier eras of our Republic. It may be trite to say that we are condemned to repeat the history we refuse to learn, but as this book is finished, the question before the nation remains whether we will persevere in order to win, or whether we will abandon those we swore to defend, abandon those who have fought by our side, as we did in 1975 in Southeast Asia, while comforting ourselves that the ensuing slaughter was inevitable.

In the current war, 9-11 was the Alpha. The Omega remains to be written.

"Dear Lord/Lest I continue/My complacent way/Help me to remember
Somehow out there/A man died for me today./As long as there be war
I then must/Ask and answer/Am I worth dying for?"

This monument is at Pearl Harbor. Eleanor Roosevelt kept this poem in her wallet during World War II, and its challenge shouts across the generations. Mrs. Roosevelt had four sons that served in the war.[536]

---

[536] Author's photograph.